# Irreconcilable

CRITICAL INDIGENEITIES

*J. Kēhaulani Kauanui (Kanaka Maoli) and*
*Jean M. O'Brien (White Earth Ojibwe), editors*



Critical Indigeneities publishes pathbreaking scholarly books that center Indigeneity as a category of critical analysis, understand Indigenous sovereignty as ongoing and historically grounded, and attend to diverse forms of Indigenous cultural and political agency and expression. The series builds on the conceptual rigor, methodological innovation, and deep relevance that characterize the best work in the growing field of critical Indigenous studies.

A complete list of books published in Critical Indigeneities is available at https://uncpress.org/series/critical-indigeneities.

# Irreconcilable

## *Indigeneity and the Violence of Colonial Erasure in Contemporary Canada*

Joseph Weiss

The University of North Carolina Press CHAPEL HILL

Set in Merope Basic by Westchester Publishing Services
Manufactured in the United States of America

Library of Congress Cataloging-in-Publication Data
Names: Weiss, Joseph, 1985– author
Title: Irreconcilable : indigeneity and the violence of colonial erasure in contemporary Canada / Joseph Weiss.
Other titles: Critical indigeneities
Description: Chapel Hill : University of North Carolina Press, 2026. | Series: Critical indigeneities | Includes bibliographical references and index.
Identifiers: LCCN 2025045097 | ISBN 9781469693729 cloth | ISBN 9781469693736 paperback | ISBN 9781469693743 epub | ISBN 9781469693750 pdf
Subjects: LCSH: Indigenous peoples—Canada—Government relations | Indigenous peoples—Crimes against—Canada | Reconciliation—Moral and ethical aspects—Canada | Haida Indians—Government relations | Haida Indians—Land tenure | Settler colonialism—Canada | BISAC: SOCIAL SCIENCE / Ethnic Studies / American / Native American Studies
Classification: LCC E92 .W45 2026 | DDC 323.1197/071—dc23/eng/20251118
LC record available at https://lccn.loc.gov/2025045097

Cover art: Maple leaf © Custom Scene / Adobe Stock.
Recycled paper © ~LENA BUKOVSKY~/ Adobe Stock.

For product safety concerns under the European Union's General Product Safety Regulation (EU GPSR), please contact gpsr@mare-nostrum.co.uk or write to the University of North Carolina Press and Mare Nostrum Group B.V., Doelen 72, 4831 GR Breda, The Netherlands.

*Dedicated to the memory of*
*Raymond D. Fogelson*

*For Bruce*

It will never be enough to recognize or reconcile or apologize or compensate for the violence and fraud committed against Indigenous peoples without abolishing the system in which that violence and fraud operate. Imperialism and colonialism must be undone, not as threads that pull at the others but a woven amalgam of ideologies and institutions that must be obliterated.

—JOANNE BARKER, *Red Scare: The State's Indigenous Terrorist*

I think for Indigenous peoples, whether we are talking about justice or solidarity or whatever, we need to start within our intelligence systems, or what Dene scholar Glen Sean Coulthard calls "grounded normativity"—the systems of ethics that are continuously generated by a relationship with a particular place, with land, through the Indigenous processes and knowledges that make up Indigenous life. For me, it's these theories and practices that form Indigenous constructions of reality, of life, and of how to ethically relate to the plant and animal nations, our families, the waters, the skyworld, communities, and nations. Decolonizing, to me, means centering grounded normativity in my life and in the life of my community, while critically analyzing and critiquing the ways in which I'm replicating white supremacy, antiblackness, heteropatriarchy, and capitalisms—structures that are ethically horrific and profoundly unjust within Nishnaabeg grounded normativity. Indigenous resurgence, in its most radical form, is nation building, not nation-state building, but nation building, again, in the context of grounded normativity by centring, amplifying, animating, and actualizing the processes of grounded normativity as flight paths or fugitive escapes from the violences of settler colonialism.

—LEANNE BETASAMOSAKE SIMPSON, "Indigenous Resurgence and Co-Resistance"

# *Contents*

# *Acknowledgments*

I've been working on this book in one form or another for the last eight years, and have in that time been helped and supported by many people, friends, family, colleagues, and loved ones from all over. My gratitude is overwhelming, and if I've neglected to mention a name here, it does not indicate any absence of appreciation.

My first thanks, as always, goes to the Haida community of Old Massett. How.aa for everything, to everyone! I am particularly indebted to the family of the late Agnes Davis—to Agnes herself, profoundly missed, Helen, Neil, Tubby, the late Roxanne, Leigh-Anne, Christine, Adam, and Robert, for giving me my first home on the islands, for their warmth and friendship, and for teaching me so much. I am also profoundly grateful to the teachers, staff, and students of the Chief Matthews School, who were my home away from home during my fieldwork and remain my most profound source of inspiration. To the late Leslie Bellis, my former principal and always friend and mentor, I miss you and I wish you could have seen this book out in the world. My thanks too to Tyler and Dana, for your friendship and insights, and for always making me feel welcome. To Sherri Burton, I am likewise ever thankful for your warmth and steadfast support, and I continue to relish our wonderful conversations—and haw.aa likewise to Alred Adams and Atticus Burton-Adams. To Karen Russ and Craig, too, many haw.aas are owed, and I'm looking forward to finally showing off that driver's license on our next visit.

I am also profoundly grateful to Jaalen and Gwaii Edenshaw, friends and fellow travelers in the complexity of it all. So too, so many haw.aas to Jaskwaan, Amanda Bedard; Haana Edenshaw; Jisgang, Nika Collison; Lucy Bell, Sdaahl K'awaas; and Gwaliga Hart, for their expertise, patience, warmth, and encouragement. So much of this book emerges out of the conversations we've had together, although it can never do justice to them. To the elders I've had the good fortune to know and learn from, I express my most profound thanks and mourn those of you who are no longer with us. To the late Primrose Adams, Merle and Knut Andersen, and the late Leona Clow, especially, my most sincere haw.aa. To other friends and colleagues on Haida Gwaii—Reg Davidson, Lisa White, Jordan Seward, Christine White, Candace Weir-White, and Elvis and Freda Davis, among many others, I am ever grateful. I would also like to acknowledge the institutional review on the relevant chapters of the book of both the Old Massett Village Council and the Council of the Haida Nation.

Over on the American side of things, my first thanks go to J. Kēhaulani Kauanui, without whom this book would quite literally not exist. It was thanks to Kēhaulani's book proposal boot camp that my initially disparate threads were woven together into something resembling coherence, and for her mentorship, friendship, warmth, and indefatigable support I am profoundly thankful. I have also been fortunate enough to work with Kēhaulani and Jean O'Brien as my series editors, and their support and hard work in helping me make this project into a book have been absolutely extraordinary. Another very important thanks goes to Khalil Johnson, my best friend at Wesleyan and one of my most significant scholarly interlocutors. This book would be much less without Khalil's keen sense of history and reality, and exceptional sense of analytical precision. Abigail Boggs has been another core friend and interlocutor, and her keen commitment to the material realities that underpin discourse has been a guiding light. I'm also grateful to Abbie, Milo, and Ben for giving me a home in Connecticut after the horrors of COVID-19 displacement. Margot Weiss has also been a constant inspiration, and I'm grateful to her for taking the time to engage with my strangest analytical departures, for her encouragement, and most of all for her friendship throughout the ups and downs of life at Wesleyan. I'm grateful too to George Bajalia, for many, many stolen cigarettes and, rather more importantly, for wonderful ideas and pushes to think differently.

I am likewise thankful to all my colleagues and friends at Wesleyan. In the Department of Anthropology, alongside George and Margot, I am grateful to my colleagues Anu Sharma, Daniella Gandolfo, Betsy Traube, Gina Ulysse, and Chloé Samala Faux, and to Allison Gallagher for her unflagging administrative support. I am equally thankful to my colleagues in my "second" academic home of Science and Technology Studies including Tony Hatch, Mitali Thakor, Elaine Gan, and Joe Rouse, and all the different members of the Indigenous Studies Research Network at Wesleyan, especially to my fellow co-coordinators, past and present, Katie Brewer-Ball, Justine Quijada, Yu-ting Huang, Roberto Saba, and some others already named. Portions of this book were completed during a fellowship at Wesleyan's Center for the Humanities, and I wish to thank Natasha Korda for her leadership of the center during my fellowship and the other fellows, Mitali, Courtney Patterson-Faye, Lori Gruen, Henry Washington Jr., Juan Esteban Plaza, Lauren van Haaften-Schick, Tori Bush, Abigail Fisher, Leila Henry, Shaoxuan Tian, and

Yiwen Huang, alongside Jess Fowler's consistent support. My thanks also to Mary-Jane Rubenstein, my institutional mentor, friend, and reliable partner in reality checks. Finally, and perhaps most importantly of all, I am grateful to my students, from whom I have learned so much and who push my work in so many different interesting directions. Particular thanks here are owed to the students in my Economies of Erasure and Toxic Sovereignties seminars, which have contributed immensely to this work in its formative stages. Thank you all!

Hilary Morgan V. Leathem has been my most patient reader and constant influence, from whom I learn immensely just about every day. I am also grateful to her for allowing me to use her photos in this book, and portions from an article we wrote together. Many of the strengths of this book (and none of its weaknesses) can be attributed directly to the keen comments and feedback of my writing group: Hannah Chazin, Andrea Ford, Eric Hirsch, Meghan Morris, Christien Tompkins, and Xiao-bo Yuan, to whom I am endlessly grateful. The work on elements of what would become this book first began while I was a curator at the Canadian Museum of History, and I am grateful to my colleagues and friends there as well. My old, dear friend Liam Begley read an earlier draft of this work, and gave me the confidence to believe it could speak beyond the narrow confines of academic prose. Finally, Bruce Miller, my college mentor and friend ever since, has been another source of support and guidance for this work, and I gratefully dedicate this book to him and to the memory of my dissertation cochair, Raymond D. Fogelson, who would have read every word of this book and, I'm sure, disagreed (affectionately) with most of them.

Many thanks are also due to the team at University of North Carolina Press and my readers at various stages of the manuscript. Mark Simpson-Vos's expert editorial work was appreciated at every stage of the process during his time at the press, alongside that of Andreina Fernandez, Tara Jordan, and the teams in copyediting, manuscript preparation, and art. I would also like to thank my three anonymous peer reviewers for the press for the manuscript and the anonymous reviewers of the initial proposal, whose productive and generous suggestions and critiques have pushed the book forward in incalculable ways.

Versions of individual chapters were presented at American Anthropological Association meetings, Wesleyan's Division II Luncheon Seminar, and the University of Victoria Anthropology Department's Anthropology Colloquium Series, and I'm most grateful for these conversations. Elements from an earlier version of chapter 1 were published in *Public Culture* as

"Settler Shock: Colonial Fetishism and the Disavowal of Violence in Contemporary Canada," and earlier versions of chapters 2 and 6 appeared as articles, respectively, in *Cultural Anthropology* and *Native American and Indigenous Studies*. Portions of the Outro originally appeared in *BC Studies* as "Sovereign Graffiti on Haida Gwaii: A Photo Essay," cowritten with Hilary Morgan V. Leathem. I am grateful to all of these venues for allowing the use of this material here. Finally, portions of this research were carried out with the support of the Wenner Gren Foundation for Anthropological Research, the American Philosophical Society, the Canadian Museum of History, Wesleyan University, and the University of Chicago, all of whom I would like to thank most sincerely.

I thank my family. My fathers, Peter Eliot Weiss and Michael Sweeney, and my mother, Kathleen Weiss, have been keen and critical readers and, more than that, wonderful parents, and my love and gratitude to them are, it goes without saying, bottomless. My godmother, Peggy Thompson, gave us a home away from home in Vancouver, and I am incalculably grateful for her constant her support and guidance. And, last but certainly not least, I thank my partner, Hilary Morgan, who's been with me through thick and thin over the course of this book—and well beyond it. We got through COVID together in a car piled with boxes and suitcases, snatching time to write when we could. I'm certain I could never have finished this without their support, encouragement, and, equally, her keen sense of what matters and what does not, whether within the academy or outside of it. My love and gratitude to them are difficult even to express, but nothing really compares to them.

# *A Note on Terminology*

Throughout this book, I capitalize the terms “Indigenous,” “Indigenous Peoples,” and “Indigenous Nations” in order to emphasize that they refer to sovereign nations and their citizens. I do not capitalize the term “indigeneity,” as that term refers to the structural status of Indigenous Peoples as “counter-analytic” to settler colonialism, as per Kauanui (2018b). Similarly, I do not capitalize the term “settler” as it likewise refers to structural status rather than political membership.

I also frequently use the terms “First Nations,” “Native,” and “Aboriginal.” In a Canadian context, First Nations is the specific legal term used to refer to Aboriginal Peoples who are distinct from Métis and Inuit Peoples within Canadian Aboriginal law, and it is also a common term of reference for both Indigenous and settler Canadians to refer to Indigenous Peoples. Aboriginal is a broader term, encompassing all Indigenous Peoples who live within the framework of Canadian settler colonialism, and, like First Nations, it has both specific legal and broader sociocultural currency as a term of reference. Native is a somewhat older reference, used both to refer specifically to Native Canadians as analogous to Native Americans and more broadly, again, to refer to Indigenous Peoples in both countries (and beyond them). While these terms are not interchangeable, they can at times be used synonymously depending on context.

Finally, as a matter of course, this book will not italicize either Indigenous names or terms in Indigenous languages, as I do not wish to normalize English as the “unmarked” language of reference. Authors’ names are referred to as much as possible using their preferred grammatical forms for both Indigenous and English names.

Irreconcilable

# Introduction

## *The Era of Reconciliation*

### "Which One Do You Mean?"

I first came to the islands of Haida Gwaii as an anthropologist in 2012, to conduct fieldwork focusing on how members of the Indigenous Haida Nation understood and experienced the Kunst'aa Guu—Kunst'aayah Reconciliation Protocol. The protocol was a treaty alternative agreement setting out limited shared governance between the Council of the Haida Nation (CHN), the provincial government of British Columbia (BC), and the federal government of Canada. Having firmly refused the "modern" treaty process in BC and, in particular, any severance of Haida Title to the lands and waters of Haida Gwaii, CHN's elected leaders and lawyers had instead negotiated an agreement in which each government would take on different duties in relationship to the islands, particularly in terms of the management of its natural resources. This agreement held in suspension the twinned questions of sovereignty and ultimate jurisdiction over Haida Gwaii, noting the Haida and Crown claims in parallel columns as simultaneously extant and mutually incompatible (Kunst'aa Guu—Kunst'aayah Reconciliation Protocol 2009, 1).[1]

This mutual suspension fascinated me. As a non-Indigenous Canadian scholar of cultural and political life with a developing understanding of settler colonialism, I wanted to understand what it meant for Haida people to live under the terms of this reconciliation protocol. It seemed paradoxical to me that the Protocol could at once recognize Haida sovereignty over their ancestral homeland and hold it in suspension, could be at once a collaboration with colonial governance and the mark of an ongoing Haida refusal to disappear politically or be fully incorporated into the settler state. I thus moved to Haida Gwaii equipped with questions that began with, I thought, a relatively simple and clear prompt for conversation: "What do you think of the reconciliation process on Haida Gwaii?"

After I'd settled into the rhythms of life in the Haida village of Old Massett on Haida Gwaii's north end, received formal approval for my research from the Old Massett Village Council, and begin to conduct interviews, however, I realized I had a problem. When I would ask my interviewees this first, most important question, they responded, to a person, "Which one do you mean?"

Having been away from Canada since the mid-2000s in grad school, I hadn't realized just how many different ways Indigenous people like my Haida friends, colleagues, and interlocutors were being promised "reconciliation." The term appeared everywhere. It was central to the Indian Residential Schools Truth and Reconciliation Commission of Canada, which regularly held events and hearings from 2010 to its closure and final report in 2015. It also named the "reconciliation" payments that were made to residential school survivors in concert with the work of that TRC. Even more, there seemed to be many different individual events and initiatives around everything from health-care management to youth activism that were described as "promoting" reconciliation, most often associated with different streams of federal or provincial funding. Reconciliation was everywhere on Haida Gwaii, to the point at which it was challenging indeed for both my Haida interviewees and I to distinguish one reconciliation initiative from another.

The confusion in 2012 has not abated more than a decade later. Quite the opposite, "reconciliation" is now ubiquitous in Canada. The term has been applied to everything from treaty processes (Penikett 2006) to a recently christened national holiday (Government of Canada 2024) and rebranding campaigns for colonial businesses,[2] served as the subject matter of an ever-growing network of corporate, school, and public workshops[3] and countless academic articles, and become a de rigueur dimension of contemporary political speech in the country in relation to Indigenous Peoples. The Canadian government has christened this an "era of reconciliation," stating in the 2017 introduction to its official webpage on First Nations in Canada, "Today the Government of Canada is working in partnership with First Nations in this new era of reconciliation to build stronger First Nations communities." This concise statement models a dominant framing of reconciliation in Canada as a series of state-driven initiatives in which Indigenous Nations are implicitly positioned as subordinate to the colonial government, in need of settler "help" in becoming "stronger" (Government of Canada 2017).

It is easy, even enticing, to lose oneself in the noise of all this reconciliation. Tempting to believe in the promise that Canada is getting better, to believe that the country is making amends for past crimes, to believe that colonialism is all in the past and what lies before the nation is a bright, shared future in which both settler and Indigenous citizens will all be equally, and enthusiastically, Canadian. But consider what those promises conceal. The Kunst'aa Guu—Kunst'aayah Reconciliation Protocol was only necessary on Haida Gwaii because the Crown denied the existence of the sovereignty of the Haida Nation over its own territories; indeed, because it denied the existence of the Haida as a polity in the first instance and had been denying that existence since the colonization of the islands and the other lands and water that would become the province of British Columbia in the late nineteenth century. The Reconciliation Protocol only existed because the political leaders of the Haida Nation refused to be reconciled to the loss of their lands and the erasure of their sovereignty. Even then, the competing sovereignty claims of the Haida and the Crown could not be reconciled with one another.

## Irreconcilable

This book is named for these irreconcilable moments in the ongoing social, political, legal, economic, and cultural landscape of Indigenous-settler relations in the territories claimed by the Crown as forming the country of Canada. *Irreconcilable* contends that the goal of settler-driven reconciliation initiatives is, precisely, to make a better Canada. This, I argue, is a fundamental problem. Reconciliation, in these frameworks, works to erase Indigenous sovereignty and, in particular, Indigenous claims to political autonomy and absolute (rather than subordinate) title over their territories. The ubiquity of reconciliation conceals the violence of ongoing settler colonial domination, making it appear as if a reconciled Canada is a commonsense good and obvious shared goal for all who live within the country, regardless of whether they only do so because their extant sovereignty has been abrogated. Canada can only become "better" by effacing those elements of Indigenous political organization, law, and social and cultural life that cannot be reconciled with the colonial nation-state, and reconciliation makes it appear as if that disappearance is inevitable and appropriate. Yet as the Kunst'aa Guu—Kunst'aayah Reconciliation Protocol also shows, and as I demonstrate throughout this book, Indigenous Peoples have not accepted and do not accept the terms of this era of reconciliation. Indeed, their experiences reveal the violence that underlies the resolution that reconciliation seemingly promises.

*Irreconcilable* traces the relationship between the settler colonial erasure of reconciliation and the ways in which Indigenous Peoples refuse to be reconciled to their dispossession or even their outright elimination. Over and over again, I argue, the seductive promises of the era of reconciliation attempt to normalize, disavow, and erase the realities of settler colonial domination; over and over again, I also show, Indigenous Peoples refuse to allow these deceptions to stand unchallenged. Furthermore, Indigenous Nations are not passively responding *to* settler colonial strategies of erasure. Rather, it is settler society that is desperately responding to the unextinguished and ongoing realities and practices of Indigenous sovereignty, community, and anticipatory world-making. Reconciliation, as I demonstrate, is not an already-given reality that Indigenous people must simply accept; rather, reconciliation is a claim, a demand, and a settler aspiration, one that is all the more fragile and precarious for all the ways in which it is presented as necessary and inevitable.

To better understand this relationship between colonial elimination and Indigenous refusal, *Irreconcilable* develops two interconnected analytical frameworks. The first locates several different examples of what I term *colonial technologies of erasure,* working from diasporic settler scholar la paperson's broader analysis of "colonial technologies" (2017). This framework highlights how colonial effacement operates within political, legal, and cultural orders in Canada. In particular, I am interested in showing how ongoing colonial efforts to make Indigenous Nations disappear as sovereign polities are normalized, so that Canadians do not have to feel unsettled by the ever-present, constitutive violence of settler colonialism (cf. Mackey 2016). My second framework looks at Indigenous practices of *generative refusal*. It draws especially on the ways in which both Mohawk anthropologist Audra Simpson (2014) and Michi Saagiig Nishnaabeg thinker Leanne Betasamosake Simpson (2021) have articulated Indigenous refusal as a mode of political and cultural praxis. Refusal, in their rendering, both contests past and ongoing settler colonialism and exceeds it, generating spaces of Indigenous resurgence, political autonomy, and world-making.

The text is structured as a dialogue between these two frameworks. Odd chapters focus on technologies of erasure, situating them within colonial legal systems, political discourse, institutional policies, and cultural logics. Even chapters offer in-depth examples of generative refusal within Indigenous lived worlds, responding to and exceeding those colonial technologies of erasure. My approach takes considerable inspiration from Métis Native Studies scholar Chris Andersen and White Earth Ojibwe historian Jean O'Brien's memorable articulation of Indigenous Studies as "methodologically promiscuous" (2016, 2). Andersen and O'Brien point out that what unifies Indigenous Studies methodologically is less any one monolithic disciplinary approach, and more the commitment to engaging theories and methods that will be of use in articulating Native and Indigenous perspectives, understandings, and commitments, on the one hand, and that might be of use to Native and Indigenous communities, on the other (2016, 3). *Irreconcilable* thus moves between methods "promiscuously" as best fits the goals of each individual chapter, incorporating elements of ethnographic analysis, historical genealogy (cf. Kauanui 2018a), political theory, and cultural studies.

In these chapters, I return repeatedly to the territories currently claimed by federal and provincial governments as the province of British Columbia, though BC is not the exclusive focus of this book. This is because the province epitomizes the precarious dynamics that underpin the era of reconciliation. Unlike other provinces in Canada, the vast majority of the lands and waters of British Columbia consist of territories that were never ceded by any Indigenous Nations.[4] As of 1763, however, British settlers were required by proclamation of the Crown to cede or extinguish Indigenous property rights, commonly now glossed as "Aboriginal title," in order to take legitimate ownership over colonial territories. I will return in greater detail to this process and the specifics—and colonial paradoxes—of Aboriginal title in chapter 1, but what is most important to understand for the book as a whole is the simple fact that this title was never formally extinguished. Instead, Indigenous Peoples were forcibly removed from their territories so that they could be occupied by settlers and then ghettoized on small reserves (C. Harris 2002; D. Harris 2008).

What this means is that the English colonization of British Columbia was essentially illegal under Britain's *own* laws (Borrows 2015, 111). The province has been defined throughout its history by what was commonly referred to, in settler discourses, as "the Indian Problem": that is, the problem of ongoing Indigenous existence in British Columbia. As long as Native people have not disappeared or been fully "absorbed" in the settler body politic, then it has been impossible for the province to escape the specter of its own illegitimacy. This has also had consequences beyond the province itself; indeed, virtually the entire apparatus of Aboriginal law in Canada has become fixated on the problem of unextinguished title in BC, particularly since the rise in the late twentieth century of legal cases brought by First Nations to Canada's courts asserting their rights over territories they never ceded to the Crown or settler society (Blackburn 2021). While these cases are usually referred to as "land claims cases," the political geographers Patricia Burke Wood and David Rossiter have asserted, instead, that it is British Columbia itself—and, by extension, settler colonial Canada—that is the "land claim," an "incomplete, unsuccessful invention" that is constantly at work justifying itself (Wood and Rossiter 2022, 7).

It is this precarity, so evidently on display in BC, that the era of reconciliation attempts to resolve. In turn, this makes the province an ideal focal point for an analysis of the dynamics of colonial erasure. Likewise, in my chapters exploring generative refusal, I center the ongoing social, cultural, and political work of the citizens of the Haida Nation. In one sense, this is because the Haida Nation has been continually engaged in the refusal of colonial domination since the advent of Euro-Canadian settlement on the islands of Haida Gwaii in the late nineteenth century, on the land and in the courts, via direct resistance, court cases, and multiple (and multiplex) political negotiations with provincial and federal governments. But even more so, I focus on the Haida Nation because this book would not exist without my experiences and relationships on Haida Gwaii. My sense of settler colonialism in Canada, my sense of what matters for Indigenous Peoples, and my sense of ethics as a settler subject have all been shaped by conversations with Haida interlocutors, friends, mentors, teachers, and Elders. This book is just one part of these ongoing conversations.

In what remains of this introduction, I expand on these different elements to lay the necessary groundwork for readers to engage the rest of *Irreconcilable*. I begin with an overview of the concept of settler colonialism and its relationship to Indigenous sovereignty, as these are foundational premises upon which my discussion rests. I then expand on the book's two primary analytical frameworks, *colonial technologies of erasure* and *generative refusal*. With these frameworks in place, I offer a more thorough discussion of the text's ethical commitments, particularly in relation to the colonial promises of closure and resolution that reconciliation offers for settler society. I end with an outline of the book's chapters.

## "Canada Invades"—Indigenous Sovereignty and Settler Colonialism

### *"Reconciliation is Dead"*

On February 13, 2020, the Unist'ot'en Camp of the Wet'suwet'en Nation published a video and an accompanying message in response to the invasion of their territory by the Royal Canadian Mounted Police. I quote the message in full:

> Canada invades. Invades on behalf of industry. Invades during ceremony. Canada tears us from our land. Tears us from our families, from our homes. Takes our drums away. Takes our women away. Jails us for protecting the land, for being in ceremony, for honouring our ancestors.
>
> On February 10, RCMP invaded unceded Unist'ot'en territory, arresting and forcibly removing Freda Huson (Chief Howilhkat),

> Brenda Michell (Chief Geltiy), Dr. Karla Tait, and four Indigenous land defenders from our yintah. They were arrested in the middle of a ceremony to honour the ancestors. Police tore down the red dresses that were hung to hold the spirits of missing and murdered Indigenous women, girls, and two spirit people. They extinguished our sacred fire.
>
> We have had enough. Enough dialogue, discussion, negotiation at the barrel of a gun. Canada comes to colonize. Reconciliation is dead.
>
> It is time to fight for our land, our lives, our children, our future. Revolution lives. (Unist'ot'en 2020)

The post was entitled "Reconciliation is dead. Revolution is alive." The Unist'ot'en Camp exists to protect Wetsu'wet'en territory from the construction of multiple oil and natural gas pipelines planned to cut directly across the traditional territory of the Unist'ot'en Clan (C'ihlts'ehkhyu / Big Frog Clan) (Unist'ot'en n.d.-a). Originally established by the Unist'ot'en Clan of the Wet'suwet'en Nation as a checkpoint at the Wedzin Kwa entrance to Unist'ot'en territory in 2009, the Unist'ot'en Camp has grown in the past decade to include housing for Clan members and visitors, a traditional pithouse, and a Healing Centre, acting as a primary home for some, a center of Indigenous community and a space for cultural revitalization and youth education (Unist'ot'en n.d.-b; cf. Barker 2021, 62–63). The camp has seen frequent and ongoing raids from RCMP officers who have arrested land defenders, destroyed structures, and threatened community members with militarized weaponry, all justified through the enforcement of colonially mandated injunctions protecting oil and gas development projects (Barker 2021, 64).

In the face of such direct and brutal colonial violence, "reconciliation" is merely "negotiation at the barrel of a gun." The Unist'ot'en's representatives connect the RCMP's actions to the systematic violence endured by Indigenous Peoples, particularly women and girls, to systematic attempts to disrupt and destroy Indigenous families, Indigenous ceremony, Indigenous culture, and Indigenous sovereign rights. All represent means through which "Canada invades," through which the settler nation-state "comes to colonize." The Unist'ot'en call instead for "revolution," the fight for their lives, lands, children, and futures.

### *A Structure of Elimination*

In emphasizing Canadian invasion in the present tense, the Unist'ot'en's Land Defenders make explicit the structural character of settler colonialism.

Settler colonial invasion, as Patrick Wolfe famously argued, "is a structure, not an event" (2006, 388; cf. Kauanui 2016). Moreover, it is a structure of elimination, in which the settler population attempts to erase the already-extant Indigenous communities that populate the territories that settlers desire to claim as their own. This elimination proceeds both through the actual extermination of Indigenous lives via war, introduced diseases, dispossession, resource starvation, and any number of other techniques of mass killing, and through the attempted erasure of Indigenous political organizations and sociocultural lifeways through often violently enforced mechanisms of forcible assimilation.

What defines settler colonialism in contrast to others forms of historical colonialism and contemporary postcolonial nation-states is that it is ongoing. The structure of elimination has never ended; Indigenous Peoples still face the "grinding gears" of settler colonialism, to borrow a phrase from Leanne Betasamosake Simpson (2022), each and every day. Elimination in this sense is embodied in the denial of Indigenous sovereignty, in the continued appropriation of their lands and waters, in the exploitation of other-than-human beings narrowly glossed as "natural resources," in the dismissals of Indigenous ways of knowing, understanding, and living, and, of course, in the covert and overt modes of racism aimed by settler society toward Indigenous people.

I use "settler" here, and throughout this book, to mark a structural relationship between settler subjects and Indigenous people, following from the usage suggested by Kanaka Maoli scholar J. Kēhaulani Kauanui (2018b). The term does not refer simply to those who were historically "active" in the process of colonial settlement, though it does include them. Rather, it indicates a structural relationship to indigeneity, which Kauanui defines as a "counter-analytic" to settler colonialism. Settlers are those who function, implicitly or explicitly, as part of the project of occupying Indigenous territories and, thereby, erasing and replacing the Indigenous Peoples to whom those territories belong. This usage characterizes settlement as an active and ongoing process, not one that has been historically "resolved" prior to the present. If we thereby understand Canada as being actively engaged in occupying Indigenous territories, then those of us who are not themselves occupied form part of the structure of occupation, regardless of our own personal experiences or politics. I use the phrase "settler subjects" in particular to indicate not only that settlers are subjects of the settler state, but that we too are subject to and defined by the violence of settler colonialism. Indeed, the popularity of reconciliation stems in part because it so effectively facilitates "settler moves to innocence" from complicity in the ongoing nature of the colonial project (E. Tuck and Yang 2012, 1).

### *"The Stubborn Insistence"*

Settler colonialism is distinctly, if not uniquely, future oriented. Because it is premised on the erasure of preexisting Indigenous polities, settler colonies fall into a perpetual deferral when they do not successfully and comprehensively eliminate the Native populations whose territories they claim (see Weiss 2018). This can justify colonial brutality. As anthropologist Elizabeth Povinelli (2011) has argued, the assertion that Indigenous people *will* disappear in the future can act as a kind of retroactive rationalization for even the worst excesses of settler violence in the present. Even such viciousness, however, is meant to mask precarity. While settler colonies might present themselves *as if* they are firmly entrenched with unchallenged jurisdiction over the territories they claim, the "problem" that Indigenous existence poses will not disappear as long as Indigenous Peoples themselves have not disappeared. This is a material problem, an issue of contested control over lands, waters, and resources. It is also a legal problem, embedded in the efforts of settler colonial laws to account for why their ongoing occupation of Indigenous territories is justified, legitimate, and inevitable. And it is a symbolic problem, as settler leaders and everyday subjects alike must reckon with the fact that they live on occupied territories that have been outright stolen or purchased or obtained under conditions of coercion, deception, and/or colonial bad faith.

Or, put more simply, settler colonialism is a claim, not a fact. As the authors of the Yellowhead Institute's "Land Back" Red Paper put it, "There is a stubborn insistence by Canada, the provinces and territories, that they own the land. For many Indigenous communities, this is a deep violation of their consent to determine what happens on unsurrendered lands, but also a violation of the broader assertion that they have jurisdiction over those lands" (Yellowhead Institute 2019, 8). Indigenous sovereignty cannot be reduced to partial rights within the framework of colonial ownership. Here is how the Council of the Haida Nation articulated their sovereignty in the Kunst'aa Guu—Kunst'aayah Reconciliation Protocol: "Haida Gwaii is Haida lands, including the waters and resources, subject to the rights, sovereignty, ownership, jurisdiction and collective Title of the Haida Nation who will manage Haida Gwaii in accordance with its laws, policies, customs and traditions" (2004, 1). Haida lands, subject to Haida ownership and jurisdiction, grounded in Haida laws, policies, and traditions.

It was this precise claim that was irreconcilable with the Crown's claim of ownership over those same islands. Even the full state recognition of Aboriginal title would not resolve this irreconcilability, as it remains a colonially determined, subordinate title to the absolute ownership and jurisdiction of the colonial state. Aboriginal title, in other words, can only ever confer limited rights to Indigenous Nations, and those always within the framework of the settler colony. The Haida Nation is by no means alone in in finding the Crown's claims irreconcilable. The "stubborn insistence" that Canada owns the land means that, for many different Indigenous Peoples, despite the fact that in "the supposed era of reconciliation there can appear to be progress," colonially driven reconciliation initiatives simply "do not go far enough" (Yellowhead Institute 2019, 8). How could they, when they seek to contain Indigenous sovereignty within colonial jurisdiction?

Moreover, the very terms under which sovereignty is understood might not be the same between colonial states and Indigenous Nations. The Yellowhead Institute's authors argue that Indigenous jurisdictions are grounded both in the refusal to cede sovereignty and in a set of ethical laws, codes, and norms around which proper relationality between humans and other-than-humans should proceed (8). These are theories of sovereignty that can be and often are fundamentally incompatible with colonial understandings, particularly around property law and the nature of ownership (Nichols 2020). This is why, in a similar sense, Goenpul scholar Aileen Moreton-Robinson (2021) has argued that Indigenous sovereignty is incommensurable with the Euro-Western Westphalian model of the concept, as each is grounded in radically different understandings of relationships to the land, the waters, and the world encompassing both humans and other beings.

As both Haida and Wet'suwet'en actors make clear, Indigenous Peoples do not passively accept the conditions of domination or the logics of colonialism. They blockade territories to protect the land, water, and other-than-human beings with whom they are in relation; they challenge colonial laws in the courts of the colony itself and in venues of international law; and they do not allow settler society to forget that it is engaged in an ongoing process of invasion. This means that the nature of sovereignty itself is in the balance in these actions. So too are ongoing questions about what it means for humans to live on this planet alongside other beings, with whom we might live or that we may destroy (see Liboiron 2021). The stakes of the era of reconciliation are high indeed, far higher than settler Canada might wish to acknowledge. Of course, this is precisely the point.

## Erasure

### *"The Real Racists"*

Shortly after publishing my first book, *Shaping the Future on Haida Gwaii* (2018), I gave a talk in the community library of the Village of Masset. It was attended primarily by settler members of the community loosely referred to as "Tow Town," who live in the unincorporated area of Tow Hill just east of Masset. The most vocal of these had attended my talk to express their unhappiness with a chapter in that book that had critiqued the ways in which Tow Town residents were themselves engaged in the appropriation of Haida lands and resources, even as they understood themselves to be participating in collective and noncapitalist ecological futures that were not in and of themselves anti-Haida or overtly colonial. The Tow Town community members in my audience disagreed with my critique, arguing that I had misrepresented the good intentions of the community's membership. I was particularly struck by one of their questions: "Why don't you criticize the real racists?" These real racists, my audience made clear, did not even live in Tow Town, but in a different community on the islands historically tied to the settler-controlled logging industry.

The Tow Town residents were not like those real racists. Real racists, for my audience, were overtly anti-Indigenous, racist in word and deed. They made it clear they did not like Haida people or want them around.[5] By contrast, while the Tow Town residents were imperfect, they acknowledged, they felt they were doing their best to be good neighbors and pointed to their many common causes with Haida people. They had attended my reading, they told me, because they were concerned that I was spreading bad feeling and opening up problems through my analysis. More than anything, in challenging my focus on settlers who *do* believe they are acting in good faith, the Tow Town residents were asking me to account for why those good intentions, those sincere beliefs in their own efforts to "be better," were not enough. What, after all, is wrong with settler good faith?

One answer can be found in the colonial dynamics of property law on Indigenous lands, which makes it possible for settlers to purchase and own land that falls on territories that were never ceded and within jurisdictions that were never extinguished (Borrows 2015). Proclamations of settler good faith—even the sincerest—mask the realities of appropriation that structure ongoing colonialism. Take what Omeshkegowuk Cree geographer Michelle Daigle has called the "spectacle of reconciliation," the "public, large-scale and visually striking performance of Indigenous suffering and trauma alongside white settler mourning and recognition." The spectacle of settler reconciliation, as Daigle aptly puts it, thus "secures, legitimates and effectively reproduces white supremacy and settler futurity in Canada" (2019, 706).

Daigle emphases dramatic and highly visible public events in her analysis, particularly those associated with the Truth and Reconciliation Commission of Canada. But the work that reconciliation does to secure and reproduce settler supremacy does not exist at that scale alone. It can also be found in the mundane contours of everyday life, in the settler sincerity of doing one's best to be a good neighbor on stolen land. Unlike the real racists who, we imagine, shout their racism out loud, the "good" settler erases the underlying structural conditions of settler colonialism through the insistence on their own good intentions, just as Daigle's spectacles stage colonial apology in order to assure the futurity of the settler state. In the process, the unsettling realities of colonial violence that maintain domination and the myriad way in which Indigenous Peoples refuse that domination are made to disappear.

### *Colonial Technologies*

Settler sincerity and the spectacle of reconciliation alike are produced through systematically interwoven colonial processes of erasure, which in this book I refer to more specifically as *technologies*. In adopting this formulation, I draw on both la paperson's (2017) and Michif scientist and theorist Max Liboiron's (2021) characterizations of "colonial technologies." "Instead of settler colonialism as an ideology, or a history," paperson writes, "you might consider settler colonialism as a set of technologies—a framework that could help you to forecast colonial next operations and to plot decolonial directions" (4) According to paperson, colonial technologies are polysemic and circulatory, traveling between overlapping spheres of domination, colonialism, and white supremacy: "Technologies are trafficked. Technologies generate patterns of social relations to land. Technologies mutate, and so do these relationships. Colonial technologies travel" (5).

The framework of colonial technologies as mobile and constitutive pushes us away from renderings of settler colonialism that confuse its structural character with stasis or rigidity. Colonialism moves and mutates, shifting opportunistically, configuring and reconfiguring relationships as forms of labor, logics, laws, and ideologies transform. Most importantly, technologies are *made*. The term's Greek root, *technê*, refers to the act of crafting, allowing us to understand technologies in the most fundamental sense as systems of made things, uniting concepts and practices in order to achieve colonial ends.

In adapting this rendering of colonial technology for a more specific theorization of erasure, I emphasize both the mutability of technologies and their ultimate nature as constructed systems. Colonial erasure does not simply exist. It must be enacted consistently, reiteratively, made and remade through means both discursive and material. The forms of erasure I expose and interrogate have ideological and symbolic coordinates—they are embedded in circulating discourses across settler colonial media and political landscapes, they are internalized as forms of settler (and, at times, Indigenous) subjectivity, and they have affective consequences. But they are inescapably material, aimed most directly at making the ongoing occupation of Indigenous lands by settler subjects appear as if it is not an occupation at all and at making the violence necessary to maintain this occupation appear as if it is not violence. As paperson forcefully asserts, what all colonial technologies have in common is their ultimate object: "Land—not just people—is the biopolitical target" (5). Though focused on domination, colonial technologies of erasure are not absolute; rather, they "tremble," as Povinelli (2016,16) might put it, always subject to being exposed and undermined no matter how fiercely they present themselves as part of the natural (settler) order of things.

This book engages three technologies of erasure in detail: *disavowal, empty signifiers*, and *colonial generosity*. These three technologies articulate closely with one another, and anchor the erasure embodied by the era of reconciliation. To disavow means to deny something that one knows to be true. Settler colonialism disavows Indigenous sovereignty; settler subjects "stubbornly insist" they own land that they in fact know they do not own. Empty signifiers refer to concepts that have been emptied of specific meaning but can be used as tools to unite political communities specifically because of their semiotic emptiness. Reconciliation itself is an empty signifier. Colonial generosity recasts domination as a gift and reframes thefts into acts of care. It is central to settler sincerity, from the mundane good intentions of everyday life to the spectacular performances of the state.

A final point that both la paperson and Liboiron make about technologies is that they are always available for appropriation or even inversion by anticolonial and antiracist actors, precisely because of their fragile, circulatory, and highly mutable nature. As we have already seen in this introduction and will see throughout this book, Indigenous responses to the era of reconciliation are not limited to "reconciliation is dead," though that is an intervention of signal importance. Rather, Indigenous people take up reconciliation strategically, making use of its emptiness for their own purposes; they invert the terms of colonial disavowal, and they offer ways for realizing colonial generosity and settler sincerity that would further Indigenous sovereignty rather than erase it. While colonial erasure might appear totalizing in individual instances, it is in fact an index of the fundamental precarity of the colonial enterprise itself. Otherwise, after all, there would be no settler anxieties about being compared to the "real racists" over in that other town, just down the road.

## Generative Refusal

### *Idle No More*

On October 12, 2012, the then–prime minister of Canada, Stephen Harper, leader of the Conservative Party of Canada, introduced the "Jobs and Growth Act," otherwise known as Bill C-45, into parliament. The proposed bill was rapidly critiqued for its erosion of environmental protections in Canada and for making it substantially easier for reserve land to be privatized, thus circumventing the previously established, relatively strenuous voting requirements for such measures within individual, federally funded First Nations (Jobs and Growth Act 2012). Perhaps the most significant response to the bill came, initially, from four Indigenous women, Jessica Gordon, Sylvia McAdam, Sheelah McLean, and Nina Wilson, who began a Facebook page in November of 2012 that they entitled "Idle No More." Idle No More—or #idlenomore, as it was often referred to, reflecting its digital origins—rapidly became an Indigenous-led mass movement in Canada, comprising everything from flash mobs, organized protests, and extensive digital activism to the public hunger strike of Chief Theresa Spence of the Attawapiskat First Nations (A. Simpson 2016).

Writing as the movement exploded, Leanne Betasamosake Simpson characterized Idle No More as an urgent next step in a long history of Indigenous activism in response to colonial, environmental devastation:

> As a Mississauga Nishinaabeg who has lost virtually all of our territory's land and waterways and who has been living without the treaty right to hunt and fish for 89 years, with less than 60 speakers left of our dialect, I cannot say this more strongly. We are the land and we need to do everything to protect what is left. We have the land today because our Ancestors . . . protected whatever they could for us. #idlenomore is standing upon the shoulders of generations of people

that were never idle because they couldn't afford to be idle. Neither can we. (L. Simpson 2012)

Settler colonialism, Betasamosake Simpson argues, is directly engaged in the destruction of Indigenous ways of living and the other-than-human beings with which Indigenous Peoples lived and continue to live. Reflecting on an encounter with a police officer who tried to arrest her and her children for "trespassing" during a ceremony at a sacred place, she writes, "Unfortunately this was not an isolated incident. In the last year alone, I have had settlers approach my family while we are harvesting rice, picking cedar, picking medicines, fishing, and finding rocks for our sweats. These interactions have yet to be friendly. Most of the time they are aggressive and racist. In all the incidences, there is an underlying assumption that I shouldn't be here in Kina Gchi Nishnaabeg-ogaming, in my territory. Being on the land, living as an Nishnaabekwe and doing things that connect my children to the land is seen as an aggressive act" (2012).

In Simpson's characterization, the heart of Idle No More is the assertion of the right to live as an Indigenous person. "For me, living as a Nishnaabekwe is a deliberate act—a direct act of resurgence, a direct act of sovereignty."

Idle No More was a direct refusal of colonial domination and the "death-making" politics—to borrow another phrase of Betasamosake Simpson's (2022)—of capitalist extraction and settler greed. At the same time, the movement offered alternative ways of imagining and understanding how life could be lived on the lands and waters claimed (and threatened) by settler colonial Canada, for Indigenous Peoples and perhaps even settler subjects. Refusals, in this sense, generated possibilities; they were aimed at futures beyond the colonial present. By early 2013, #idlenomore was all over the digital landscape, including my own social media. I remember in particular one post by a Haida friend, a photo of her newborn grandchild. The caption was simple: "This is my grandson. He is why I am Idle No More."

### *Blockades*

This relationship between the refusal of colonial domination and world-making is at the heart of the notion of generative refusal that I explore in this book. I draw heavily here on Betasamosake Simpson's recent *A Short History of the Blockade*, which originated as part of the CLC Kreisel Lecture Series at the University of Alberta. In her discussion, Betasamosake Simpson situates Indigenous blockades—sustained spaces of resistance against colonial excoriation and expropriation on Indigenous territories without Indigenous consent—as a model of generative refusal: "Indigenous blockades are indeed a refusal of the dominant political and economic systems of Canada. They are a refusal to accept erasure, banishment, disappearance, and death from our homelands. They are indeed an amplification and centring of Indigenous political economies—Indigenous forms of governance, economy, production, and exchange. They are indeed a resurgence of social and political practices, ethics and knowledge systems, and in this way they are a generative refusal" (L. Simpson 2021, 10; cf. A. Simpson 2014).

Indigenous refusal is never *just* negation. Indigenous activists are engaged in the systematic rejection of Canadian colonial domination, of erasure, of the expectations of their own death or disappearance. But this rejection is achieved precisely *through* what Betasamosake Simpson terms "resurgence" in this quote and later refers to more broadly as affirmation—through systematic engagement with Indigenous ways of knowing, thinking, acting, and being, activated in spaces and through strategies that oppose colonial domination. "Blockades," as Betasamosake Simpson writes, "are both a refusal and an affirmation. An affirmation of a different political economy. A world built upon a different set of relationships and ethics. An affirmation of life" (2021, 56).

It is this orientation to life as it should be lived—to *world-building*—that defines Betasamosake Simpson's twinned framing of Indigenous refusal and affirmation. She situates both her discussion and the Indigenous blockades she explores within a broader commitment to dialogical and respectful world-building practice that is always in opposition to the violence of colonial domination: "This land has taught me that Nishnaabeg life is continual, reciprocal, and reflective. Sometimes, it is a critical engagement with my ancestors, those yet to be born, and the nations of beings with whom I share land. It is a living constellation of co-resistance with all of the anti-colonial peoples and the world they build. This land has taught me that Nishnaabeg life is a persistent world-building process, despite of and in spite of the constant imposition of the colonial machinery of elimination" (2021, 3–4). Note that Betasamosake Simpson does not limit the world-building relationships with which she is concerned to human actors alone. Rather, she sketches out a world of relationships between humans, nonhumans, and the land, all of whom could be engaged together in respectful and generative ways of living. Being Nishnaabeg is what grounds these relationships for Simpson, but she is also careful to situate this perspective as just one of many possible articulations of Indigenous values, laws, and ethics, "in the spirit of Indigenous internationalism," as she terms it (12).

### *Grounded Normativities*

In conversation with Yellowknives Dene political theorist Glen Sean Coulthard, Betasomosake Simpson has used the term "grounded normativity" to refer to these "systems of ethics that are continuously generated by a relationship with a particular place, with land, through the Indigenous processes and knowledges that make up Indigenous life" (L. Simpson 2016, 22).[6] Grounded normativity is not simply and never exclusively *responsive* to the conditions of colonial domination, even though it might refuse them. Indeed, the stories that Simpson draws on her analysis of blockades go back to time immemorial, the ways in which beavers and humans—among other beings—formed relationships with each other. The term she uses more frequently to characterize the work of the blockade is in her Nishnaabe language, Nbwaakawin, "the practice of knowledge" (13): "A beaver dam, a blockade: / Life-giving. / Generative. / Affirmative. / A world-building place, governed by deep relationality. / An expansive fantastical sharing of space. / A network of life generating blockades that built and maintained the ecosystems that Nishnaabeg, Nehiyawak and Dene, for instance, lived as part of for thousands and thousands of years" (15–16). Nbwaakawin entails its own universe of understandings, values, and practices, which are, moreover, just one of the "Seven Grandfather Teachings" in Nishnaabeg tradition, only one aspect of the Nishnaabeg ethical systems from which Simpson has learned and upon which she draws.

Yahguudang, a Haida term that can be translated as "respect," does similar work to Nbwaakawin. Here, for instance, is one way that Haida curator and scholar Jisgang, Nika Collison, has summarized the concept: "One of the main laws of the Haida Nation is yahguudang, respect, meaning respect for all things: land, water and air; the Supernatural; our Ancestors, and each other. It is only when we show such respect that we can be worthy of respect ourselves. From this law, and many others of our Nation, comes the privilege of responsibility. As museum professionals and as human beings, we carry the responsibility to affect societal change by mainstreaming Canada's dark history with Indigenous peoples, while actively working to set things right" (Collison 2017).

Yahguudang, in Jisgang's formulation, explicitly refuses settler erasure; but, just as with Nbwaakawin, its significance is neither defined by its response nor limited to the conditions of colonial domination. Rather, yahguudang is the ethical ground for proper relationality, which compels responsibility—which, Jisgang is clear, is a privilege, not a burden or mere obligation—and forms the basis, in turn, of self-respect. It is a value that guides Haida policymaking and proper behavior in everyday life, a means of understanding how human nations can engage with each other and how different communities of being can show respect to each other (cf. Blackman 1992; Krmpotich 2014).[7]

The point is not, of course, that Nbwaakawin and yahguudang are identical or that they should be identified with each other. Rather, what I want to articulate here is that both guide different modes of Nishnaabeg and Haida life as it should be lived, expressing how these ways of living are always more than just resistance or refusal, and how these ways of being give meaning, revitalize traditions, and build better lives for humans and nonhumans. In this sense, I would suggest, we can think of both terms as "cognates" with each other. In classic anthropological (and jurisprudential) terms, a "cognate" is someone who is kin, who is family. It is in this sense that I use the term, rather than the more technically linguistic sense of words that share their derivations. Nbwaakawin, yahguudang, and so many other ideas are kin, part of an Indigenous network of relationships that are working together to build a better world both against and beyond colonial erasure.

This book emphasizes the generative aspect of generative refusal. The chapters focused on generative refusal are situated in the complex lived worlds of Haida people, past and present. They are not meant to represent any single, unified Haida "perspective," though they do explore commonalities of Haida experience under the ongoing conditions of settler colonialism. More importantly, though, they are about the social, political, and cultural worlds Haida people build, worlds that need not be monolithic in order to push beyond the constraints of colonial domination. Each of these chapters demonstrates the refusal of a particular technology of erasure, but they are even more concerned with the ways lives are lived and futures made through those moments of refusal.

## The Desire for Resolution

It is worth making clear that my goal in this book is explicitly not to advance the goal of reconciliation in Canada. I offer no suggestions for how reconciliation can be achieved, nor do I suggest that a "reconciled" Canada is either a necessary or desirable future for either Indigenous Peoples or settler subjects. Instead, I take inspiration from Unangax̂ scholar Eve Tuck's embrace of irreconcilability as productive, a means of pushing away from settler colonial desires for closure, resolution, and compatibility (2010, 640). The desire for resolution is at the heart of the era of reconciliation. A reconciled Canada is a Canada that would no longer be unsettled, that could be secure in its legitimacy. It would be a Canada that could finally fulfill the promise of being a "just society," in the famous words of the late former prime minister Pierre Trudeau.[8] My point is that we must refuse these promises entirely in order to recognize the ways that erasure and violence are co-constitutive of settler colonialism. We should not be imagining a better future for Canada; rather, we should work to imagine better futures in which Canadian colonialism has been abolished.

I write these words as a settler Canadian myself, whose background is in anthropology, who grew up on unceded xʷməθkʷəy̓əm (Musqueam), Sḵwx̱wú7mesh (Squamish), and Sel̓íl̓witulh (Tsleil-Waututh) territory, and who has worked with the Haida Nation and been a guest on their sovereign, unceded islands for more than a decade, the entirety of my professional life. As a Canadian settler subject, I am intimately familiar with the seductive quality of the settler promise of reconciliation, the imagined future in which Canada is always getting better and, thus, can be taken as fundamentally legitimate (and essentially good) in the present. As a professional settler scholar, I am equally familiar with the seductive quality of the critique of reconciliation, which offers non-Indigenous people like me the opportunity to separate themselves out from those naive Canadians who don't recognize that settler colonialism is ongoing and that reconciliation is itself a means of continuing domination. Both of these antithetical framings allow settler Canadians to feel as if they act in good faith, either with or against the colonial state; both of those framings allow for settler closure.

In emphasizing irreconcilability, I hope to push away from any such promises of closure, whether in the triumphant liberal or equally triumphant critical mode. *Irreconcilable* likewise does not attempt to adjudicate which Indigenous engagements with the era of reconciliation are more effective, whether it is "better" to forge negotiated futures under the concept's sign or to condemn reconciliation entirely. I wish instead to force reconciliation open, to make its erasures visible, and to offer some examples of how it can be refused and how alternative futures can be made that are not reconciled to the perpetual maintenance of settler colonialism. It is the structures of settler colonialism themselves that must be overcome, not simply made better or more humane.

## Outline of the Book

*Irreconcilable* proceeds from this introduction in three parts: "Disavowal," "Empty Signifiers," and "Colonial Generosity," named for the different technologies of erasure each part explores. This ordering is not arbitrary. Rather, these different technologies are nested within each other, with disavowal as the most foundational and colonial generosity resting on the other two. A full sense of the argument thus requires engaging the text linearly. That said, each chapter also has its own distinctive methodological and analytical commitments, including legal history (chapter 1), ethnography (chapter 2), cultural studies and political theory (chapter 3), semiotics and performance studies (chapter 4), museum studies (chapter 5), and ritual analysis (chapter 6), among others.

The first section, "Disavowal," engages erasure as constitutive of the settler colonial project, showing how disavowal structures Canadian law and the logics of military occupation and, in turn, how Indigenous people refuse those settler deceptions. Chapter 1, "'Harsh Realities' and Legal Fictions: Aboriginal Title and Colonial Disavowal in British Columbia, Past and Present," focuses on the concept of Aboriginal title in order to show how disavowal operates at the heart of Canadian law. Structured primarily as a synoptic history of Aboriginal title from the Royal Proclamation of 1763 to the Delgamuukw v. British Columbia decision of 1997, the chapter argues that the subordinate status of Aboriginal title to the Crown's jurisdiction is a legal fiction imposed on Indigenous people through violence. This imposition, I demonstrate, is recurrently disavowed throughout the history of British Columbia, which in turn forms the foundation for other genres of colonial disavowal.

Chapter 2, "'Not Built to Last': The Presences and Absences of Military Occupation on Haida Gwaii," moves the reader for the first time in the text into a sustained engagement with Haida Gwaii and the citizens of the Haida Nation. It aims to bring the reader directly into the social realities of the social world of military-Indigenous relations sketched out in chapter 1 through its focus on the history and afterlife of Canadian Forces Station Masset, a military base that was established on Haida Gwaii in the middle of the twentieth century. Canadian Forces Station Masset was officially decommissioned in 1997 and its buildings abandoned by Canada's Armed Forces. The understanding of both Haida and their settler neighbors was thus that the army was gone, leaving only ruins and ambivalent affects in its wake. The chapter is in part about those ruins and the conflicting, sometimes contradictory affects that both military presence and absence engendered for members of the Haida community. However, the military had not actually left; rather, it remained in concealment, continuing to monitor the territory it had occupied. What is at work in this strange juxtaposition of absence and presence, I argue, is the deliberate production of a paradox, a constitutive contradiction that serves to reinforce the structures of settler domination even as it mitigates the visible presence of the forces of occupation. Or, put another way, a long-term, durable, and yet simultaneously phantasmagoric mode of colonial disavowal. The affects of ruination engendered by the military's departure, I contend, form part of these processes of settler concealment and deception, allowing the reader to better understand how disavowal as settler social and political strategy plays out for Indigenous communities in day-to-day life.

The next section, "Empty Signifiers," explores how the era of reconciliation relies on emptying concepts and even legal and political processes of meaning so that they can be taken up toward essentially colonial political ends, though, I contend, this also makes these empty signifiers available for Indigenous resignification. Chapter 3, "'So-Called Reconciliation': Empty Signifiers and Settler Political Community," argues that the settler discourse of reconciliation in fact works to *empty* the signifier of reconciliation, voiding it of any concrete meaning that would entail structural transformation. Moreover, it shows how the empty signifier of reconciliation draws a circle around the Canadian political community that excludes Indigenous sovereignty and overt resistance against colonialism, labeling it, in Lenape scholar Joanne Barker's (2021) provocative formulation, as "indigenous terrorism." This enables settler reconciliation to *target* Indigenous sovereignty as an obstacle and enemy to Canada even as it continually reinscribes its good intentions for Indigenous-settler relations.

Chapter 4, "'Our Drums Are (Not) Silenced': Refusing the Ruse of Liberal Fairness in the Commission of Inquiry," grounds the critiques of chapter 3 through a case study: the hearings of the Joint-Review Panel (JRP) on the Enbridge Gateway Pipeline that took place on Haida Gwaii between 2012 and 2013. Such hearings have become a primary mechanism through which "the rubber hits the road," so to speak, in terms of how reconciliation is actually *enacted* in Canadian spaces. In particular, the article takes up the consistent critique leveled against the panel that its procedural form silenced Indigenous voices while rhetorically performing the claim that the hearings represented a sincere engagement with Indigenous perspectives. It links the JRP to a long history of commissions in British Columbia that engaged in this precise mode of procedural silencing, epitomized by the reserve allocation commissions of the late nineteenth and early twentieth centuries. It thus argues that the commission form is a powerful tool for colonial domination, masking its domination in the language of equity and fairness. However, the chapter then demonstrates the ways in which Haida participants in the JRP process refused this precise equation, reshaping the "stage" of the hearings in order to make their views known. The language of fairness, even the very idea of a "hearing" itself, are remade through these actions, demonstrating both the semiotic fluidity of the commission of inquiry form—in particular, its capacity for reappropriation—and the skillful navigation of the language *and* limits of liberalism by Indigenous actors.

The final section of the text, "Colonial Generosity," explores the ways in which notions of care, fairness, and equality can be put to use as grounds for the justification of colonial violence and appropriation. Repatriation—the return of goods, belongings, or people to their home nation—appears in this section as both an exemplar of these problematic strategies of disavowal and a means through which Indigenous people refashion social and political futures and, in particular, redefine the relationships that *should* exist between settler states and Indigenous Nations. Chapter 5, "'Objects with Invalid Title': Myths, Fantasies, and Other Liberal Fictions of Legitimate Museum Acquisition," turns to the repatriation of Indigenous cultural belongings from settler state and private museums, one of the most visible and significant ongoing concerns in Canadian-Indigenous relations. It begins with an overview of the repatriation policies of some of Canada's more significant museums—the Canadian Museum of History, the Royal British Columbia Museum, and the Royal Alberta Museum—each of which has been noted for being progressive in relation to repatriation claims. The chapter demonstrates how this "progressiveness" arrives at its limit with the concept of "fair purchase"—items that were recorded as having been sold by Indigenous actors of their own free will, particularly as the concept has been applied to material collected prior to the mid-twentieth century. The chapter argues that "fair purchase" inscribes a liberal, entrepreneurial subject into the colonial archive, whose ability to sell freely and fairly was not impacted by the decimation of colonially introduced diseases, the implementation of oppressive, anti-Indigenous laws and policies, or the very violence of colonial settlement. In so doing, it argues, it naturalizes colonial laws as essential arbitrators of value and legitimacy, making the violent bases of these laws disappear.

Chapter 6, "'Giving Back the Name with Respect': Repatriation and Refusal between Canada and the Haida Nation," turns to a very different rendering of the concept of reconciliation, one articulated not by settler institutions but, rather, by Haida political leaders. On June 17, 2010, representatives of the Council of the Haida Nation held a ceremony to formally return the "Queen Charlotte Islands," a name that had been colonially imposed on Haida Gwaii, their ancestral homeland and sovereign territory, since the nineteenth century. This ceremonial return is analyzed as a process through which the Haida Nation can incorporate settler governance into a regime of respectful relations that functions on Haida terms. Framed simultaneously as the rejection of an unacceptable imposition and a respectful act of relationality in its own right, the ceremony offers a searing critique of colonial domination and invites settler powers into an alternative modality of relationship based in mutual understanding and respect. It is repatriation freed from the monopoly of the settler state, one that attempts to communicate mutuality rather than the liberal generosity of an occupying power. Through this process, I argue, the Council of the Haida Nation constitutes itself concurrently as a particular kind of political entity with clear traditional antecedents and essentially equal—if not superior—relationships with foreign governing powers.

The book ends with an "Outro" and then a short coda rather than a conclusion, marking the open-ended nature of its analysis of irreconcilability in the era of reconciliation. Entitled "Irreconcilable Images, Irreconcilable Futures," the outro ends the book by returning one final time to Haida Gwaii and the ruins of Canadian Forces Station Masset. In particular, it contrasts the appropriation of a Haida design by former Liberal prime minister Justin Trudeau as a tattoo on his own body with graffiti that has now been painted on the ruins of the military base in the town of Masset, painted by both Indigenous and settler high school students. Trudeau's tattoo, the conclusion argues, figures the colonial erasure at the heart of Canadian multiculturalism, in which the country's leader can literally inscribe a proprietary Indigenous design on his body without either permission or proper relationality. He can thus display his seeming affiliation with indigeneity while erasing Indigenous rights *to* their own possessions. This contrast sharply with the messages of Haida sovereignty, respect for others, and self-love that the student graffiti foregrounds, helping us, in turn, understand the fragility of these forms of appropriation and to work against their looping, reiterative erasures. The coda that follows ends the text with a discussion of the significance of the Gaayhllxid/Gíhlagalgang "Rising Tide" Haida Title Lands Agreement, which was signed between the province of British Columbia and the Council of the Haida Nation in April of 2024.

# PART I | Disavowal

CHAPTER ONE

# Harsh Realities and Legal Fictions

## *Aboriginal Title and Colonial Disavowal in British Columbia, Past and Present*

### A Matter of Law

In his 2022 decision in the case of Thomas and Saik'uz First Nation v. Rio Tinto Alcan Inc.—a case in which two Dakelh First Nations sued the Rio Tinto Alcan corporation for the impact on fish stocks of the construction and operation of a hydroelectric dam in their traditional territories—the Honourable Mr. Justice Nigel P. Kent posed a question that has always been at the core of settler colonialism in the province of British Columbia. "One might rightly ask," the justice writes, "if the land and its resources were owned by Indigenous peoples before the arrival of Europeans, how, as a matter of law, does the mere assertion of European sovereignty result in the Crown acquiring radical or underlying title? How and why does pre-existing Indigenous title somehow become subordinate?" (Thomas and Saik'uz First Nation 2022, para. 196).

The fact that Justice Kent even poses the question in these terms here represents a stark transformation in the logics of Canadian colonial law, one that builds on decades of court cases in which Indigenous plaintiffs have attempted to assert their sovereignty and their jurisdiction over their own traditional territories in the courts of British Columbia. In the first instance, it takes as given the existence of Indigenous, or Aboriginal title, a subordinate title to the underlying title of the Crown—that is, the colonial government of Canada—but, nonetheless, a legal formation that grants the existence of at least limited Indigenous land rights without the settler colony. And yet, unextinguished Aboriginal title was only recognized in British Columbia at the tail end of the twentieth century, a result of the iterative changes to Canadian legal understandings brought on by those many court cases.

More radical is Justice Kent's dismissal of the legitimacy of both "the doctrines of discovery and *terra nullius*" as "legally invalid" (para. 194), an assertion that was, in 2022, virtually without precedent in Canada's courts. The doctrines of discovery and *terra nullius* are foundational to the legitimacy of Canadian colonialism. They refer, respectively, to a set of ideas articulated in a series of late-fifteenth-century papal bulls that stated that land discovered by European powers would fall under their sovereign dominion and the accompanying premise that land occupied by Indigenous Peoples was "empty land" because it was not "properly" cultivated according to European agricultural imaginaries, as per John Locke's *Second Treatise on Government* (e.g., R. Miller 2019; C. Harris 2002). If Native people(s) did not truly own their land, then it was ripe for European possession, and the process of violent conquest could be recast as a simple and straightforward assertion of legitimate jurisdiction over land that was otherwise not truly occupied (Tully 1995). This idea, Justice Kent asserts, has no legal validity.

Likewise, he suggests, it makes little sense to imagine, on the one hand, that Aboriginal title exists as subordinate to the Crown's radical title when, on the other, this title only "crystalized" when the Crown asserted its own sovereignty over the lands and waters over which Indigenous Peoples were understood to have only partial title. "Some argue," Justice Kent concludes, "in my view correctly, that the whole construct is simply a legal fiction to justify the de facto seizure and control of the land and resources formerly owned by the original inhabitants of what is now Canada" (Thomas and Saik'uz First Nation 2022, para. 198).

Though Justice Kent ultimately decided the case in favor of the corporate defendants, his written decision seems at first glance to puncture the entire legal and ideological edifice on which the legitimacy of settler colonialism in British Columbia rests. If "the whole construct" from the doctrines of discovery and *terra nullius* to the subordinate nature of Aboriginal title is "simply a legal fiction," then, we might wonder, what ground does Canadian colonialism have left to stand on? How could Justice Kent's decision not represent a sea change, a signal moment in the history of Canada in which, at last, the fictional nature of colonial legitimacy stands exposed? Such is not, however, the nature of settler colonial domination in the era of reconciliation.

In the paragraphs that immediately follow this eviscerating critique of colonialism, Justice Kent instead reasserts the inevitability of ongoing colonial domination in the territories Canada continues to claim as its own. He reasoned:

> [201] Still, regardless of any legal frailties underlying the Crown's assertion of sovereignty over British Columbia in 1846, the plaintiffs' claims confront certain harsh realities, unpalatable though they may be to many.

> [202] First and foremost is the fact that the system of law and government imported by settlers into British Columbia and superimposed upon Indigenous peoples has become firmly and intractably entrenched. It is the foundation for Canadian society as it exists today. The laws relating to ownership of land are the basis for this country's wealth and the very foundation for its economy. It is these same laws which provide legitimacy to this Court.
>
> [203] As the Court noted in Delgamuukw, "we are all here to stay," and while the legal justification for Crown sovereignty may well be debatable, its existence is undeniable and its continuation is certain. (Thomas and Saik'uz First Nation 2022, paras. 201–3)

Even though Crown sovereignty is, in essence, fictional, it remains a "harsh reality" for Justice Kent: "We are all here to stay." Justice Kent's seemingly paradoxical logic is, I argue in this chapter, an instance of colonial disavowal. Disavowal, following political theorist Kevin Bruyneel, is "an active form of deflection from the implications and obligations to attend to what one knows" (2021, 3). To disavow is to know something is not true—Crown sovereignty, for instance—but to believe in it anyway, because otherwise the whole colonial order might fall apart.

If not for Justice Kent's disavowal, then what Mohawk anthropologist Audra Simpson terms the "meta-claims of the state" might no longer make sense, the stories that Canadian institutions and individual citizens can tell about themselves in which settler states such as Canada are peaceful, legitimate political entities that govern with the consent of their citizens and Indigenous Peoples are "citizens" of the settler state like any other (2016, 9). In these tellings, the reality that Indigenous Nations are occupied polities that can, and do, refuse the occupation of their lands and waters and resist, sometimes forcefully, the forces of colonialism is made to disappear. "This disappearance," Simpson writes, "keeps things in their place, the narratives, the politics, the distributions in power that allow for land to still be taken, for Indigenous identities as well to be violated and stolen because it is presumed that Indigenous peoples are not here to claim each other, to stand up for each other and themselves" (10).

Thus, even Justice Kent's seemingly unequivocal condemnation of the legal basis of settler colonialism in British Columbia is folded back into that very project, representing yet one more means through which settler authorities reify colonial occupation and disavow its contingency. It becomes fodder for the discursive project of the era of reconciliation, one more means to compel Indigenous Peoples to accept their own domination because it is inevitable, a "harsh reality" that is, at worst, unpalatable to some. The work of the court, for Justice Kent, is precisely reconciliation: "The task of the Court is therefore to somehow reconcile continued settler occupation and Crown sovereignty with the acknowledged pre-existence of Aboriginal societies. In my view, such reconciliation will not likely entail wholesale evisceration of common-law concepts such as private ownership of land or the enforceability of contractual obligations" (Thomas and Saik'uz First Nation 2022, para. 203). This legal reconciliation cannot be reconciled, however, with its own contradictions. Nor can it be reconciled with the ongoing actions of Indigenous Peoples who, as Simpson reminds us, are not willing to simply take these fictional assertions as the harsh realities that Justice Kent takes as inescapable.

This chapter explores these legal irreconcilabilities in British Columbia. In it, I make three interrelated claims. First, I follow Justice Kent's initial critique in maintaining that settler colonialism in Canada is based on legal and ideological fictions and, thus, is an unstable formation. Second, I suggest that the need to maintain those fictions in the face of contradictory realities generates colonial paradoxes such as the ones that Justice Kent grapples with: for instance, that British Columbia is at once occupied illegally and that this illegal occupation is itself part of the basis for the ongoing legal system of the settler colony. Third, I argue, faced with this and other such colonial paradoxes, settler authorities such as Justice Kent at once acknowledge and dismiss them via disavowal, the assertion that irreconcilable contradictions are not *really* contradictions and, thus, can somehow be reconciled in such a way as to maintain the colonial order of things. Disavowal acts here as a technology of erasure that maintains settler colonialism as inevitable, as a "harsh reality" that we cannot imagine living without. Ultimately, however, disavowal cannot sustain the contradictions of colonial (il)legitimacy, and it exposes, rather than conceals, the actual harsh reality that Canadian domination is maintained not via any inherent right or any unimpeachable legal jurisdiction but, rather, through the simple and brutal monopoly on force.

I lay out this this argument initially through a historical sketch of the constitution of Aboriginal title in the territories now claimed as the province of British Columbia. In this sketch I touch on the history of settlement in the province and some of the most significant cases that have shifted how colonial law apprehends this title over the course of the twentieth century, but only in so far as these different historical and legal moments help define the operation of colonial disavowal. I thereby show how disavowal is a technology that is at once protean and opportunistic and, yet, at the same time remarkably and constitutively consistent over the past two and a half centuries. The deception embedded in the development of the category of Aboriginal title in turn acts as a foundation for other modes of colonial disavowal, which I highlight in the final third of the chapter with an analysis of Canadian federal and provincial apologies and articulations of shame over colonial violence that is always presented as part of a "dark" past that the nation-state has now transcended. Before proceeding, though, it is useful to offer an expanded articulation of how I am using the concept of disavowal in this analysis.

## "I Know Well, But"

In *Settler Memory: The Disavowal of Indigeneity and the Politics of Race in the United States*, political theorist Kevin Bruyneel places disavowal at the heart of his analysis of settler societies' selective remembrance of indigeneity. "Settler memory," Bruyneel writes, "refers to the way in which a settler society habitually reproduces memories of Indigenous people's history and of settler colonial violence and dispossession, and in the same moment undercuts the political relevance of this memory by *disavowing* the presence of Indigenous people as contemporary agents and of settler colonialism as a persistent shaping force" (2021, xiii).

Bruyneel's goal is to capture the slippery quality of the "settler" aspect of settler colonialism in the United States, how Americans can figure themselves as legitimate inheritors of the country's Indigenous past while simultaneously erasing the ongoing work of colonialism in the present. Accomplishing this substantial collective doublethink, Bruyneel suggests, requires that Americans disavow indigeneity. Bruyneel's characterization of disavowal as an "active deflection" from engaging with what settler subjects in fact already know (3) is in many senses similar to its classic formulation in Freudian psychoanalysis, pithily represented by French psychoanalyst Octave Mannoni with the phrase "I know well, but all the same." It refers to the patient's capacity to know something is not true, but to believe in it nonetheless (2003, 70).

Bruyneel makes clear, drawing on the writing of James Baldwin, that the problem of disavowal is political rather than epistemological (or, for that matter, psychoanalytic).[1] That is to say, disavowal is a response to a "threat white people sense will be posed to their individual and collective identities, power, and status if they were to act upon what they know" as opposed to a simple question of knowledge, of what a white subject actually knows or does not know in white supremacist society (3). Bruyneel applies Baldwin's analysis to the dynamics of settler colonialism, which, he suggests, are bound up in white supremacy but not reduceable to it.[2] What is denied in settler colonial society, Bruyneel argues, is the ongoing existence of Indigenous Peoples themselves, the fact that the colonial state has not successfully erased or replaced the Indigenous communities whose territories the settler colony continues to occupy. A liberal commitment to greater "awareness" of colonialism would not resolve the issue; settler disavowal is active, a choice made at the intersections of social and psychic life to deliberately deny the evident realities of Indigenous existence under settler colonialism. This is disavowal par excellence: "I know well" that Indigenous Peoples are actually not extinct, "but all the same" I will believe that they are, in order to justify my own sense of myself and my nation.

Disavowal is not a problem of knowledge. The question of how much information to which a given settler subject might have access in relation to Indigenous existence is effectively immaterial; disavowal operates to refuse what one knows, not in the vacuum of simple ignorance. But what is the status of this refusal? Bruyneel, following Baldwin, understands it as active, which might imply that disavowal is at the very least intentional, if not always conscious. This is an important point, particularly given the implicit claim Bruyneel is making as a settler scholar that it is possible for settler subjects not to disavow indigeneity or colonial violence, a conviction and positionality that I share. Were this effacement completely unconscious it would give settler colonial domination a totalizing quality that belies its own instability, rendering it an ontological rather than historical formation. This is an approach Bruyneel rejects.

The intentionality of disavowal in Bruyneel's formulation does not, however, render it monolithically stable and consistent for settler subjects. We might thus productively complement Bruyneel's analysis with anthropologist Eva Mackey's characterization of "settler anxiety," which she defines as a "defensive hardening of unexamined self-evident assumptions" (2016, 36). This anxiety emerges in Canada, Mackey writes, because "Indigenous people making *a priori* claims to land, sovereignty, and ways of being indicates that the settler project is not complete, reveals settler certainties as fantasies of entitlement, and shows how the precarious and illogical claims to settler sovereignty must be constantly reinvented and defended" (35–36). When confronted with the fundamental instability of the settler colonial project, Mackey contends, settlers' taken-for-granted assumptions about reality are necessarily unsettled and, in response, they respond defensively.

It is precisely the instability of settler colonialism as a formation built on "precarious and illogical claims" that compels disavowal, the attempt to stabilize an unstable structure by maintaining that the foundational (in every sense) problem of colonialism's illegitimacy is not really a problem at all. In Freudian psychoanalysis, disavowal, which is similarly both foundational (in this instance, to childhood development) and unstable, relies on a fetish to act as a kind of stabilizing force so that the subject can function psychologically (Freud 1961). But what could stabilize the settler anxieties that Mackey writes about? One answer, as we see throughout this book, is the promise of the era of reconciliation: The problems of colonialism are no longer really problems, and they will all be reconciled as Canada moves toward an integrated, multicultural future as sovereign Indigenous polities are reconciled to their own political disappearance. Such an imagined reconciliation is particularly tempting because it enables the disavowal of the harshest reality of all: Negotiations between Indigenous Peoples and settler authorities always come, as the Unist'ot'en Land Defenders remind us, "at the barrel of a gun" (Unist'ot'en 2020). Canadian settlers enforce their domination over Indigenous territories and people through military and martial forces, in the present just as in colonial history.

## "Under Our Protection"

### *The Royal Proclamation of 1763*

The concept of Aboriginal title in Canada, by most settler accounts, originates in the Royal Proclamation of 1763, issued by King George III after Britain's victory in the Seven Years War and its consolidation of New France into the British colonial territories that would become the provinces of Quebec and Ontario in Canada. Issued to sediment British jurisdiction over those territories, the Royal Proclamation also contained the first formal British acknowledgment of what eventually be termed, first, "Indian" and then Aboriginal or Indigenous title (Wood and Rossiter 2022, 8; cf. Borrows 1997). The relevant passage in the proclamation reads as follows: "And whereas it is just and reasonable, and essential to our Interest, and the Security of our Colonies, that the several Nations or Tribes of Indians with whom We are connected, and who live under our Protection, should not be molested or disturbed in the Possession of such Parts of Our Dominions and Territories as, not having been ceded to or purchased by Us, are reserved to them, or any of them, as their Hunting Grounds" (George III 1763, 5).

While the term "title" is not used in the proclamation in relation to Indigenous Nations, the framework it sets out is precisely the subordinate structure that Justice Kent criticized more than two hundred years later. The several "Nations or Tribes of Indians" have what land that has not been "ceded to or purchased by Us . . . reserved to them" as their "Hunting grounds." But this is not a recognition of autonomous Indigenous sovereignty. Rather, the proclamation clearly positions Native Nations as under the "Protection" of the British Crown, and those lands are reserved, the Proclamation later states explicitly, under the "Sovereignty, Protection, and Dominion" of the Crown. Taken on paper, the Royal Proclamation seems to state clearly that Native Tribes or Nations must cede or sell their land for it to be acquired for colonial settlement but, at the same time, that this is a specific allowance made by the Crown *for* those tribes, not in any sense an inherent Indigenous right.

As Anishinaabe/Ojibway legal scholar John Borrows has argued, the text of the proclamation was not an invention of British imagination in a vacuum. Rather, Borrows details, it was the product of extensive and complex negotiation between British and Indigenous actors in the mid-eighteenth century. Indigenous actors were not passive "victims of a greater power," but participated directly in the negotiations that led to the proclamation and the Treaty of Niagara, which Borrows characterizes as the "other half" of the Royal Proclamation (1997, 155). The contradictions of the Royal Proclamation were thus in direct response to the exigencies of those negotiations, as British officials wished to expand their own power in their putative colony but also pacify Indigenous Peoples and convince them that their own territories were not under threat of arbitrary seizure. The proclamation thus had two inherently contradictory objectives. First, British colonists wished to "convince First Nations that the British would respect existing political and territorial jurisdiction by incorporating First Nations understandings of this relationship in the document . . . , implying that no lands would be taken from First Nations peoples without their consent" (160). Second, and in direct contradiction, the proclamation was a clear and explicit attempt by the Crown to "exercise sovereignty over First Nations" (161), signaled both by the language of care and protection and by the assumption that the Crown *already* had jurisdiction over the territories "reserved" to Indigenous Nations.

The Royal Proclamation is thus an exercise in disavowal, asserting British sovereignty over Indigenous Peoples while at the same time seeming to assure them that they will retain their political autonomy. This is particularly evident in the way in which the proclamation treats Aboriginal rights to land, as Borrows articulates:

> These rights and their potential removal were affirmed by three principles or procedures: 1) colonial governments were forbidden to survey or grant any unceded lands; 2) colonial governments were forbidden to allow British subjects to settle on Indian lands or to allow private individuals to purchase them; and 3) there was an official system of public purchases developed in order to extinguish Indian title. In implementing these principles an area of land was designated as First Nation territory. The boundaries were determined by past cessions and existing First Nation possessions. These principles codified pre-existing First Nation/colonial practice and reflected some First Nation preferences in maintaining territorial integrity and decision-making power over their lands. These principles simultaneously worked against First Nation preferences by enabling the Crown to enlarge its powers by creating a process to take land away from First Nations. (160)

There was no preexisting legal basis for the Crown's assertion of jurisdiction over the territory of these First Nations; indeed, the Treaty of Niagara, which immediately followed the Royal Proclamation in 1764, affirmed that the relationships between First Nations and the Crown were a "multination alliance in which no member gave up their sovereignty" (161). And yet, the proclamation laid out a set of structures and processes through which Aboriginal land rights were always-already given as subordinate to the absolute title of the Crown, and, further, asserted that these rights could be extinguished through a set of processes laid out by that same Crown. Native people were thus rendered colonial subjects in a document that disavowed that very process as it was happening.[3] By the time of Canada's confederation in 1867, political geographers Patricia Burke Wood and David Rossiter write, "Indigenous peoples were no longer regarded as a constitutive political community by the colonial government." Rather, they had been "reduced to 'subjects of the Crown' without any consensual legal basis," paving the way for the "second-class and depoliticized status of Indigenous people in the *Indian Act* of 1876" (2022, 9).

### *"The True and Absolute Lords"*

While the Royal Proclamation's assertion of a limited form of Aboriginal title represented a form of colonial disavowal that concealed colonial attempts to erase Indigenous sovereignty, the proclamation was itself disavowed in the early years of the "settlement" of what would become the province of British Columbia. This settlement process began—at least formally—with the signing of the Oregon Treaty, in 1846.[4] Said treaty "resolved" the question of sovereignty over the Oregon Territory, officially dividing it between two contesting parties, the United States and the British Empire, assigning Vancouver Island and the mainland north of the Forty-Ninth Parallel to Britain.[5] As geographer and historian Cole Harris points out, the Oregon Treaty made no mention of Indigenous Peoples (2002, 15). The British Crown then officially granted Vancouver Island to the Hudson's Bay Company, recognizing the company as "the true and absolute lords and proprietors of the same territories, limits, and places, and all other premises (saving always the faith, allegiance, and sovereign dominion due to Us, Our heirs, and successors for the same" (quoted in C. Harris 2002, 16). The only mention made of Indigenous Peoples in the grant from the Crown was, simply, that the colonization of Vancouver Island should be conducive to "their protection and welfare" (16).

Much as in the Royal Proclamation, the language of imperial care masked the fact that the Crown was assuming it had sovereign jurisdiction over lands and waters that belonged to other people. Such an assumption was only possible, legal scholar Kent McNeil has suggested, due to the normative presumptions of the doctrines of discovery and *terra nullius*, which had themselves been codified legally in the United States by Chief Justice John Marshall. "Discovery of parts of North America," McNeil writes, "gave the discovering nation an underlying title to the land and an exclusive right to purchase the Indian's right of occupancy" (2016, 704). However, in the case of what would become British Columbia, even that "right of occupancy" was predominantly ignored. This, Cole Harris argues, was a more specific response to the recent Treaty of Waitangi in Aotearoa (New Zealand), which many in the British Colonial Office had come to feel had recognized too many rights and too much authority, relatively speaking, for the Māori. Given this risk, these colonial officials felt, they must avoid any policies that "might turn out [an] impediment in the way of colonization" (2002, quoted on 16). The simplest and most expedient route to colonization, then, lay in ignoring even the possibility that Native Nations had any preexisting land rights whatsoever, a position well supported by contemporary understandings of Indigenous people as "savage" and incapable of understanding property laws or possessing land accordingly (Bhandar 2018).

The Royal Proclamation thus posed a problem for these early colonial authorities, as neither Vancouver Island nor, indeed, the entirety of what would become the province of British Columbia had been ceded or was in the process of being ceded by any Native Nations through treaty or sale. In other words, the Crown had granted possession to the Hudson's Bay Company of territories over which it did not, in fact, have legitimate possession, as no Indigenous Nations had ceded their land to the Crown by treaty or any other means. The British Colonial Office at the time simply punted the issue, so to speak, notifying the company that "in parting with the land of the island Her Majesty parts only with her own right therein, and that whatever measures she was bound to take in order to extinguish the Indian title are equally obligatory on the Company" (quoted in C. Harris 2002, 16). Ultimately, however, with the exception of the "Douglas Treaties," a small group of treaties signed on Vancouver Island in the 1850s and not subsequently honored, neither the Hudson's Bay Company nor the early settler governments of British Columbia that followed entered into any treaties or processes that would fulfill the terms of the Royal Proclamation and formally extinguish Aboriginal title anywhere in what, in 1871, became the province of British Columbia in the newly confederated country of Canada.

One can put this starkly. Under the terms of Britain's own laws, the colonial occupation of British Columbia was illegal (e.g., Borrows 2015, 111). Colonial land grants could not be given to territories that had not been sold or ceded by Indigenous people; however, colonial authorities proceeded as if this was not an issue, and that there was no Aboriginal title to lands to begin with. It was simply assumed that first British and then Canadian settlers had a right to the lands they were colonizing, and that despite Britain's own laws, Indigenous Peoples did not. "At its most basic level," writes Harris, "the settler discourse surrounding the Native Land question [in the 1860s] was simple and pervasive." While there was a certain degree of settler disagreement over the terms of colonial land grants *to* settlers, "The proposition that almost all provincial land was unsettled and unused . . . was not debated. Natives were wanderers, primitive people who did not know how to use land effectively" (2002, 46). In other words, most settlers took for granted that the land was freely available to become their property, and that, in turn, once it had become their property, it was theirs by law. Conversely, Native people had no corollary right to preempt land except by special dispensation of the Crown (Bhandar 2018, 60).

This double move acts as a foundation for what critical theorist Robert Nichols has termed the "recursive dispossession" of Indigenous Peoples: "For instance, in a standard formulation one would assume that 'property' is logically, chronologically and normatively prior to 'theft.' However, in this 'colonial' context, theft is the mechanism and means by which property is generated, hence its recursivity. Recursive dispossession is effectively a form of property-generating theft" (2020, 9). Unable to claim their land as their own or even to (re)acquire it under colonial laws, Indigenous Peoples become understood as "original owners" only ever *retroactively*, once their territories have already been appropriated (8).

There is a complex, nested structure of disavowal at work here. The Royal Proclamation, in the first instance, was already at work disavowing Indigenous sovereignty, making it appear as if the Crown had already gained jurisdiction over territories that had never been ceded to it. This assumption of jurisdiction was maintained in the colonization of what would become British Columbia, but even the limited Aboriginal title recognized in the proclamation was disavowed for the sake of settler convenience. The future province was thus made available for settlement, but on the basis of systematic fictions that were not even internally consistent, much less in conversation with any of the actual Indigenous Nations whose lands and waters were being stolen.

And just as in the present, these Indigenous Peoples did not passively accept either the theft of their lands or the disavowals that made those thefts appear legitimate in settler eyes. The 1860s marked the beginning of the survey, demarcation, and "allocation" processes that would eventually create the reserve geography of British Columbia—allocation here marked in quotes to signal that, in effect, First Nations were being constrained to tiny portions of their own land through settler fiat. From the beginning of this process, Indigenous Peoples contested, opposed, and refused the legitimacy of settler surveys and policies. As one missionary wrote to the governor of British Columbia at the behest of a Nicola chief, the "Indians . . . never will be reconciled to receive in peace and content the land as now offered for their acceptance and enjoyment" (quoted in C. Harris 2002, 62). Indigenous Peoples, in other words, found their spatial restriction to small reserves an irreconcilable prospect, one that was ultimately forced on them through the threat and deployment of force of arms. The sheer frequency with which gunboats were deployed by colonial agents in order to "pacify" recalcitrant Native communities led one historian to coin the term "gunboat diplomacy" in reference to the colonial policies of the period (Gough 1984, e.g. 17), a euphemism that could itself be read as a disavowal.

Through these twinned processes of colonial purchase and reserve allocation, the lands and waters of the Northwest were sedimented under settler colonial law as the province of British Columbia, an ostensibly legitimate territory split between settler private land holdings and Crown land, including the territory "granted" to Indigenous Nations as reserves. In 1927, furthermore, a federal government committee concluded that "Crown sovereignty in BC was certain and Indian Title nonexistent" (Wood and Rossiter 2022, 31), bringing the federal position on the absence of Aboriginal title in the province in line with both the de facto position of the early colonial bureaucrats and the policies of the provincial government they ultimately built.

This, in brief, is the settler edifice to which Justice Kent was referring in his 2022 decision: "First and foremost is the fact that the system of law and government imported by settlers into British Columbia and superimposed upon Indigenous peoples has become firmly and intractably entrenched. It is the foundation for Canadian society as it exists today. The laws relating to ownership of land are the basis for this country's wealth and the very foundation for its economy. It is these same laws which provide legitimacy to this Court" (Thomas and Saik'uz First Nation 2022, para. 202). While Indigenous Peoples did not reconcile themselves to this edifice, by the turn of the twentieth century the only space left available for contestation that would not immediately be met with military force was in the arenas of the settler colony itself, from attempts at negotiation at the hearings associated with reserve allocation (more on these in chapter 4) to political organizing within and between Nations (see Tennant 1990) and, finally, the landmark land claims cases of the late twentieth century into the present. It is to those cases we now turn, and the attempts of settler lawyers and judges to reconcile the irreconcilable through disavowal.

## The Crown's Pleasures and Burdens, or, Plus ça Change . . .

In 1967, Frank Calder and a group of his fellow Nis*g*a'a elders sued the provincial government of British Columbia, alleging that their Aboriginal title to their lands had never been lawfully extinguished. The subsequent court case, Calder v. Attorney General of British Columbia, was a landmark in the history of Canadian colonial law. While the Nis*g*a'a Chiefs case was dismissed in the BC Supreme Court and the Court of Appeals, the Supreme Court of Canada, reviewing the case on appeal, affirmed in principle that Aboriginal title existed in British Columbia, the first such affirmation in Canadian legal history. The court split, however, on whether or not Nis*g*a'a title itself still existed, with three justices maintaining that it had never been extinguished by treaty or other lawful means, and three others arguing that Canadian Confederation and colonial control over Nis*g*a'a land by definition had extinguished their title. The case was ultimately dismissed by the seventh justice on a technicality (Calder v. Attorney General of British Columbia 1973).

Wood and Rossiter describe the *Calder* decision as "both decisive and indecisive. It confirmed in Canadian law the existence of Aboriginal title, but it made no definitive declaration as to what this title meant" (2022, 70). This ambiguity, it should be clear, was not an issue with the submissions by Frank Calder and his fellow chiefs, as summarized in the *Calder* decision: "The Nishgas claim that their title arises out of aboriginal occupation; that recognition of such a title is a concept well embedded in English law; that it is not dependent on treaty, executive order or legislative enactment (1973, 318). This "aboriginal occupation" was expanded on by Calder himself, in his testimony:

> Put it this way, in answer to your question, from time immemorial the Nishgas have used the Naas River and all its tributaries within the boundaries so submitted, the lands in Observatory Inlet, the lands in Portland Canal, and part of Portland Inlet. We still hunt within those lands and fish in the waters, streams and rivers, we still do, as in time past, have our campsites in these areas and we go there periodically, seasonally, according to the game and the fishing season, and we still maintain these sites and as far as we know, they have been there as far back as we can remember. We still roam these territories, we still pitch our homes there whenever it is required according to our livelihood and we use the land as in times past, we bury our dead within the territory so defined and we still exercise the privilege of free men within the territory so defined. (349)

Equally importantly, and reiterated throughout *Calder*, was the simple fact that the Nis*g*a'a had never ceded any of this territory, never accepted the reduction of these territories to the reserves "granted" by the Crown, and at no point had given up their right to sovereignty or self-determination. But these claims posed problems when translated into the terms of Canadian property law, even if the Supreme Court had recognized the existence of Aboriginal title in principle. Did title confer fee simple ownership of land? If not, how could "use rights" and "occupation rights" for Aboriginal people be defined, and by whom? And what to do about the fact that the Nis*g*a'a claim represented far more territory than had been "set aside" for them by the provincial reserve allocation processes of the late nineteenth and early twentieth centuries?

Answers to some of these questions came twenty years later, in the Supreme Court's 1997 decision on the case of Delgamuukw v. British Columbia.[6] Building on *Calder* and the growing body of land claims cases brought to provincial and, ultimately, federal courts by First Nations plaintiffs, *Delgamuukw* began as a case brought against British Columbia by a group of Gitxsan and Wetsu'wet'en hereditary leaders, summarized here in the Supreme Court's decision:

> The appellants, all Gitksan or Wet'suwet'en hereditary chiefs, both individually and on behalf of their "Houses," claimed separate portions of 58,000 square kilometres in British Columbia. For the purpose of the claim, this area was divided into 133 individual territories, claimed by the 71 Houses. This represents all of the Wet'suwet'en people, and all but 12 of the Gitksan Houses. Their claim was originally for "ownership" of the territory and "jurisdiction" over it. (At this Court, this was transformed into, primarily, a claim for aboriginal title over the land in question.) British Columbia counterclaimed for a declaration that the appellants have no right or interest in and to the territory or alternatively, that the appellants' cause of action ought to be for compensation from the Government of Canada. (Delgamuukw v. British Columbia 1997, para. 7)

While the First Nations plaintiffs' claim was defeated both at trial and at the British Columbia Supreme Court, the federal Supreme Court accepted part of the plaintiffs' appeal, holding that Aboriginal title "is a burden on the Crown's underlying title" rather than the trial judge, Justice McEachern's, finding that Aboriginal rights "existed at the pleasure of the Crown, and could be extinguished by unilateral acts" (quoted in Borrows 1999, 541).

As Borrows points out, while this decision was heralded as a significant sea change in Canadian law and a significant step in the recognition of Aboriginal rights in the country, it had remarkably "conservative foundations." The Supreme Court "did not substantially depart from the previous courts' reliance on assertions of British sovereignty in grounding its discussion of Aboriginal title," nor did it "specifically recognize Gitksan and Wet'suwet'en ownership or jurisdiction over their territories" (Borrows 1999, 542). Indeed, the way in which the Supreme Court asserted the right to "transform" the Gitxsan and Wet'suwet'en assertions of sovereignty, ownership, and jurisdiction into one merely of Aboriginal title, which could then be (re)defined as a subordinate title to the Crown, points to that same systematic disavowal we have seen at work in Canada since the Royal

Proclamation. Indigenous Peoples were not sovereign entities that had been unjustly conquered; rather, though they preexisted colonial settlement, their rights and title were still granted *by* those same settling powers, meaning that their preexistence was effectively irrelevant, despite being the ostensible basis *of* their own (limited) title.

This is the paradox to which Justice Kent pointed in 2022 even as he echoed the 1997 Supreme Court's ultimate political conclusions, quoted here: "Ultimately, it is through negotiated settlements, with good faith and give and take on all sides, reinforced by the judgments of this Court, that we will achieve what I stated in *Van der Peet, supra,* at para. 31, to be a basic purpose of s. 35(1)—'the reconciliation of the pre-existence of aboriginal societies with the sovereignty of the Crown.' Let us face it, we are all here to stay" (Delgamuukw v. British Columbia 1997, para. 186).

As with the Royal Proclamation, the paradoxical nature of the *Delgamuukw* decision can be seen in the ways in which it specifies the relationship of Aboriginal title to land as property. As defined by *Delgamuukw,* Aboriginal title is sui generis, which means, per Kent McNeil's roughly contemporaneous analysis of the decision, that it is "an interest in land that is in a class of its own." Unlike conventional fee simple property ownership, Aboriginal title "cannot be sold or transferred," and it can only be held "by a community of Aboriginal people, not by individuals" (McNeil 1998, 3). In other words, Aboriginal title is *not* ownership, as we might understand it by the terms of common law property, even though what the *Delgamuukw* plaintiffs were claiming was, precisely, ownership rights over their land.

In even more seemingly explicit contradiction, Aboriginal title represents an "exclusive right to land," encompassing "a full range of uses that need not be linked to past practices" (4). However, this exclusive right was limited by the Supreme Court to reflect its own understandings of Indigenous relationships to their respective territories: "Lands held pursuant to Aboriginal title cannot be used in a manner that is irreconcilable with the nature of the attachment to the land which forms the basis of the group's claim to Aboriginal title" (Delgamuukw v. British Columbia 1997, para. 124; cf. McNeil 1998, 4).

It is the courts themselves, furthermore, that are vested with judging whether a given usage of land would fall within the proper boundaries of this privileged attachment to land, not the Indigenous Nation that actually holds this ostensible attachment to the land against which they can be judged. This, for McNeil, presents the worrying possibility that "Aboriginal peoples may be prisoners of the past" (1998, 5); more critically, we might view it as an instance of what anthropologist Elizabeth Povinelli (2002) famously termed "the cunning of recognition," in which Indigenous Peoples are compelled to perform according to a colonial vision of Aboriginal authenticity in order to receive recognition for rights that they, ostensibly, already hold inherently (cf. Coulthard 2014). The *Delgamuukw* decision, in other words, did not offer a legal framework for Indigenous autonomy from settler colonialism. Rather, it offered a framework for Indigenous subordination that was, in many respects, remarkably familiar even as it was presented as something radical and new.

The *Delgamuukw* decision could be said to have set the stage for the era of reconciliation. It confirmed that both federal and provincial governments could not ignore Aboriginal title, which, in turn, led to the development of what has been called the "modern" treaty process in British Columbia and the ratification of the Nisg̱a'a Final Agreement, the first treaty signed in the province since the 1850s (Penikett 2012; Woolford 2006). As the Supreme Court made explicit in its decision, "reconciliation" was needed in Canada between "the pre-existence of aboriginal societies" and the "sovereignty of the Crown." However, as Borrows reminds us, there was little, in fact, that was new in this seemingly epochal shift. Like the Royal Proclamation, *Delgamuukw* understands Aboriginal title as being secondary, a "burden" on the Crown's absolute title. The *Delgamuukw* decision explicitly dismisses the possibility of either full Indigenous ownership or jurisdiction, just as the Royal Proclamation did, masking its disavowal through a fiction of Indigenous title as dependent on the Crown sovereignty that it preexists. This is why it is the courts that retain the power to evaluate whether or not Indigenous uses of their own territories are consistent with their own cultural practices and values.

Put another way, the purportedly radical nature of *Delgamuukw* is itself a disavowal, a way of making ongoing domination appear as if it has shifted its terms when, in fact, the fundamental (and fundamentally fictional) structure of settler colonialism remains fully intact. The cases that have followed in *Delgamuukw*'s wake, including, notably, Haida Nation v. British Columbia (Minister of Forests) and Tsilhqot'in Nation v British Columbia, have further specified the duties and obligations that Aboriginal title imposes as a "burden" on the Crown. *Haida* established that the Crown had a legal "duty to consult with Aboriginal peoples and accommodate their interests" prior to exploiting or authorizing the exploitation of territories that fell within their title claims. This duty was "grounded in the honor of the Crown," and applied even when an Aboriginal title claim had not been "proven" in a Canadian court: "The foundation of the duty in the Crown's honour and the goal of reconciliation suggest that the duty arises when the Crown has knowledge, real or constructive, of the potential existence of the Aboriginal right or title and contemplates conduct that might adversely affect it" (Haida Nation v. British Columbia 2004, para. 35).

*Tsilhqot'in* further specified the nature of this duty to consult, offering a legal mechanism through which the Crown could determine whether it had adequately fulfilled said duty and could thus override Aboriginal title in the public interest. At the same time, however, the Supreme Court ruled that the Tsilhqot'in Nation did have Aboriginal title over the full expanse of the territories they had historically occupied, representing the first such ruling in Canada (Wood and Rossiter 2022, 185). Even then, the Aboriginal title recognized in the *Tsilhqot'in* decision did not include private property (Borrows 2015, 92).

What these cases have not done is fundamentally transform the nature of Aboriginal title as subordinate to the Crown. The *Delgamuukw* decision and its successors have accomplished an extraordinary (and extraordinarily colonial) sleight of hand. By rejecting the initial disavowal *of* the terms of the Royal Proclamation in British Columbia and firmly establishing the category of Aboriginal title in the province, Canada's Supreme Court has made it appear as if it is engaged in a fundamental transformation of Canada's law and its very nature as a settler colony. But this too is disavowal. In fact, what has happened has been, effectively, a *restoration* of the original terms of the Royal Proclamation, including its assumption of Indigenous Nations as always-already existing within the framework of colonial jurisdiction and Crown sovereignty. We are right back where Canada started, so to speak, but in such a way as to make it appear as if this represents a new era of Canadian jurisprudence and Indigenous-settler relations, an era in which, as the justices of the Supreme Court point out repeatedly in their judgments, "reconciliation" is required between Indigenous Nations and settler sovereignty. Or, rather, Indigenous Nations must reconcile themselves *to* settler sovereignty.

## "A Sad Chapter in Our History"

One thing about the discourse around the *Delgamuukw* decision and the cases that have followed that is markedly different from the language of 1763 is the recurrent invocations of social transformation and, especially, liberal progressivism. *Delgamuukw* was heralded by both Indigenous and settler actors as "a blow to colonialism" and a "new beginning" in relations between Indigenous Nations and the settler state (quoted in Borrows 1999, 543). Similar excitement was generated around more recent decisions such as *Tsilhqot'in*. In each case, we see media reporting on how these cases have transformed Canada (e.g., Canadian Press 2024b)[7] alongside dark warnings from conservative Canadian institutions, politicians, and experts around how the country is losing its way, showing "a reckless disregard for public opinion and popular sovereignty," in the words of one furious respondent to *Delgamuukw* (quoted in Borrows 1999, 543). In short, the string of legal decisions since *Delgamuukw* (if not *Calder*) are usually read as an index of Canadian transformation, of rapid shifts in the country toward greater equity that are, for the most part, a good thing for the status of Canadian, liberal multiculturalism.

Such discourses add temporality as an additional dimension to the structure of disavowal that this chapter has been unfolding. The disavowal of *Delgamuukw* does not just offer renewed legal substance to the assumption of Crown sovereignty over Indigenous Peoples; it does so in such a way as to make it appear that it is correcting previous colonial errors and helping settler Canada progress toward a more legitimate, more just future in which Indigenous Peoples and settler society have been reconciled—legally, politically, and morally. Pioneered (if you'll pardon the expression) in the courts, this temporal framework has moved rapidly and effectively into Canadian political and civil discourse, demonstrating the extent to which Canadian legal institutions form part of a unified and mutually reinforcing colonial apparatus.

Consider, in this regard, the genre of the colonial apology, and the concomitant gesture of sincere regret over Canada's "bad" past. In 2008, then–prime minister Stephen Harper issued an apology "to former students of Indian Residential Schools." Spanning from the late nineteenth to the mid-twentieth century and justified as necessary for the assimilation of Indigenous children into "civilized" society, the residential school system was systematically violent, leaving survivors with lasting traumas from physical, emotional, and sexual abuses, to say nothing of the essential violence of the project of assimilation itself. In part due to missionary pressures, school attendance was compulsory for Indigenous children after 1894, and thus a vast number of those children were effectively kidnapped by colonial authorities from their parents to be placed at the different residential schools that had been established throughout the country.[8]

Prime Minister Harper's apology begins by stating that the "treatment of children in Indian Residential Schools is a sad chapter in our history." Sedimenting this temporal structure, the apology recurrently relies on the formulation "we now recognize" as it condemns the abuses of the schools, all strictly in the past tense. It then moves toward a future orientation: "There is no place in Canada for the attitudes that inspired the Indian Residential Schools system to ever prevail again. You have been working on recovering from this experience for a long time and in a very real sense, we are now joining you on this journey." Prime Minister Harper's apology then details the Indian Residential Schools Settlement of 2007 and the establishment of the Indian Residential Schools Truth and Reconciliation Commission as part of that settlement, each presented as part of "healing, reconciliation, and resolution of the sad legacy of Indian Residential schools."

The apology ends by encompassing its ostensibly Indigenous audience, who have been referred to as "you" throughout the apology, in the "all of us" of the future, reconciled Canada: "It will be a positive step in forging a new relationship between Aboriginal peoples and other Canadians, a relationship based on the knowledge of our shared history, a respect for each other and a desire to move forward together with a renewed understanding that strong families, strong communities and vibrant cultures and traditions will contribute to a stronger Canada for all of us" (Harper 2008).

Harper's gesture of encompassment here is familiar from the Royal Proclamation and onwards. The well-being of Indigenous people is the responsibility of the Crown, and though Canada might have failed them in the past, it is better now and will be able to establish a better country for all of its citizens, Indigenous or otherwise. The apology includes no mention of Indigenous sovereignty. The problems with residential schools are described primarily in terms of individual "abuse and neglect" and being "inadequately controlled," and the ways in which the schools formed part of a broader colonial structure of elimination are elided. The apology gives no indication that there could be any future for Indigenous Peoples *but* as citizens of Canada, whether reconciled or otherwise. Indeed, to borrow a phrase from Kanaka Maoli scholar J. Kēhaulani Kauanui's analysis of the United States' Apology to Native Hawaiians in 1993, it "affirms the endurance" of Canadian sovereignty in the very gesture of apology itself (2014, 115).

One of the fundamental fictions of settler colonialism in Canada is that it is not essentially and continuously violent. This, recall, is crucial to the state's "meta-claim," in Audra Simpson's (2016) terms, of Canada as being a just society. And yet, in late 2019, the *Guardian* published an article entitled "Exclusive: Canada Police Prepared to Shoot Indigenous Activists, Documents Show." Said documents, which came from an RCMP strategy session, argued for "lethal overwatch," or officers being prepared to use deadly force, to dismantle the Unist'ot'en Camp, a blockade established by members of the Wet'suwet'en Nation in opposition to pipeline development in northern

Canada. The camp was raided on January 7, 2020: "The documents show that ahead of the raid, the RCMP deployed an array of surveillance, including heavily armed police patrols, a jet boat, helicopter, drone technology, heat-sensing cameras and close monitoring of key land defenders' movements and social media postings. . . . Armed RCMP officers can be seen patrolling the area, and three police trailers are tucked away in the woods alongside the access road. Drones and helicopters often circle overhead. CGL has also retained two private security firms that track Indigenous people's movements" (Dhillon and Parrish 2019). The threat and actual application of overwhelming violence is a consistent and significant colonial strategy for reminding Indigenous populations that, in the first and final instance, they are subject to the military force of an occupying power—the "most unambiguous form of exceptional relations, that of warfare" (A. Simpson 2014, 152). As one article in the *Tyee*, a regional and independent Canadian newsmagazine, pithily and effectively put it, "When Indigenous Assert Rights, Canada Sends Militarized Police" (Nikiforuk 2019).

The "sad chapter" displaces that violence to a past that has now been transcended, disavowing the harsh reality that it is still happening, that colonial domination has not changed in force or character since 1763. While court decisions abstract these realities into questions of property rights and the proper contours of consultations, colonial apologies and articulations of shame can engage the violence of domination directly, acknowledging it as constitutive of Canada while simultaneously asserting that it is no longer real, no longer there, regardless of any ongoing situations of lethal overwatch facing Indigenous activists.

Perhaps this is why the contrite language of Canada's dark past has now become almost as common in Canadian public discourse as invocations of reconciliation itself. In late May of 2021, as many as 215 potential unmarked graves were identified on the grounds of what was Kamloops Indian Residential School, at one time the largest residential school in Canada (Pruden 2021).[9] Soon after the discovery, Justin Trudeau—who defeated Stephen Harper in 2015 to become the next prime minister of Canada—tweeted that the bodies were a "painful reminder of that dark and painful chapter of our country's history." (Venn 2021). Then–Conservative leader Erin O'Toole echoed Trudeau's language, characterizing the residential school system as a "dark and painful part of the Canadian story." It is "our duty," O'Toole suggested, "to heal the wounds from this horrific part of our history" (Zimonjic 2021). Both echo the framing of Harper's apology: The residential schools system represented a prior era of Canadian history, and it was a bad one.

However, by force of official (settler) acknowledgment, we mark that chapter as closed even as new "discoveries" of colonial violence come to light (cf. Weiss 2015). In this discourse of the "shamed state" as Elizabeth Povinelli has put it, the state recognizes past violence and in so doing displaces ongoing forms of violence into that past, now superseded by the liberal state (Povinelli 2002).

Which is not to say that such attempts at disavowal go unchallenged. Take, for instance, Inuit member of parliament Mumilaaq Qaqqaq's June 3 response to Trudeau's tweet: "Colonization is not a dark chapter in Canadian history. It is a book that the federal institution continues to write" (Venn 2021). The colonization of Indigenous Peoples, Qaqqaq asserts, is ongoing. The methods might have transformed over time, but it has not, in any sense, ended. Qaqqaq's refusal of the dark chapter metaphor pointedly identifies the disavowal at the heart of the formula. The "sad chapter" formulation acknowledges that a history of violence against Indigenous Peoples existed as part of Canadian colonialism. In so doing, it represents colonial violence as of the past, no longer part of Canada's story except as something to be shamefully memorialized. Contemporary violence cannot exist; thus, the redolent irony (much remarked upon in social media responses to Trudeau) that the head of the Canadian state was apologizing for a "dark chapter" in Canada's history even as his government was pursuing legal action against survivors of the Kamloops Residential School (Barrera 2021). These are obviously contradictory positions for a representative of Canada. Like the subordinate nature of Aboriginal title, this is a paradox that cannot be reconciled; it can only be disavowed.

## Harsh Reality

Supreme Court decisions on Aboriginal title, royal proclamations, and federal apologies are just a few examples of the means by which disavowal is mobilized in Canada as a means to make the paradoxes of settler colonialism appear as if they can be reconciled. Or, more precisely, these disavowals are part of systems of compulsion that attempt to force Indigenous Peoples to reconcile themselves *to* settler colonialism as an ongoing inevitability. Colonial disavowals attempt to make it appear as if settler colonialism is an ontological precept of existence, not a historical imposition. The settler colonial state has always asserted jurisdiction over Indigenous territories; dispossession has always been an act of care for those under the protection of the Crown.

But this is not true. And from the Indigenous leaders who negotiated the Treaty of Niagara in 1764 and the chiefs who contested the "allocation" of reserves in British Columbia in the nineteenth century to Frank Calder and Chief Delgamuukw, Earl Muldoon, all the way until Mumilaaq Qaqqaq, among so many others, Indigenous Peoples have refused the closed circle of disavowal. They have refused to let the fictions that founded colonial legitimacy be reified; they have contested the idea that subordination is care, respect, or reconciliation itself. Justice Kent, like the Supreme Court justices who decided *Delgamuukw* before him, presents the notion that "we [settlers] are all here to stay" as a harsh reality, an inescapable fact to which Indigenous Peoples must reconcile themselves. But we might invert this framing, borrowing Kauanui's characterization of the double structure of an "enduring indigeneity": Indigenous Peoples continue to endure as sovereign Nations, while the settler state must continue to endure the claims by Indigenous Nations that undermine the ongoing legitimacy of that state (2016). This endurance is the true harsh reality for settler colonialism. However vigorously justices, politicians, or other colonial leaders disavow the fictional quality of the fictions that founded their own legitimacy, they cannot sustain these deceptions when Indigenous People refuse to be reconciled to them. All that is left is the violence of settler domination, an unacceptable truth for the era of reconciliation.

CHAPTER TWO

# Not Built to Last

## *The Presences and Absences of Military Occupation on Haida Gwaii*

### Absence and Presence

It took a long time for the swimming pool to close in the Village of Masset. The pool had been the single most important feature of Masset's recreation center, which the community had inherited when the military base was decommissioned in 1997. But the only way to heat the swimming pool was with diesel fuel, and by 2013 that had become entirely cost prohibitive for the Greater Masset Development Corporation, an organization administered jointly by the settler village of Masset and their immediate neighbors, the Haida First Nations community of Old Massett. Left without any other option, the pool was shut down and the recreation center closed for good. Only the shell of the building remained, the last remnant of Canadian Forces Station Masset, left hollow and abandoned in the center of town.

The shuttering of the rec center appeared to many in both Masset and Old Massett as an unhappy epilogue to more than fifty years of sustained military presence on the islands of Haida Gwaii, ancestral home and unceded territory of the Haida Nation. The Base, as CFS Masset was popularly known, was gone, and with it all the resources it had brought to the two communities. Other than ruins, all that remained was a radio outpost a few kilometers north of Masset, which, it was popularly understood, was remotely operated. Except, as it turns out, military presence was not gone from Haida Gwaii, as Marlene Liddle and her family discovered. One day in July, when Liddle and her family were out berry picking on their traditional territory, they were surprised to discover a sign on their recently renovated outhouse. The sign, written and placed by a member of Canada's Department of National Defense (DND), informed the Liddle family that their outhouse had been built on DND land and was thus an "illegal building, . . . built without the approval of the Minister of National Defense, and violated [sic] the Canadian Environmental Protection Act." Unless the family took down the offending building, the note informed them, it would be "removed on their behalf" (Peerless 2013).

And yet, the offending outhouse was not new, even if it had been newly renovated. Indeed, one incarnation of the outhouse or another had stood in this same place for the last fifteen years. The military had been notorious for interfering with Haida resource gathering on land the DND had claimed for its own, and Marlene Liddle and her family had wasted little time in returning to berry picking and other forms of food gathering when the military, ostensibly, left in 1997. And there was material evidence of that departure. As the buildings that had made up the Base gradually decayed and the facilities it had left shut down, it seemed to both Haida and their neighbors that the military were gone for good. Even the "private married quarters," midsized houses built for military officers and their families, had been sold to Masset's residents as civilian housing. The ruins of the base were a material reminder of the military's absence, their skeletal frames signaling Masset's postmilitary present to new arrivals and residents alike. As, it turned out, however, that absence was an illusion, or perhaps even a deception.

What does it mean when ruins lie? In his ethnographic exploration of the afterlives of material and social destruction in Argentina, Gastón Gordillo characterizes the rubble left behind by the multiple histories of conquest and violence in the Chaco as "the material sedimentation of destruction" (2014, 10). A focus on rubble, Gordillo argues, allows us to "examine space negatively: by way of places that were negated to create the geographies of the present" (11).[1] As Gordillo makes clear throughout his ethnography, such acts of negation are productive, making possible particular political, social, and temporal realities via the "material and affective erasures of traces from the past," most often "shaped by orders to remember given by dominant social actors" (207). Destruction, then, is a performative action, a means of making erasure real, and the rubble left behind acts as a "topography of oblivion" for these ongoing social projects of selective memory (ch.8; cf. Trouillot 1995). Or, put more simply, to destroy material traces is to suggest that those who inhabited said matter are, themselves, gone. Such modes of "ruination," as Yael Navaro-Yashin has argued, leave profound and often deeply ambivalent affective traces—"the subjectivities and residual affects that linger, like a hangover, in the aftermath of war and violence," as she elegantly puts it (2009, 5). Humans, these authors argue, feel haunted by what has come before, the ghostly doubling of an effaced past that has constituted the present by its absence but at the same time cannot truly be said to have disappeared (cf. Leathem 2019).

Except, on Haida Gwaii, the military never actually left. This does not mean that both Haida and non-Haida alike did not experience the military as gone: Quite the opposite, as I will show, the military's departure and the subsequent erosion of the facilities it left behind generated a series of affects that resonate with Gordillo's and Navaro-Yashin's accounts of ruination. Indeed, this is precisely the point. Ruination made it appear as if the military had left Haida Gwaii, concealing the fact that the army was still actively occupying Haida territory. This, I argue, is no coincidence. Rather, what is at work here is the deliberate production of a paradox, in Kanaka Maoli scholar J. Kēhaulani Kauanui's sense: a constitutive contradiction that serves to reinforce the structures of settler domination even as it seems to mitigate the visible presence of the force—and the forces—of occupation (2018a). By erasing the overt forms of military power, colonial governments thereby render covert the ongoing maintenance of settler domination. Here is one means through which the violence of settler colonialism is maintained in the same moment as it can be disavowed, a structure in which the military can act and yet remain invisible.

The deceptive ruins of the military on Haida territory help us understand the work of colonial disavowal in the era of reconciliation. As we saw in chapter 1, settler domination in British Columbia was established at the barrel of a gun; however, as time went on, the overt threat of military force was gradually effaced through a series of legal mechanisms that made it appear as if Indigenous Peoples had consented to their own domination. But that consent was, as Audra Simpson (2017) argues, a colonial ruse. As the ongoing RCMP action against the Unist'ot'en blockade on Wetsu'wet'en territory further reminds us, when Indigenous Peoples make clear that they have not consented to colonial action on and exploitation of their lands and waters, settler police and military forces take action. This capacity for force, however, must remain concealed for settler Canadians to continue to act as if they are living in a just society; the ongoing fact of colonial military capacity must always, somehow, disguise itself so that the violence that undergirds colonialism can be disavowed.

Thus the haunting power of the absent presence of the military on Haida Gwaii. Despite the ideological elegance of such a phantasmagorical formation, however, the military cannot simply disappear from the islands, nor could it ever. Instead, its legacy remains complex and ongoing, even as the base itself might have been left to slowly and performatively go to ruin. In navigating this legacy, Haida people hold the military to account, puncturing its attempts at disappearing even as these same Haida also negotiate the complex feelings that emerge from living with an ongoing colonial occupation. As we shall see, while Haida people like Marlene Liddle refuse the right for the military to continue to occupy their lands, there is also an ambivalence to these refusals that, for some, points to alternative possible forms of relationality between Indigenous people and settler subjects.

My goal in this chapter, accordingly, is to hold together the very real affects of ruination on the part of Haida people with the contention that this ruination was a deliberate and deceptive means through which a particular kind of military presence disguised the ongoing quality of its occupation of Indigenous territory. In this way I offer a case study of the impact of colonial disavowal "on the ground," as it were, exploring the ways that settler disavowal of the constitutive violence of colonial domination comes to be embedded in the relationships between Indigenous Peoples and settler subjects. While in chapter 1, I focused on disavowal as it emerged primarily in legal and political discourses, here I explore disavowal as shared social reality in day-to-day life, one with very real consequences for how Haida and settlers can engage with each other in the context of settler colonialism.

I begin with the Base itself, situating CFS Masset in the history of Haida Gwaii, with a particular focus on the experiences of Haida people. I then turn to the idea that, despite its seeming permanence, the Base was "not built to last," as one former employee put it. Instead, the military adopted a series of strategies designed to mitigate the possibility of its personnel forming durable relationships with Haida people or, to an extent, their settler neighbors, taking the ruination of the swimming pool as my central, epitomizing image. I query the nature of these paradoxical "imperial durabilities," borrowing Ann Laura Stoler's language (2016), keeping in mind the particular irony that CFS Masset's occupation of Haida land was, from a military perspective, an almost incidental epiphenomenon of the need to maintain radio surveillance during the Cold War. Finally, I return to the Liddle family's "illegal outhouse," suggesting that the fact that the military remains on Haida Gwaii despite its performance of departure offers us a potent metonymy for the shifting means through which settler colonial states such as Canada conceal the violence that remains at the heart of their ongoing occupation of Indigenous territories.

## "Three Communities"

I first became interested in the legacy of the military base on the north end of Haida Gwaii during a conversation with David Armstrong, a well-respected senior member of Old Massett's community.[2] We'd been talking "on the record" about changes in the Haida community for a dozen or so minutes when Armstrong turned the conversation to the Base:

DA: I mean, when I was growing up around 1970 the military showed up. *I mean the military was always here, but small scale, and all of a sudden there were three thousand of them. So it made it three communities instead of two, and they drove the wedge in more, well I guess we all* did cuz it's, when they had the rec center and they had their own CANEX, the food store.

JW: Yeah, I remember hearing about that, that they had their own grocery store that no one else could use.

DA: Unless you worked for them or else you were military and that, that was hard on the kids cuz, I mean, all these kids were going to the gym and swimming pool and if your parents didn't work for them you couldn't go. *And that really segregated the place.*

JW: Yeah, that's really rough.

DA: And the military the first thing they were told when they arrived here is they're not to go down to the village.

JW: Huh.

DA: So, and that, I mean, *they've downsized them quite a bit and it's changed, it's back to two communities now not three* [emphasis added].

Armstrong's concise narrative of the social changes brought by the military reconfigured my understanding of the social terrain of the two Massetts. The "settlers" of settler colonialism were not, for Armstrong, a homogenous mass, a single, cohesive body to be endured by the Haida. Instead, when the military "showed up"—and note again the fact that even before their arrival en masse, the military "was always here"—it made "three communities instead of two," interposing itself between the Haida of Old Massett and the historically settler community of the Village of Masset.

Relationships between the two Massetts were already markedly segregated before the establishment of CFS Masset in the Village of Masset. Haida Gwaii has been Haida territory since time immemorial, but living conditions were fundamentally transformed in the late nineteenth century with the arrival, on the one hand, of settler missionaries and, eventually, homesteaders, and the decimation of epidemic diseases such as smallpox on the other. Haida are matrilineal, with territorial and resource rights allocated to individual matrilineal clans and adjudicated through the feasts now commonly glossed as "potlatches" (e.g., L. Bell 2016; Collison 2011).[3] However, the reserve allocation process in British Columbia ignored clan rights, superimposing colonially mandated boundaries in perpetuity over a flexible system of interclan territorial negotiation. The reserve of Old Massett was thus by definition a hybrid space when it was officially constituted by British Columbia's Joint Reserve Commission in 1882, with a population composed of the survivors of many different clans who had joined together in a single, central location in order to survive (Weiss 2018, 7). The creation of these reserves on Haida Gwaii was justified, as elsewhere in British Columbia, by the assertion that the islands had been claimed as Crown land and that Canada, as the Crown's representative, had jurisdiction over the lands and lives of Haida Gwaii's Indigenous population. This was despite the fact that no treaties had been signed (or even proposed) and Aboriginal title had never been extinguished on the Islands, just as in the vast majority of the rest of British Columbia. Nonetheless, the Haida communities were allocated small patches of land on their ancestral territory and expected to allow for colonial settlement and resource extraction throughout the islands.

The Village of Masset was founded a few decades later by a group of settler homesteaders who appropriated territory just a few kilometers east of the reserve. Even its name represents a kind of founding theft, as I have chronicled elsewhere: "In 1907, when the site for the future settler village was first surveyed, the town site was given the name Graham City. However, when the city planners discovered that the postmaster for the Haida community then called Masset was leaving, they applied for a post office in their townsite and claimed its name was Masset. Effectively, the city planners had stolen both the post office and the name Masset from their soon-to-be neighbors" (2020, 67).

What followed over the course of the twentieth century was the systematic establishment of settler domination over the island's resources and territories. Alongside the centralization of services in the settler community and the regular refusal by most banks and businesses to serve "Indians," settler fishermen monopolized control of commercial fishing, establishing themselves as leaders of fishing crews that, at best, included Indigenous employees, and attempting to push independent Indigenous fishermen out of business (see Weiss 2018, 53–57; Stearns 1981).[4] This was the landscape in which David Armstrong grew up, and the social world where the military "showed up" in the late 1960s.

The Base as it was remembered by Armstrong's generation was opened in a lavish ceremony in 1968. It was not, strictly speaking, the first military base on Haida Gwaii. Rather, the Base's first incarnation was Naval Radio Station Masset, established during World War II, operating directly within the Old Massett reserve as a relatively minor naval listening station aimed primarily at the Pacific theater of operations. But the Base was different when it was (re)opened. While it retained its function as a listening station—albeit one now firmly entrenched in the geopolitics of the Cold War—the "new" Canadian Forces Station Masset was heralded at the time as also inaugurating a major transformation in military-civilian relations in Canada. CFS Masset was to be the first "open-concept" military base in the country, "devoid of fences and sentries" and, instead, "enmeshed" in the life of the two Massetts (McMullen 1998, 3).[5] And enmeshed it very quickly became. At its peak of operations in the 1970s, the Base included almost three hundred military personnel split between barracks—the core of the ruins, post-1997—and the aforementioned "private married quarters," built in residential circles near the Base's primary facilities. These houses, typically two-storied affairs with nicely painted exteriors, spread out around the Base in miniature neighborhoods, offering an almost suburban veneer to the barracks' stark brown walls and flat, squat roofs.

The Base provided employment for many, developed local infrastructure, acted as a local hospital, and hosted leisure activities like dances, arts and crafts groups, and community events. Indeed, the very layout of Masset as I encountered it was shaped by the presence of the Base, its residential circles radiating out from the center where the Base once sat, with easy proximity to the local elementary school (constructed, I learned, with military support to educate Haida and non-Haida students along with the children of military personnel). Even the asphalt roads that connected the Masset area to the southern towns on Haida Gwaii's largest island were laid by the military, a road that passed by the golf course put in by the military for recreation. And while there might not have been fences, the military was ubiquitous, patrolling "its" territory and making sure that "intruders"—particularly local Haida out resource gathering—were quickly removed. Another irony of the "open-concept" military base was that, as the barracks were positioned within the Village of Masset, this meant that the military police patrolled the town itself, though ostensibly only when issues involving the military occurred. As we shall see, this was a porous boundary.

As Armstrong details, with these transformations came shifts in the forms of segregation—the "wedge," as Armstrong puts it—that were already present between the Indigenous and settler communities on island. The modes of division that the Base brought unfolded in parallel with these already-ongoing dynamics, but their terms were distinctive: If you worked for the Base, you and your family had access to discounted groceries, to military dining messes, to programming aimed at military families, and, of course, to the rec center and its facilities, especially the all-important swimming pool.

And many Haida did indeed work for the Base.[6] Over the course of my research, I spoke with former cooks and drivers, former janitorial workers, and even former radio operators, all of whom formed part of the substantial support staff that the Base relied on in order to operate at its peak. Many Haida elders whom I have known draw military pensions for this work.

These facts mean that the terms of inclusion and exclusion from Armstrong's three communities might be more complicated than they at first appear. While his initial two communities seem to map fairly coherently onto the categories of Indigenous and settler, the fact that the privileges carried by the military extended to its nonmilitary employees makes such binaries messy.[7] This meant that some Haida had access to facilities that Haida did not; so, too, some Haida shared that access with some of the non-Haida residents of Masset who were also working for the Base. Likewise, some Haida shared with their non-Indigenous neighbors the *absence* of privileged access—more expensive groceries, fewer (if any) recreational facilities, no space to teach their children to swim. Note Armstrong's discursive shift as he tells the story: "And *they* drove the wedge in more," meaning the military, transitions to "well I guess we all did," distributing the responsibility for community polarization among all three categories of actors, Haida, settler, and military alike.

Armstrong was not the only person to elaborate on these tensions. Consider, for instance, how divisions in Haida community over the military emerge in Haida artist and political leader Fred Willis's comparison between life now and life with the Base:

> FW: Like I said, eh, there's more sense of freedom again, being able to walk where you want, when you want. You go do your seasonal things in that area, . . . which I've been doing and I never did stop, even though they came after us, I never did stop. I always reminded them, "You're on Haida territory, it's Old Massett's territory you're on." They never understood that kind of thing, because they'd never dealt, a lot of them had never dealt with First Nations before, let alone stepped on somebody's territory, and had somebody say something about it without due process, eh? Ask first, that kind of thing. So.
>
> JW: Which makes a lot of sense. So, like, would they ever, I'm just thinking in terms of resource gathering, would they ever intervene when elders were out gathering?
>
> FW: Yeah, it didn't matter who it was. Their orders were to go out and remove people from that area, and so they did. So yeah, some of our

elders were—that's when we really really started to hear about it, more often than not, was because the elders were the ones who were most upset about it.

JW: Yeah.

FW: And then of course there were some [Haida] that would, that, you know, basically joined them, if you will, eh? Like did and said and worked with them, and so they were side by side, a lot of them, and so now we have Haidas on that side and Haidas on this side, so it created a conflict for sure, for sure. Plus they took our women! That's why I say it's now [with the departure of the military] a little more serene for me, anyway.

Willis begins with a confident assertion of Haida sovereignty in the face of military occupation and his own commitment to resource gathering even when faced with opposition from the Base: "Even though they came after us, I never did stop." Haida sovereign rights, for Willis, necessarily entail the right of Haida to gather resources on their clan's territories and to retain the power of permission over who can and cannot gather on Haida land; to disrupt these rights is a violation. "Ask first, that kind of thing?" Indeed, in the face of this opposition, Willis remembers reiterating Haida territorial sovereignty to these invaders, whom he figures as disconnected from any experience with Indigenous communities whatsoever, much less any specific knowledge about or respect for the Haida people whose lands they were occupying.

And yet, as he continues, Willis turns to the Haida who "basically joined them," those who worked with and stood by the Base's employees even as, in Willis's view, Haida elders in particular were impacted by the military's refusal to allow them to gather resources or even simply to be present on their traditional territories. Unlike the military, which "never understood that kind of thing," these Haida, presumably, would have known better, and yet chose nonetheless to ally themselves with, in Willis's reading, the agents of military occupation of their own land. Here the clear lines of "us" and "them" break down, as different Haida position themselves and are positioned separately in an ongoing space of at least imminent conflict. This sense of division was as much true for Haida who worked for the Base as it was for Willis and those who share(d) his position. Former Haida Base employees with whom I spoke expressed to me their frustrations with friends and family who didn't understand their choice of employment or, even more distressingly, were resentful of the financial benefits and privileged forms of access that military employment brought. Some friends even recalled seeing physical altercations between Haida on different sides of this divide.

We also should not neglect Willis's exclamation near the end of our excerpted conversation: "Plus they took our women!" One of the most dramatic and yet simultaneously most intimate consequences of the sustained presence of military officers was the relationships—and sometimes marriages—that developed between military personnel, their families, and Haida community members. As Willis emphasizes, there were—and are—undeniably gendered dimensions to these discourses, with the narrative of "theft" in particular mapping onto older, typically colonial, and certainly problematic discourses that frame women as male possessions.[8] And yet, men as well as women made frequent reference to intimate and sexual relations with military folk as a major axis of Haida-Base sociality (cf. Enloe 2000). One reason for this, as was reiterated to me frequently, was in order to avoid intimate relations with kin. Haida clan and moiety membership is reckoned matrilineally, and the Eagle and Raven sides are formally exogamous. As my friends pointed out, sometimes in jest, sometimes seriously, entering into a relationship with a military officer or their children guaranteed you wouldn't wind up "dating your cousin," opening up the field of potential partners—both casual and long-term—considerably.

The impact of the Base means that, on Haida Gwaii at least, the boundaries between inclusion and exclusion did not devolve comfortably into clear lines between Indigenous and settler, between Native and military. Whether one reads the Haida people who worked with the Base as co-opted by it, as Willis intimated, or follows the opposing position that those Haida who did not work with the Base were jealous of the resources it offered to employees, as others suggested to me, we arrive in each case at the Base as a complex site of relationality, striated by flows of power, by access and exclusion, and by gender and intimacy. In these senses Haida experiences with the Base echo ethnographies of other military bases in North Carolina (Lutz 2002) and South Korea (Schober 2016).

At the same time, the fact that Armstrong nonetheless characterized the islands as being divided into "three communities" matters. There was real and ongoing pressure to keep the three communities conceptually separate, even if they could not be separated economically or socially in any real material sense. Even the Haida people who did have connections to the Base through their own work or that of a family member sometimes found themselves excluded from military-sponsored events and organizations through the force of social pressure and hostility, echoing the forms of segregation that Haida were already subjected to in settler Masset. There was a sense from many who had lived through the military era that the bars were not safe spaces, as fistfights were perceived to break out often between Haida and army personnel. These antagonisms were ritualized regularly in local sports events, in particular the annual "tug of war" challenges that were a fixture of my conversations about life during the Base era. In these "games," participants were separated into Indigenous, military, and Masset resident teams, formalizing Armstrong's three communities not only as socially visible, but in a sense as implicitly obvious. Such performative attempts aimed to make clear what was unclear, grouping communities into clear and legible lines even as their forms of sociality cut across them in complicated, intimate, and uneasy ways.

## "Poof, It Was All Gone"

While there might have been very little that was simple about the entanglements of military, civilian, and Haida during the Base era, one thing seemed obvious to most Haida and settler civilians alike: The Base was there to stay. It is not difficult to understand why this would be the case. The military paved the roads, provided medical services, built a school, radically expanded the infrastructure of Haida Gwaii's north end, and even put in a golf course. They were engaged in the ongoing, material, and irreversible transformation of Haida Gwaii's landscape, and so too its social landscape, reshaped simultaneously by military employment, by the privileges of CANEX and rec center access, and by the more intimate ways through which military personnel were building relations (and sometimes families) with Haida people. The presence of the military, this is to say, appeared *durable* in Stoler's sense, a "hardened," "tenacious," and "enduring" fact of life on the islands. "Imperial durabilities," as Stoler frames her analytic, are charged with suffering, but they also speak to the ways that subjects of empire can "endure" against ongoing colonial violence and domination and the "damage and disability" that it brings with it (2016, 7). In this instance, the specificity of settler colonialism gives a particular cast to what is durable in the maintenance of domination—precisely, in the case of settler colonialism, the expectation that domination has "come to stay," to paraphrase Patrick Wolfe (2006). Dealing with the Base was an inescapable, ongoing reality for Haida people, whether they were navigating the opportunities it afforded or experiencing the many constraints and limitations that the military imposed.

And then, in 1997, CFS Masset was decommissioned and the military "left." From a Canadian defense perspective, the end of the Cold War in the late 1980s meant there was simply less need for a well-staffed training base so close to Russian waters. While interlocutors who were working at the Base during that time described a gradual winding down of military operations, marked especially by decreases in active personnel and training activities, others who were not Base employees and thus not privy to these more gradual shifts described feeling that the Base's decommissioning was abrupt and unexpected.

Though this might have been an untampered relief for those Haida like Fred Willis who had avoided the Base as much as possible, for many others the Base's departure was met with considerably more ambivalence, especially given the speed at which the military's departure seemed to occur. For Daniel Montgomery, the son of a Haida woman and a non-Haida military officer, this ambivalence was especially sharp. While Montgomery's parents met on Haida Gwaii, he did not spend his earlier years there. Effectively, he could not have; not only did military deployment rules mean that army families *had* to move every few years (a point to which we will return in detail), but the terms of Canadian Native law before the 1980s meant that Montgomery's mother had lost her Indian status, and thus her band membership and right to reside on reserve, on her marriage to a non-Haida man.[9] It was only after the end of the marriage of Montgomery's parents when Montgomery was a youth that he came to live on the islands full time. Reflecting on his experiences with the Base, Montgomery shifted affective registers. He spoke with considered enthusiasm about the income the Base brought into the community despite its complications, the ways meeting families from all over the country expanded his own horizons, and the benefits of meeting potential partners who were definitely not his cousins. "I think, I was sad to see it go," Montgomery told me. "I enjoyed it, it was a good experience for me, met my first love through the military. . . . So, yeah, I miss it, I think it was a sad thing when that happened."

But, and here Montgomery shifted, "I mean, good and bad, I've had some bad experience with the military." He then told me the story of being detained by military police one evening because he was out walking after dark. Apparently, he later learned, there had been an assault reported, and Montgomery, a dark-skinned Haida man walking alone after 10:00 p.m., seemed to the military police precisely the kind of person to interrogate about the matter. This was despite the fact that, from Montgomery's perspective, the military did not have the jurisdiction to detain civilians on such matters:

"They were patrolling around the area, and I was in the wrong place at the wrong time. . . . I of course wasn't who they were looking for, but it was quite, really, you guys aren't even police, how can you do this? So we got through that, but it was traumatizing at the time." Crucially, Montgomery noted, the military officers who detained him weren't people that he knew.

As he turned toward the Base's eventual decommissioning, Montgomery's reflections became more critical:

> The houses were all still there, but the people who filled the houses weren't there. It was over a couple of years, I guess, but it sure didn't seem to take long for them to move out. . . . Once a decision was made, it seemed like it was just, "poof," it was all gone. And then what really seemed to, you know, we always had the barracks, it was kind of sad to see that go, nothing really came out of that, you know? I understand that it was an older building. Like that's almost kind of sad, it's almost like we just got, I'm not going to say left their garbage, but the equipment was old, the swimming pool was old, the barracks was old. So, I guess in that way, it almost feels like we kind of got used, you know, kinda. So that's probably my most negative thing towards it, just saying, "Yeah, you came, you saw, you took what you had to take and you just left," and all we got left was some old houses and a run-down barracks that had to be torn down.

He was sad to see the Base go, but also sad to see what it had left behind. The military was too "militant," as Montgomery put it, about "defending" what they took to be their territory, but when they left, what was most insulting is that they left nothing behind but ruins, material reminders of the *lack* of commitment to making life better on island for Haida and non-Haida alike. Ambivalence can be productive, argue Ciara Kierans and Kirsten Bell, because it "*destabilizes* the very categories it is built upon" (2017, 39; emphasis original). Ambivalence, that is to say, is unsettling, casting critical purchase on the conflicting emotions that constitute it precisely because the paradox—the military as a force that provided and would be missed, the military as an active agent of violent domination—cannot be resolved. And, for Montgomery at least, the legacy of the military was full of contradictions that were not easily reconciled.

Montgomery's ambivalent comments echo the theories of ruination with which we began this chapter, aptly embodying the "subjectivities and residual affects" of Haida people dealing with the aftermath of the Base as social phenomenon and material presence. These feelings had their corollary in the rec center's swimming pool, whose maintenance became the predominant fiscal priority of the Greater Masset Development Corporation. Founded in partnership between Old Massett and Masset, the GMDC's mandate was to manage the lump sum that the military left to the two communities as part of the Base's decommissioning process.[10] Over the next decade, it invested a significant percentage of its funds to maintaining the recreation center—and, especially, its swimming pool—as a public facility. This seemed an obvious choice at the time. As I noted earlier, the two Massetts are fishing communities. Haida people have been fishing for salmon, halibut, and other seafood since time immemorial, and marine resource gathering is perceived by many, if not most, as an essential dimension of what it means to be Haida. So, too, fishing income was and remains crucial to many Haida families operating within the settler capitalist economy. Fishing was likewise central for the Haida community's nonmilitary settler neighbors, who relied primarily upon (and monopolized) commercial fishing for much of their community's income. In this context, a controlled environment in which it was possible to safely teach children how to swim took on tremendous importance for Haida and non-Haida alike at the same time as it offered a valuable means of exercise and recreation for the two small towns.

But these facilities were *old*, as Montgomery emphasized to me: run down, destined to be nothing but garbage. Eventually, it simply became financially impossible for the GMDC to maintain them, and the rec center was shuttered. Moreover, the efforts to keep the facilities open as long as possible had essentially wasted much of the money that the military had left. All this, and all the frustration, ambivalence, and betrayal that it represented, sedimented the idea that what was left of the Base was mere rubble, without any more value for the community or social significance except as a reminder of a prior era, a "space negated to create the geography of the present," as Gordillo might put it. This was certainly my experience of the Base when I first began spending time on Haida Gwaii in 2012. I recall walking around the brown, hollowed-out shells of the barracks in the center of Masset and wondering what they could even be, as by then they had been stripped of any identifying features or labels. When I asked, people referred to the military presence as having been "a long time ago," a part of the community's history. They were long gone, now.

## "Not Built to Last"

As potent as the appearance of durability was that the Base gave, however, and as resonant and complex were the emotions generated by the Base's decommissioning and its aftermath, what must be emphasized is that these very forms of ruination were *anticipated* by the military. They were, put simply, part of the design of CFS Masset itself. Take the swimming pool. As Ted Andrews, a former Base employee told me, none of the military facilities were "built to last." In particular, the fact that the swimming pool relied on a steady source of diesel fuel to be heated meant that the costs to keep the pool operating without the deep pockets of Canada's Department of Defense were exorbitant. The military, Andrews explained, didn't think of its facilities as permanent structures—they were constitutively temporary, to be kept as long as their function was needed, but not preserved past that point. The funds given to the two Massetts by the Department of Defense were nonrenewable, and the portion that had been sunk (quite literally) into the swimming pool could never be recovered or put to other uses. This is not necessarily surprising, in and of itself. After all, the Department of Defense had (and has) a network of bases all throughout Canada, meant to respond to particular threats and needs as might be necessary. The significance of one station or another can always be understood as relative to that broader scale of operation. The fact that this *necessarily* erodes both the spatial and social specificity of military relationships *within* a given context would, by this logic, be a desirable consequence of the structure of military durability.

Similarly, while the military presence on Haida Gwaii was, in aggregate, constant, individual military personnel were rarely given permanent postings at the Base. Instead, personnel were deployed on the basis of an approximately five-year rotation, which meant that, with the exception of some key higher-rank personnel, no soldier resided in the Masset area for more than a few years at a time.[11] Thus, while the Base itself could be understood as a permanent fixture of the north end of Haida Gwaii, its constantly shifting personnel undercut the possibilities for durable relationality between Haida people and any individual soldiers or their families. These rules applied just as much to personnel with Haida spouses, who had to uproot their lives on island if they wished to remain with their partners. For the military, then, social relationships, just as much as material structures, were not built to last.

The colonial durabilities of military occupation appear paradoxical here. As we've seen, the military reiterated its presence on Haida Gwaii in the most visible and dramatic of ways, restructuring social and physical geographies alike, meeting elders with guns as they picked berries, and arresting young Haida men when they were in the wrong place, at the wrong time. Why, then, did the military seem so systematically to emphasize the temporary nature of its own occupation? One answer lies in the nature of occupation itself. The forces of occupation are precisely that, *forces*, people acting upon other people. These people thus contain within themselves the imminent potential to enter into relationships with those they occupy. So, too, because the Base relied on the labor of nonmilitary employees, this meant that Haida could be employed by the military for much of the lives, forming durable—and, as we've seen, often fraught—attachments to the military community even as it acted to deny the sovereignty of Haida actors on their territories. Such modes of attachment are developmental, even linear, building and growing as relationships are made, attachments formed, and social (and physical) worlds transformed. There is a *mutuality* here, one that might make it difficult, for instance, to bring one's firearm to bear on a grandmother by her berry patch. The structures of military deployment cut against this form of durability, consistently reforming the social composition of the Base's personnel so that, while the institution remained—including the ways in which Haida were recruited to it—individual relationships between Haida and non-Haida would always be temporary. The social content of occupation is perpetually foreclosed even as the material fact of occupation is, just as perpetually, reinforced. That is to say, the actual social relations that constitute military relationships with the Haida—and form by definition the social terrain upon which occupation occurs—are eroded and erased so that, in turn, military violence can be wielded against Indigenous community members as if they exist outside of any social or affective relationships with military personnel. Indeed, the rendering absent of military presence could even be understood to reinforce this power, offering us (the fantasy of) a despatialized and nonsocial military force that can operate anywhere without any ongoing commitments to the peoples or communities against which they operate.

The durabilities of domination, then, need to be carefully managed, because affective ties, social relations, kin-making, and all the other ways in which military personnel, Haida people, and their settler neighbors build community together are *also* durable, at least in potential, and can precisely rupture such fantasies of military totality. The very fact that people like Daniel Montgomery experienced such ambivalence at the military's departure points to this. Undercutting these social durabilities requires what we might almost think of as a premeditated plan for ruination, an anticipated foreclosure that leaves no space for ongoing relationality. The military was always going to leave, even as it made it appear as if it was there to stay. Disavowal, in this sense, is built into the structure of the military base itself, at once permanent and temporary. Except, as Marlene Liddle and her family discovered, the military did not, in fact, ever give up its occupying presence on Haida Gwaii.

## Ghostly Militaries and Durable Domination

Despite the ruination of CFS Masset, the military remained on the islands and continued to monitor the territory it claimed as its own. But there had certainly been a shift in approach with the closure of the Base. I was told on a number of occasions that the military personnel who remained on island had been ordered explicitly not to wear their uniforms, effectively "blending in" with the local population. These claims were coming from local residents and former base personnel, not active-duty officers, so they exist at the level of local rumor rather than, necessarily, military policy.[12] Nonetheless, the idea that the military had remained in concealment couples resonantly with the experiences of Marlene Liddle and her family. Recall that Liddle did not encounter any actual soldiers when her outhouse was declared illegal. Rather, her family returned to the presence of a note placed—one almost wishes to say surreptitiously—while they were in the woods resource gathering. Compare this experience with Fred Willis's stories of elders being forcibly removed and the frequent refrain of guns being leveled at berry pickers that dotted my conversations with older Haida who had lived through the Base era. For Liddle's family, rather, there was an almost ghostly quality to military presence, making its claims known without direct, human interaction.

We must remain clear, however, that the performance of a disappearance, or the assumption of a ghostly quality, is not actual absence. The military personnel who put that note on the outhouse were not ghosts, and they maintained the same capacity for violence they had when they made their presence overt. The ruination of the base was itself a form of disavowal, a means through which the military could deny its ongoing presence on Haida lands. What Liddle's experiences show us, moreover, is that what is held to be most durable under the conditions of colonial occupation are not the material sedimentations of the military or, especially, their potentially unsettling social relations with Indigenous civilians. What is durable is the maintenance of domination itself. This was certainly not lost on Marlene Liddle. "Regardless of the DND having a 'lease' or 'license of operation' over that area," Liddle wrote to the local paper in response to the notice,

> "for the radio station or 'elephant trap' or whatever you want to call it I am hereby giving notice that as a Haida I will not be pushed out, or

bullied out of accessing an area that my family and generations before me have accessed for pleasure, and for food gathering![13] . . . Your 'occupation' of my traditional lands have altered the appearance and use on a much larger scale than my little outhouse ever will! Your 'golf course' has ruined our berry picking areas, and our access to a large swath of land that covers acres. I think that we have a bigger issue that needs to be discussed, not only with myself, but with our community as a whole." (Peerless 2013)

For Liddle, in other words, the note on her outhouse was an extension of the Base itself, an instrument of settler violence and domination on Haida traditional territory—altering Haida land and restricting Haida access to resource-gathering areas that had been used for generations. The ruins of CFS Masset did not mean, then, that the military was gone. Really, they did not mean anything at all for Marlene Liddle, since the "issue" that the Base had always represented remained ongoing.

Instead, Liddle's argument centers the violence of occupation. The purpose of the military's presence on Haida Gwaii was never, in the first instance, *to* dominate Haida territory. Rather, it did so as a matter of course, a taken-for-granted privilege of the settler appropriation of Indigenous lands. As Marlene Liddle, Fred Willis, and David Armstrong all describe, this privilege was maintained by force of arms, always ready to be pointed at Haida who "trespassed" on lands the military was occupying. We should take Marlene Liddle seriously, in turn, when she invokes a "bigger issue" in need of discussion. Indeed, one could extend her critique to the mechanisms of settler colonialism more broadly—the occupation of Indigenous territories via legal means that ignore Indigenous claims to sovereignty and land title; the transformation of the lands and waters in sometimes devastating ways that ignore long histories of Indigenous rights, resource practices, and care for human and nonhuman beings; and, of course, the many different means of violence through which colonial domination is effective and maintained (see Kauanui 2016; Wolfe 2006). The military is metonymy here, the literal occupying force that instantiates and undergirds settler colonialism at its most basic level.

Military violence is at the heart of settler colonialism. Consider, for instance, Audra Simpson's reflections on the so-called Oka Crisis, which occurred when a country club in the Quebec town of Oka extended its golf course directly onto the land of the Mohawk community of Kanehasatà:ke in the early 1990s. After months of peaceful protest to this latest iteration of centuries of land expropriation produced little result, as Audra Simpson narrates, "the Warrior society convened at Kanehasatà:ke with AK-47 assault rifles," intending to directly block the theft of their land. In response, Quebec's provincial government and the federal government of Canada deployed a total of 2,650 troops to end what had been declared a "crisis" in settler media. There were only fifty-five Mohawk Warriors. "This," writes Simpson, "was the most unambiguous form of exceptional relations, that of warfare" (2014, 151–52). Similar shows of violence occurred throughout Canadian history, just as they continue into the present, as the 2018 and 2019 deployments of the RCMP (armed with assault rifles, sniper rifles, and helicopters) to "remove" Wet'suwet'en elders and activists from their own land demonstrate (Dhillon and Parrish 2019; NetNewsLedger 2020; Nikiforuk 2019).

This colonial capacity for immediate and overpowering military intervention on Indigenous lands and in Indigenous communities undergirds the many "diverse forms of violence—from cultural repression to labour coercion to sexual exploitation," as Penelope Edmonds and Amanda Nettelbeck put it, that together constitute imperial and colonial domination in settler contexts (Edmonds and Nettelbeck 2018, 6).[14] Dispossession, as Leanne Betasamosake Simpson writes of her Michi Saagiig Nishnaabeg Nation, "was accomplished and is maintained through land theft as a result of unethical treaty making and the murdering, disappearing, assimilating and erasing of Michi Saagiig Nishnaabeg bodies and presence from the north shore of Ontario" (2017, 41). All of these are essentially violent processes, but, echoing both Weber and Agamben, it is the colonial monopoly on "legitimate" violence that makes them possible by rendering Indigenous bodies perpetually vulnerable *as* Indigenous bodies, bodies that always carry the potential to be excluded from the circle of settler society and legitimately killed as its inconvenient excess (A. Simpson 2014, 152–57; cf. Agamben 1998; Weber 1994). Or, put another way, the distinctively military capacity to, at any moment, slip Indigenous subjects from the category of "(partial) citizen" to "enemy" is one means through which colonial legitimacy is *produced* in the first instance, allowing military interventions to be read by settler citizens as the maintenance of civil order rather than the exertion of colonial (and colonizing) force. We will return to this slippage in greater depth in chapter 3.

What the Oka Crisis, the attacks on Wet'suwet'en protestors, and the many other cognate moments in which police and military force are deployed to "address" Indigenous protest has in common are their *visibility*. These are the flashpoint moments, the overt expressions of military violence that remind both Indigenous and settler citizens alike of the capacity of the settler state to enforce its territorial authority. In order to remain marked as "exceptional," however, such violence must become invisible in the course of everyday life. Here is where the particular configuration that was CFS Masset can give us specific insights into the broader nature of colonial occupation. Unlike an RCMP raid on an Indigenous camp, the Base was not *aimed* at the Haida community. As a naval listening station, it was focused on the Cold War, and the everyday ways in which it *happened* to dominate Indigenous territories and attempt to regulate Indigenous lives could be understood as a mere epiphenomenon of everyday military practice. The Base, in other words, was not commissioned, explicitly, to dominate Indigenous populations but, rather, did so as a matter of course. And this mundane quality, this everyday domination, erases itself even as it proceeds, even as it eventually erodes even the possibility for alternative modes of relationality.

And, of course, the Base was itself exceptional rather than typical as a military base. It was meant to be "open-concept," after all, a striking move away from the model of army facilities as being spaces of fear surrounded by barbed wire fences. Yet, as we have seen, there was tremendous insecurity about this very openness. Both the Base's facilities themselves and the Base's personnel policies undercut the idea that anything could be durable in the military's relationship to Haida Gwaii except for the simple fact of occupation itself. And for those purposes, a Base in the center of town was simply far too visible. The ruination of the Base works as itself a form of disavowal, concealing through the very appearance of disappearance the ongoing conditions of occupation to which Marlene Liddle pointed so effectively in her letter (cf. Leathem 2019).[15]

## "They Sure Thought We'd Miss Them"

One night, over dinner with Haida friends in their house in the Village of Masset, which was once one of the private married quarters, we began to chat about the legacy of the Base and my research. After reflecting on her own experiences over many years of engagement with the personnel of CFS Masset, Primrose Adams, Elder and Matriarch, responded pithily, "They sure thought we'd miss them. We didn't."

There are many ways to read Adams's quip. One, as Marlene Liddle discovered, would be quite literal—how can one miss the military when they have never, actually, left? But we might also see in Adams's statement an almost sympathetic understanding that military personnel too were engaged in relationship building with Haida, that they too were subject to the ambivalences of bonds that were "not built to last." As I've argued, the dangerous possibility of military-Indigenous relationships is mutuality, the ways in which military personnel could find themselves in relationships with Haida people in which both care and respect are entailed. Even beyond the unsettling promise of such relationships, however, the idea that at least some military personnel hoped to be appreciated for the work they understood themselves to be doing for the Haida community, even if that work was ultimately Janus-faced, would not be particularly surprising. Adams nods to this in her quip, positioning the military as actively desirous of affective ties, of wanting to be missed. For non-Haida, just as much as Haida, relationships are meant to be durable even when, structurally, they are foreclosed: thus, the hope that Adams reads into the military officers by saying, "They sure thought we'd miss them." In this we see the ways in which the military's policies also do a kind of affective violence to its own personnel, preventing them from building relationships with Haida people even if they might wish to do so. All that is left is for them to hope to be missed.

Ruination, particularly in Navaro-Yashin's reading, is inextricable from loss. What has been lost on Haida Gwaii is not the violence of military occupation. Such violence cannot be escaped under the ongoing structures of settler colonialism. But what the ruins of the Base—literal and figurative—represent is the loss of the potential for something otherwise to colonial hegemony, the potential for relationships that might be more entangled, more complex, perhaps even relationships that could open up the space for dialogue, for mutuality. This loss is worth mourning, at least for Daniel Montgomery and those Haida who find the legacy of the Base irreconcilable. And, one imagines, it might be worth mourning for those military personnel who did wish to make Haida Gwaii home, for whom the golf course, the swimming pool, and the other transformations that CFS Masset brought with it were also part of making the islands into a more suitable home for cosmopolitan Canadian military officers.

Primrose Adams, by contrast, was not ambivalent in our conversation. There was an affective charge, a sharpness, to Adams's quip that text does not convey perfectly: "*They* sure thought *we'd* miss them. We didn't." Adams here claims the power to reject, to refuse, an ongoing affective relationality with the military, and she claims it on behalf of her Haida community more generally. Regardless of what the military might have wanted, it was an aggressive presence on Haida land and the changes it had brought were neither asked for nor, necessarily, desired. For Adams, who experienced Haida

Gwaii's entire military era over the course of the twentieth century, there is nothing there worth missing, either by her or by Haida people more generally. While she hints that military personnel might regret this loss even though they engendered it, Primrose Adams is certain that the Haida community has no reason to regret the loss of relationality with the forces of occupation. Haida people, for Adams, have no need to ever reconcile themselves to the presence of settler military forces. Indeed, as the continuing pseudophantasmic presence of military personnel on Haida Gwaii reminds us, the promise of relationality, of an "open-concept" military base embedded in the community, was always illusory, always a means of disguising the violence of settler colonialism. Even the sincerest of affects are eroded by this ongoing violence.

Primrose Adams's quip both encapsulates the tremendous ambivalence of Indigenous-settler relation building under the conditions of ongoing colonial occupation and articulates a precise form of refusal. For Adams, the ground upon which relationships might be built cannot be determined by settler subjects, regardless of their desires to that effect. Instead, it is up to Haida people to determine their own orientations to settler society. Echoing Fred Willis's call for the military to "ask first" before they step on Haida territory, Primrose Adams refuses the idea that the military has a right to expect to be "missed" when it is a force of occupation. In so doing, she also refuses the disavowal of violence that such an expectation makes possible.

# PART II | Empty Signifiers

CHAPTER THREE

# So-Called Reconciliation

## *Empty Signifiers and Settler Political Community*

### "Unity"—A Parable for Reconciliation in Canada

I was puzzled when I spotted the notice depicted on the next page in the elevator of a luxury apartment building in downtown Edmonton near the end of 2021. Addressed primarily to the residents of the building, the notice's particular combination of earnest vagueness caught my attention. What, I wondered, is "the" healing process with "our" Indigenous communities? (Note the possessive "our" here.) Had the building's managers taken other measures to engage with local Indigenous Nations, or was this a more general reference to the ubiquitous usage of reconciliation that had come to define settler media representations of contemporary Indigenous-state relations? If that was the case, and this name change was meant somehow to acknowledge either local First Nations or Edmonton's status as a community encompassed by Treaty 8, then why was the building's name being changed to something as achingly generic as "The Residences on 104th"?[1]

I did, at the very least, find a few answers to these questions. The undefined "neighborhood renaming process" to which the sign referred was, in fact, a reference to the recently successful campaign to rename Oliver Square, the small retail hub in which the newly (re)minted Residences on 104th were located. Frank Oliver, for whom the area had been named, was the founder of one of Edmonton's earliest newspapers and, in his later life, a politician who was appointed minister of the interior by Wilfred Laurier in 1905. In that role (and throughout his life), Oliver advocated for stringent restrictions on immigration, particularly in relation to Black immigrants, and engaged in systematic attacks on Native communities in order to further curtail Indigenous land rights of any kind (see Donald 2004).[2] Though the Oliver Community League that championed removing Oliver's name from his eponymous square emphasized his complicity in these different forms of settler colonialism and antiblack racism as the reason for its campaign, it was the commercial real-estate company BentallGreenOak, "in consultation with local business owners and community leaders," which arrived at the former Oliver Square's new name: Unity Square. Its press mailer reads, "Welcome to

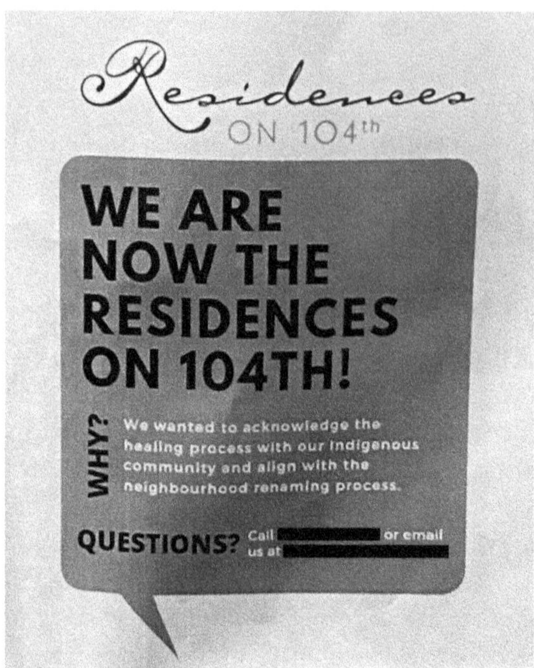


"The Healing Process." Photo by author, November 2021.

Unity Square, where the awesome power of community connects" (CBC News 2021).

While it remains unknown to me to what extent those community leaders included First Nations or Black participants, the fact that the chosen name is bereft of any specific mention of either Indigenous Peoples or Black Canadians is telling. So too is the choice of the term "unity" to replace the name of a historical politician whose perspectives and policies white settler Canadians now understand to be intolerant and intolerable. Oliver's name inscribed a specific historical violence onto the space of downtown Edmonton, offering an uncomfortable reminder that Canada was built on colonial dispossession coupled with fundamentally racialized immigration policies. "Unity," by contrast, inscribes very little at all; it is a generic statement that indexes no necessary commitments to any particularly political causes or transformations in Canadian society. The reader of BentallGreenOak's mailer is simply meant to understand that "community" has an "awesome power," which somehow exists in relation to "connection," which are both themselves forms of unity. It's a kind of semiotic tautology, in which any of the specific references to actual people that *inspired* the name change in the first place have disappeared. Put another way, because "unity" only really indexes itself, it could mean anything at all that a given reader might wish it to mean without actually committing itself to any one particular interpretation.

There is another important dynamic within this small story. Just as the mailer for Unity Square's renaming does not specify the "awesome power of community," the building announcement with which we began assumes that there *is* a healing process with "our Indigenous communities" that is already ongoing within which this renaming can form part and that building residents will immediately understand. It presents an implicitly settler "we"—an already given sociopolitical community—that is engaging in healing with *our* Indigenous communities—the possessive marking the gradual inclusion of the Indigenous outside inside the settler inside, encompassed, of course, within the grammar of settler possessiveness.[3]

The availability of this unspecified "healing process" to be invoked by building managers without further comment, I would suggest, is a consequence of the broader settler discourse of reconciliation in Canada, encountered here less in the spectacular mode of public events and settler performance marked by Michelle Daigle as "the spectacle of reconciliation" (2019) but, rather, in the aching banality of something that is already so taken for granted that it has come to mean nothing, very much, at all. In invoking the idea of banality, I signal a certain affiliation with Hannah Arendt's famed argument in *Eichmann in Jerusalem*, and, in particular, Judith Butler's reading of the text. Arendt, as is well known, located the "banality of evil" in its unthinking, routinized quality; banality itself was a failure to think. "In a sense," as Butler puts it, "by calling a crime against humanity "banal," [Arendt] was trying to point to the way in which the crime had become for the criminals accepted, routinised, and implemented without moral revulsion and political indignation and resistance" (2011, 1). Crucial to understand here is the fact that banality is neither natural nor inherent; rather, thinking, as Arendt understands it, is effectively evacuated from systems of action so as to render them unavailable for moral or ethical consideration. They are, in a sense, made into objects of unthinking. Reconciliation, I suggest in this chapter, is similarly *made* banal for settler Canadians.

In particular, what I am interested in investigating are some of the ways in which settler discourse renders reconciliation into an empty signifier, a term whose semiotic underdetermination plays a central role in its ability to bind together highly disparate meanings within the formation of a political community (Laclau 2005). The empty signifier is a productive concept to help us better understand the era of reconciliation, a technology of erasure in which the very invocation of reconciliation works to erode the concept's ability to be precise and meaningful. In this chapter, I argue that mainstream, typically settler representations of "reconciliation"—and a semiotic universe of associated terms such as "healing" and "unity"—mean, precisely, nothing. And this, I contend, is precisely the point. The forms of settler discourse I explore in this chapter *empty* reconciliation of any possible meaning, insulating the term from entailing any specific commitments, transformation, or even social action as such on the part of colonial governance or, for that matter, settler subjects in their day-to-day lives. My point, I should add, is not that *all* settler political speech is empty of determinate meaning; rather, what I explore here are ways in which colonial discourses are always at work attempting to empty out this very meaning. It is tendency, a pattern, an act, and a process in, through, and with language.

Though they might be attempts to void determinate meaning, however, empty signifiers do real social and political work, binding together communities through their ability to embrace the empty signifier's curious mix of redolent effect and semiotic indeterminacy. Reconciliation, as Haida curator Jisgang, Nika Collison has put it, is *useful* to settler society, "commodified by the Western world in certain circles to further certain agendas" (Collison and Levell 2018, 78). And this usefulness, I suggest, is constitutive rather than merely instrumental; in emptying reconciliation and them mobilizing it as an empty signifier, settler discourses of reconciliation work to reconstitute the sociopolitical order in Canada a way that "includes" both settlers and Indigenous subjects, but always, already, on settler colonial terms. The empty signifier of reconciliation thus forms the second technology of erasure this book explores, one that partakes in the active deceptions of colonial disavowal we have previously explored and, at the same time, works to form settler political community precisely as if it *is* legitimate and unified.

What, then, happens to those Indigenous people (and Peoples) who do not wish to form part of this reconciled "unity?" Not only are they cast out from "reconciled" Canadian society, but the trick of the empty signifier is to make it appear that these Indigenous actors have arbitrarily rejected the very possibility of a better life for both Indigenous people and settlers alike. It is *their* fault they do not want reconciliation. Joanne Barker's figure of the Indigenous terrorist (2022) here fuses with Audra Simpson's poignant question of what it means when Indigenous people "refuse the good" (2014, 1). Not only does this imaginary of the Indigenous "enemy" constitute the boundaries of contemporary Canadian political society via its putative refusal of the good-faith efforts of Canadian settler subjects, but the Indigenous enemy does so in a way that naturalizes its own exclusion. Why *wouldn't* an individual or a community *want* to work toward reconciliation, toward unity, toward healing? Thus, Canadian settler subjects can sincerely believe they are working toward reconciliation—an undefined but affectively charged "good"—while in fact working to draw ever tighter the limits on what forms of Indigenous politics can be recognized by the settler state and what political actions should be cast out as the work of the terrorist, the enemy of the state. Put simply, reconciliation is not done *with* Indigenous Peoples; it is done to them.

In order to better demonstrate these claims, this chapter examines a number of sites at which settler discourses empty the signifier of reconciliation. I begin by nuancing my terms, in particular putting Argentinian political philosopher Ernesto Laclau's rendering of the concept in conversation with Lenape Indigenous Studies scholar Joanne Barker's analysis of the Indigenous terrorist as colonial state shibboleth. I then turn to a few different theaters of Canadian reconciliation, each of which turns on higher stakes—and more evident modes of erasure and exclusion—than were present in my initial example of Edmonton's newly minted Unity Square. First, I consider the nested denials of responsibility that have characterized the responses of settler political leaders to the ongoing police actions against Wet'suwet'en Land Defenders in relation to the recent spate of acts committing federal and provincial Canadian governments to implementing the United Nations Declaration on the Rights of Indigenous Peoples (UNDRIP). Second, I examine the controversy surrounding Conservative senator Lynn Beyak's dismissal of the abuses of Canada's residential schools program in relation to the recent settler-led "Freedom convoy" protests that dominated Canadian media attention for much of the early months of 2022. Finally, I follow former Liberal prime minister Justin Trudeau on a seemingly very poorly timed visit to the beach.

## The Political Community of Empty Signifiers

### *Populist Reason and Semiotic Emptiness*

In 2005's *On Populist Reason*, Ernesto Laclau characterizes the core of political communities as being a set of relations among differences—in particular, different forms of social demand (73). While some of these demands *can* be fulfilled via already-present institutional frameworks, the demands that are left unfulfilled—what Laclau terms "democratic" demands—can gradually be connected together as part of a "chain of equivalence," linked not by their individual denotational signifieds but, rather, by the simple fact of being unfulfilled (74). What enables these demands to cohere together, for the chain to stabilize, is the emergence of an "empty signifier," one particular demand within the chain that comes to synecdochally represent its entirety. As part of this process, the empty signifier is gradually stripped of any determinate meaning, coming to act instead purely as a means of signifying the chain as a whole.

This signifier becomes "increasingly full from an *extensional* point of view, for it represents an ever-larger chain of demands," but "*intensionally* poorer, for it has to dispossess itself of particularistic contents in order to embrace social demands which are quite heterogeneous" (96, emphasis original). Or, put another way, signifiers are quite literally *emptied*. The "people," "popular identity," "justice," and "freedom" are all terms that can occupy (and have historically occupied) this space of signification. Affect is crucial here; as Laclau argues, it is the ability of a political community to "invest" affectively in a particular empty signifier as a marker of collective identity that gives populist movements their power, precisely because they are *not* premised on any one individual demand (115).[4] The less clearly we are able to define *how* to "make America great again," to give an example that will be immediately familiar to most of my readers, the easier it is to believe in the idea, even as it structures radically different individual demands.

Laclau's theorization of the constitutive value of empty signifiers resonates with prior theorizations. Most notable among these are Stuart Hall's classic characterization of race as a "floating" or "sliding" signifier that can shift scale and position within discursive chains toward different political ends (2017) and Claude Lévi-Strauss's similar reading of mana as a "floating signifier."[5] That is, mana, as Lévi-Strauss defines it, "is a symbol in its pure state," whose "zero symbolic value" makes it "liable to take on any symbolic content whatever" (1987, 64). In both theorizations, the semiotic indeterminacy of "floating" signifiers offers a kind of coherence to otherwise incoherent discursive systems. As Lévi-Strauss puts it, they enable "symbolic thinking to operate despite the contradiction inherent in it" (63). But there is a political specificity to Laclau's rendering that differentiates it from either Hall's or Lévi-Strauss's arguments, one that makes Laclau's formulation both particularly useful and particularly troubling for our purposes.

This is because politics, for Laclau, cannot cohere without the projection of some kind of oppositional force. The populist movements with which Laclau is concerned form because a given "people" makes demands upon a "power" of some kind that is unable (or unwilling) to fulfill those demands. There is an enemy against which populism can fashion itself and thereby claim to represent a political totality that is constitutively unfulfilled. "A demand," Laclau writes, "is always addressed to somebody" (86). Because Laclau's oppositional framing is premised on deficiency in relation to institutionalized power, there is little room in his account for the application of populist reason to already well-instituted political communities—institutions, after all, do not make demands; they are subject to them. The work that empty signifiers do to bind political communities, however, need not be limited to thinking through populist movements in opposition to an already-institutionalized state. In Canada, we in fact see the reverse: the deployment of semiotic emptiness in order to make an already-constituted political community appear (and feel) *as if* it is remade anew, without thereby losing the oppositional character of the political body itself.

### *The Limits of Canadian Political Community*

In 2015, in a speech marking the release of the Final Report of the Truth and Reconciliation Commission of Canada, Justice Murray Sinclair, the commission's chair, told his audience that he stood before them, "hopeful that we are at a new threshold of a new era in this country." A "period of change," Sinclair continued, "is beginning, that if sustained by the will of the people, will forever realign the shared history of indigenous and non-indigenous peoples in Canada." In response, then–recently elected Liberal prime minster Justin Trudeau reiterated the prior government's apology for the abuses of the residential school system and affirmed that his government would "respect and renew its relationship" with Indigenous people in Canada. "We will remember," Trudeau asserted, "that reconciliation is not an Aboriginal issue, it is a Canadian issue" (Mas 2015).

While Trudeau's intention in the latter statement may have been to signal an understanding that "reconciliation" is the responsibility of settler as well as Indigenous Canadians, I think we can also take the framing of "reconciliation" as "a Canadian issue" quite literally. If, as I am contending, reconciliation is an empty signifier in Laclau's sense, then two consequences follow. First, reconciliation would work to bind a political community together by unifying seemingly very disparate demands, ideas, and positions and simultaneously symbolizing that unity. Second, it would do so in relationship to an oppositional group, something against which the political community can define itself. If that political community, as Trudeau suggests, is "Canada," then what might be the oppositional group? My contention in this chapter (and throughout this book) is that it is Indigenous Peoples themselves that are the secret "enemy" to the settler vision of reconciliation—and to the Canadian political community it constitutes.

In order to better understand this seemingly contradictory claim, it is helpful to turn to Joanne Barker's (2021) analysis of the figure of the "Indigenous terrorist." Drawing both on twentieth- and twenty-first-century discourses of the political-cum-cultural figure of the "terrorist"—which itself encompasses communists, Middle Eastern "jihadists," and other, interrelated figures—and the actual history of counterterrorist strategies being applied to Indigenous communities and organizations by the United States and Canada, Barker makes the compelling argument that colonial state authorities "slide," to borrow Hall's term, Indigenous Peoples into the category of terrorist whenever they are perceived as resisting or opposing the settler state.[6] Indeed, such a position as alter to the state can itself be understood as the normative space that Indigenous Peoples have occupied historically, given the simple fact that settler colonialism is premised on the erasure of an already-present and ongoing Indigenous sovereignty. It is thus relatively easy to (re)position Indigenous actors and communities in the role of "enemy of the state" when their goals do not align with colonial (or imperial) priorities, since Indigenous Peoples never quite "belonged" to the state to begin with (cf. Rifkin 2009).

But not all Indigenous people. Echoing Audra Simpson's influential characterization of Indigenous refusal as "refusing the good" (2014, 1), Barker argues that Indigenous Peoples are continually faced with the choice between defending their sovereignty, their territories, and their responsibilities to maintain proper relationships with other communities of beings and being "good" citizens within the framework of a colonially constituted and imperially instituted liberal multiculturalism. As Barker writes, focusing here on state attacks on the #NoDAPL protests:

> This was not a war of words, as social and news media often portrayed it. It was a struggle over the state's modes of objectification, which sought to transform Indigenous people into the particular kinds of subjects—terrorists—over which it had absolute authority, not just "here and now" but across state borders and in perpetuity. This required not merely a "casting out" into rightlessness, as Sherene H. Razack argues in relation to Muslims, but a particular kind of inclusion—one demanding that Indigenous peoples reject their sovereignty and self-determination and subject themselves entirely to the legal terms,

> material conditions, and political interests of the United States and Canada. In short, they were required to let go of their Indigeneity, even as that Indigeneity was used to represent the state's embodiment of the values of a multicultural democratic society. (2021, 22)

Reconciliation—the empty signifier—is the mechanism that makes this "particular kind of inclusion" possible in Canada. Reconciliation does not align Canadian settler society to Indigenous Nations. It demands the alignment *of* those nations to the political goodwill of the liberal state, which can encompass everything except Indigenous sovereignty itself. Sovereignty is the irreducible difference, in Laclau's terms. It is the element that cannot be equivocated within the chain of equivalence. Reconciliation, however, is framed *so as* to include all, meaning that when Indigenous Peoples continue to refuse the state, they are refusing the good of multicultural democracy itself. They cannot thus be anything but terrorists, the paradigmatic enemy, outside of the political community that reconciliation has (re)constituted.

A tremendous political sleight of hand is thereby accomplished. As I have argued elsewhere (2015), there has been no "break" in Canadian governance from the country's confederation in the late nineteenth century to the present. But the ideological demands of portraying oneself as a morally legitimate nation-state have most certainly changed. Crucial among these is a commitment to multiculturalism, to the "tolerance" of difference, and to the vision of the nation as an unproblematically transparent unity of citizens who are able to live a good life together despite, across, and because of their respective differences (cf. Brown 2006).[7] One consequence of this shift has been policies of "recognition" across settler states that purport to recognize Indigenous "difference" while in effect strictly limning that difference in ways that can only ever reinforce the maintenance of colonial authority and domination (Coulthard 2014; B. Miller 2003; Povinelli 2002). But recognition cannot, in and of itself, encompass the colonial complexity of a country such as Canada, which ranges from provinces such as Ontario or Alberta, whose lands were negotiated in the context of historical treaties, the explicitly Inuit territory of Nunavut, the more limited incarnation of a similar framework in the Yukon, or the almost totally unceded Indigenous lands that represent the vast majority of the province of British Columbia, especially given the perceived failures of the modern treaty process in this province. Thus the promise of the era of reconciliation is that these complexities *will* be resolved, that there will be political unity in a Canada that remains Canada (which is to say, fundamentally colonial in its character), and thus that the political community can be reformed in the present so as to include Indigenous Peoples without friction, as transparently valued members of that polity.

In the process, Canada appears to have been remade, as if it is a new country, a new political community, one that is no longer tied to the violence of its colonial past. As a colonial technology of erasure, the empty signifier makes possible settler disavowal on a vast scale. Not only does it offer language through which the settler colony can justify virtually any action as being in some sense in the best interests of Indigenous Peoples, however violent that action may be, but it presents those peoples as effective enemies of the state should they refuse to be reconciled to their own domination. The fact that colonial violence *is* ongoing, however, whatever else may be said within the era of reconciliation, leaves open an incoherence in which the actual, material violence of Canadian state actors is at once ever present and consistently denied even as it is happening. It is to this incoherence that I now turn.

## "So-Called Reconciliation"

September 30, 2021, marked the first "National Day for Truth and Reconciliation" in Canada, a newly created national holiday intended for the "public commemoration of the tragic and painful history and ongoing impacts of residential schools," as stated by the official website of Heritage Canada, an organ of the federal government. This commemoration, the site continues, "is a vital component of the reconciliation process" (Government of Canada 2024). In his official statement for the day, then–Prime Minister Trudeau emphasized this same idea, suggesting that it was only by together "facing these hard truths, and righting these wrongs, that we can move together toward a more positive, fair, and better future." Furthermore, Trudeau (2021) claimed, "the Government of Canada has been working in partnership with indigenous peoples [*sic*] to close the gaps that still exist for far too many—and together we've made real progress."

Trudeau's statement goes on to elaborate the degree to which the federal government has fulfilled or is committed to fulfilling the recommendations set out by the TRC's final report and other measures Canada has taken, including, in particular, passing the United Nations Declaration on the Rights of Indigenous Peoples Act. This act, in the words of Justice Canada, "provides a roadmap for the Government of Canada and Indigenous peoples to work together to implement the Declaration based on lasting reconciliation, healing, and cooperative relations" (Department of Justice Canada n.d.). The reader will not be shocked, at this point, to learn that the act itself does not provide further specificity on what, precisely, this roadmap will include, though it does "affirm" that the United Nations Declaration on the Rights of Indigenous Peoples is a "universal international human rights instrument with application in Canadian law," commits Canada to rendering its law "consistent" with UNDRIP, and states that the promised roadmap should "address injustices" against and "promote mutual respect and understanding as well as good relations" with Indigenous Peoples (United Nations Declaration on the Rights of Indigenous Peoples Act 2021).

This is just one link, as it were, in reconciliation's chain of equivalence. There are many others in Canada, from the "Indigenous Strategic Plans" of major Canadian public universities (e.g., University of British Columbia 2021) to the Hudson Bay Company's controversial sale of orange shirts, worn to commemorate the horrors of the residential school system (Cram 2021).[8] It is, however, the ways that gestures to UNDRIP as part of "the" reconciliation process on the part of Canadian governments work to conceal the ways in which federal and provincial governments are in fact in violation *of* UNDRIP's terms that I wish in particular to emphasize in this section. The claim to "consistency" with UNDRIP, in other words, allows Canada's myriad *in*consistencies with the declaration to disappear. Here, the federal government's recent act joins British Columbia's 2019 provincial "Declaration on the Rights of Indigenous Peoples Act," which similarly established UNDRIP as "the Province's framework for reconciliation," mandating "to bring provincial laws into alignment with the UN Declaration" and requiring the Province to "develop and implement an action plan, in consultation and cooperation with Indigenous Peoples, to meet the objectives of the UN Declaration" (Government of British Columbia 2024a). Indeed, the two government bodies echo each other almost precisely, give or take the substitution of "roadmap" for "action plan" or the more proper capitalization of "Indigenous Peoples" in the province's text.

Given this shared provincial and federal commitment to developing a framework for implementing UNDRIP, it is useful, at this juncture, to highlight a few of the Declaration's provisions, namely, Articles 18 and 25; Article 29, subsection 1; and Article 32, subsections 1 and 2. Article 18:

> Indigenous peoples have the right to participate in decision-making in matters which would affect their rights, through representatives chosen by themselves in accordance with their own procedures, as well as to maintain and develop their own indigenous decision-making institutions. (UNDRIP 15–16)

Article 25:

> Indigenous peoples have the right to maintain and strengthen their distinctive spiritual relationship with their traditionally owned or otherwise occupied and used lands, territories, waters and coastal seas and other resources and to uphold their responsibilities to future generations in this regard. (UNDRIP 19)

Article 29, subsection 1:

> 1. Indigenous peoples have the right to the conservation and protection of the environment and the productive capacity of their lands or territories and resources. States shall establish and implement assistance programmes for indigenous peoples for such conservation and protection, without discrimination. (UNDRIP 21)

Article 32, subsections 1 and 2:

> 1. Indigenous peoples have the right to determine and develop priorities and strategies for the development or use of their lands or territories and other resources.
>
> 2. States shall consult and cooperate in good faith with the indigenous peoples concerned through their own representative institutions in order to obtain their free and informed consent prior to the approval of any project affecting their lands or territories and other resources, particularly in connection with the development, utilization or exploitation of mineral, water or other resources. (UNDRIP 23)

The emphasis in UNDRIP, as these articles make quite clear, is on the rights of Indigenous Peoples to determine what happens on their territories and what forms of resource extraction (if any) take place on those territories, and that free and informed prior consent is required for any projects that might take place on those lands.

Now, consider the Unist'ot'en Camp. As I note in this book's introduction, the Unist'ot'en Camp was established in 2007 by the Unist'ot'en Clan within the Wet'suwet'en Nation, with approval from all five of the Nation's clans, and has grown in size, scale, and significance until the present (see Barker 2021, 62–63). The camp's formal goal is to protest and, if necessary, prevent access to Coastal Gaslink and other energy development projects that seek to build on—and potentially damage—Unist'ot'en lands. As Leanne Betasamosake Simpson argues, the camp, and other similar blockades, are spaces of both refusal *and* affirmation, sites in which colonial extractivism and settler power can be opposed and interrupted and, simultaneously, world-building spaces for vital and ongoing Indigenous life (e.g., 2021, 10). Most of all, however, the Unist'ot'en Camp is a sovereign space, an articulation of the rights of the Unist'ot'en Clan to determine what happens on its own territory, an important dimension of Wet'suwet'en governance that would, at least in theory, be affirmed by the UNDRIP articles I have quoted above. And yet, in 2018, Coastal Gaslink Pipeline Ltd. filed an injunction against the camp, specifically naming community leaders and elders in their filings. RCMP raids against the camp followed, and continue into the time of this writing in early 2022. The scale and severity of these raids are stunning, as I have detailed in previous chapters, including permission to use "lethal overwatch," extensive military and surveillance equipment, media blackouts, systematic arrests, and, most recently, demands that Indigenous activists "prove" their indigeneity by providing information on blood quantum, despite this not being a requirement of Wetsuw'et'en Band membership or, for that matter, the nation's traditional laws.

My point here is a relatively simple one. This approach to "dismantling" the Unist'ot'en Camp is not in line with UNDRIP. This would not be de facto a problem for the Canadian settler state, given the conditions of disavowal I have pointed to earlier in this book, *except* for the fact that both the federal government of Canada and the provincial government of British Columbia have explicitly committed themselves to implementing UNDRIP as their framework *for* reconciliation. Two things are thus simultaneously true. First, these different governments and their agencies are authorizing, funding, and enacting ongoing violence against Indigenous land defenders. Second, they are espousing a set of documents that recognize Indigenous rights to sovereignty, to territorial protection, and to free, prior, and informed consent to any processes of resource extraction on or any ecological risk to their territories. Just as we saw in the previous chapters, the settler state here again engages in a colonially productive paradox, holding together contradictory positions so as to disavow the maintenance of colonial domination in the era of reconciliation.

Marking this seeming contradiction, one finds a remarkable pattern in the ways these different government agencies respond to the question of whether they are *responsible* for the ongoing violence against Wetsu'wet'en Land Defenders. Consider, for instance, the actions of deputy premier and solicitor general of British Columbia Mike Farnworth, who has authorized increased police presence in response to Wet'suwet'en Land Defenders for three straight years. When asked to comment on this decision in December of

2021, Farnworth's office responded, simply, that "enforcement decisions are made by police. Politicians do not direct police operations in B.C." This is one of many such statements made by the Horgan government to the effect that the provincial government does not directly interfere in police decision making. In the meantime, the federal government has suggested that it is not their place to interfere in a dispute between the province and the Wet'suwet'en Nation. And, all the while, the RCMP themselves have suggested they are simply enforcing court-mandated injunctions and are not themselves a decision-making entity. The irony of it all is made clear in a comment from Grand Chief Stewart Phillip of the Union of British Columbia Indian Chiefs: "We're deeply concerned with the current practice of the Horgan government to weaponize the use of injunctions to authorize these highly militaristic raids on Indigenous territory. It does not bode well for the future of so-called reconciliation" (Forester 2021).

Reconciliation is *always* "so-called reconciliation." It encompasses a political community that exists, by its very nature, in order to refuse Indigenous sovereignty. This refusal is rooted in the structural and historical conditions of colonial Canada. After all, it is in part the fact that the colonially constituted system of band governance in Westsu'wet'en territory has *not* opposed the pipelines in the same terms that enables the casting of the Unist'ot'en Camp as an illegitimate space of Indigenous terrorism. Thus can the Government Operations Centre—part of Canada's Department of Public Safety—argue that there is "no indication that ongoing protests and blockades have been endorsed by local band councils or First nations chiefs," despite the presence of multiple hereditary chiefs *at* the Unist'ot'en Camp. Thus can this same report characterize one of these same chiefs as an "aboriginal extremist" and characterize the camp as a threat to Canada's "national interest" (quoted in Barker 2021, 65). The "threat" here is not just the refusal *to* reconcile; it is the revelation of the discursive emptiness at the heart of reconciliation itself.

As long as Indigenous Peoples refuse colonial domination, settler Canadians will always be confronted by the violent realities of domination that underlie the veneer of liberal multiculturalism. The brilliance of reconciliation as a hegemonic formation is that it makes those Indigenous Peoples appear to be themselves responsible for the violence that is done against them. After all, they have refused the good. And yet, these Indigenous "terrorists" do not disappear, acting instead as a continual reminder that reconciliation is empty, a colonial performance that reconstitutes the settler state in its own image and must continually endure, as J. Kēhaulani Kauanui might put it,

Indigenous sovereignty (2016). Even the most pernicious and potent discursive strategies cannot erase the material realities of Indigenous action, as much as they might attempt to recast those actions as crimes against the common good. But what if Indigenous politics—and indigeneity itself—could be emptied of signification?

## The Political Community of Reconciliation

### *"The Good, as well as the Bad"*

In January 2021, Lynn Beyak announced her retirement from Canada's Senate. Beyak, who had been appointed in 2013 by Conservative prime minister Stephen Harper, was retiring three years earlier than the Senate's mandatory retirement age of seventy-four. Her early retirement generated little surprise from the Canadian public, given the controversy of her tenure as a senator. More specifically, by the time of her retirement, Beyak had become notorious as "the senator who defended residential schools," to borrow a phrase from the CBC headline announcing her retirement (Tasker 2021). Since 2017, Beyak had delivered a series of speeches and public statements pivoting on the "well-intentioned nature" of the residential schools system, which was too often "overshadowed by negative reports" of violence and abuse in the schools (quoted in Carleton 2021, 1). Her speech announcing her retirement exemplified this position:

> "Some have criticized me for stating that the good, as well as the bad, of residential schools should be recognized. I stand by that statement. Others have criticized me for stating that the Truth and Reconciliation report was not as balanced as it should be. I stand by that statement as well," Beyak said in the press release.
>
> "And finally, I have been criticized for offering concerned Canadians a space to comment critically about the Indian Act. My statements and the resulting posts were never meant to offend anyone, and I continue to believe that Indigenous issues are so important to all of us that a frank and honest conversation about them is vital." (Tasker 2021)

Beyak's speech—and broader position—was roundly criticized by settler and Indigenous politicians, leaders, and scholars alike. These critiques point—quite legitimately, I think—to Beyak's racism, including comments about the "dirty" appearance of an Indigenous man at one of her (multiple) federally ordered antiracism training sessions; to her willful erasure of the myriad abuses that occurred individually and systematically at residential schools in Canada; and, perhaps most broadly, to her attacks against "truth and reconciliation in Canada," as the title of an article by settler historian Sean Carleton (2021) frames it.

However, I am less convinced that Beyak's position is genuinely *in opposition* to the empty signifier of reconciliation in Canada. After all, note the ways in which Beyak frames her comments not as racism—that is to say, not as deliberately hateful speech—but, rather, as a framework for a conversation about issues important to "all of us," an implicitly settler majoritarian claim. In response, Carleton's article carefully analyses the discursive tropes on which Beyak and her supporters rely in order to oppose the "denialism" they represent with facts and reasoned inquiry, rather than merely dismissing it as "ignorance" (e.g., 2–3). Beyak's comments are thus shown as false on their own merits, allowing a better and more reasoned approach to truth and reconciliation in Canada and less space for Beyak-style denialism. It reconstitutes a better and more reasoned "all of us" from which figures like Beyak should learn, and allows fair ground for their dismissal if they do not.

And yet, I want to emphasize the *civility* of this response. Beyak was not arrested, not branded a radical nor subjected to police violence. The question turned instead, merely, on whether Beyak was "ignorant" and thus could be educated, or whether she was acting in genuinely bad faith and would thus, at worst, face suspension from the Senate. And, crucially, in response, Beyak consistently attempted to include herself *in* the circle of reconciliation, making appeals to equity, to balance, to reason, to the space of rational debate and discussion. Beyak's failure was thus, in a sense, simply one of rhetoric, as her position ultimately could not be absorbed within the chain of equivalence. But Beyak's fundamental *belonging* within the political community was never in question—at worst, she was simply a bad faith actor requiring community discipline. Even within the context of Carleton's critical article, however, Beyak has continually been afforded the privilege of personhood and political membership in Canada. This is quite different than, say, the RCMP's response to the Indigenous "extremists" against whom reconciliation itself is positioned. Wetsu'wet'en Land Defenders are not "bad faith" actors who can be rationally debated within mainstream settler discourse; they are threats that must be eliminated for the good of Canada itself.

There is, in addition, one particular—and perhaps, almost peculiar—element to which I wish to point in the Beyak controversy. It was reported that, at multiple points during the first session of her antiracism training at the Ontario Federation of Indigenous Friendship Centres, Beyak "claimed

Indigenous ancestry because her family had adopted a First Nations child," and "'consistently referred' to her Métis status and her 'Indigeneity' during discussions about the place of Indigenous peoples in Canada" (Tasker 2021). In so doing, Beyak engaged in the discursive production of what Barker has termed "the Kinless Indian": "The Kinless Indian is the Indian without any but an invented relationship to Indigenous people, often cultivated through family or local folklore. This Indian allows the imperialist not merely to follow or be cured by an Indigenous shaman but to claim an Indigeneity all its own. The imperialist is thus not only saved but absolved of any responsibility for any benefit from or complicity with state violence against Indigenous people by suggesting that, all along, they were in fact, if secret, the Indigenous" (2021, 70–71).

By folding herself into the category of indigeneity, Beyak implicitly suggests not only that she cannot be engaging in racist or anti-Indigenous speech or practice but, more significantly, that her positions represent an authentic articulation *of* an Indigenous politics. The issue, in other words, is not simply that of "appropriation." It is, rather, the constitutive erasure of an indigeneity that opposes the settler state through the assimilation of whiteness itself into indigeneity. If Lynn Beyak is Indigenous, and as an Indigenous person is arguing that residential schools were not so bad, that colonialism was "good intentioned," then, by implication, those Indigenous people who *do* argue that residential schools were systematically violent and that settler colonialism is indeed ongoing can be recast as "extremists," particularly when they take action to oppose the settler state of which Beyak, as a Senator, formed an explicit part.

From this perspective, Beyak does not oppose reconciliation. She *is* reconciliation, a signifier emptied of any elements that could threaten colonial hegemony or, for that matter, white supremacy. Beyak sketches the limit of what the chain of equivalence can include, by both her inflammatory statements and her "race-shifting," in Circe Sturm's (2011) terms: her claims to an invented indigeneity. In so doing, she naturalizes the *real* opponents to reconciliation as those Indigenous actors who nonetheless claim their sovereignty, regardless of—and often in opposition to—even the most fulsomely articulated expressions of the good faith of the colonial state. Barker argues that the Murderable Indian—the Indigenous terrorist—and the Kinless Indian—the race-shifter—work in tandem to erase Indigenous sovereignty and, thus, indigeneity itself. The latter reconfigures the space of indigeneity *within* the political community so as to be meaningless, while the former represents the right of the state to kill any Indigenous life that opposes colonial domination. As Barker puts it, "Together, the Murderable/Kinless Indian disciplines Indigeneity into a position of death for the taking" (2021, 111).

### *"Freedom"*

If Lynn Beyak represents the limit of what modes of political speech can be included within the discursive emptiness of reconciliation within a relatively civil framework, the so-called Freedom Convoy that occupied Ottawa between January 22 and February 23 in 2022 staged those limits in a far more visible and violent fashion. The convoy's stated goal, as per January fundraising material from some of its primary organizers, was to protest "against the COVID-19 vaccine mandate introduced Jan. 15 by Canada on cross-border truckers," though its explicit demands rapidly expanded to encompass the end of all vaccine mandates in Canada (Aiello 2022). While the group claimed to represent an international coalition of long-haul truckers and their allies, a statement released by the Canadian Trucking Alliance condemning the occupation noted that more than 85 percent of truckers were fully vaccinated and complying with federal and provincial COVID-19 restrictions, and that the organization as a whole did not support the convoy (Canadian Trucking Alliance 2022). In truth, the convoy was a disparate assemblage of different communities of protestors, at least some of whom had strong ties to white supremacist organizations and far-right conspiracy networks of various kinds (Gilmore 2022). What united the convoy, at least to many observers, was a commitment to Whiteness (with a capital "W"), with American confederate flags and swastikas on display at various moments during the Ottawa occupation (e.g., Crawford 2022). It was quickly associated with parallel white supremacist demonstrations in the United States—and, indeed, included some shared participants (Coletta and Timsit 2022)—and widely identified as a fundamentally racist space of sustained violence against the residents of Ottawa and the other Canadian communities in which allied convoys attempted to establish similar occupations.

The convoy was extraordinarily disruptive, making the city of Ottawa close to impassable for a month, harassing residents, disrupting medical and other critical supply chains, and defacing local monuments. The police response to the convey was, however, markedly muted, and it was not until February 14, after more than two weeks of sustained convoy occupation, that then–Prime Minister Trudeau invoked the Emergencies Act in order to authorize measures to remove the convoy. It was not lost on either many

Indigenous people or even settler Canadians that this was a radically different response than that typically adopted against Indigenous blockades, including the Unist'ot'en Camp, which faced rapid and overwhelming military, police, and private security opposition. As Indigenous scholars Joyce Green and Gina Starblanket wrote in an op-ed in the *Regina Leader-Post*, "Indigenous people everywhere are shaking their heads. If only we got that kind of support and concern the "truckers" get when we challenge the many forms of injustice that Canadian freedom is built upon. The indulgence for these "truckers" to date is a far cry from official and popular responses to our public critiques and protests. As Canada contemplates the "freedom convoy" and its claims of oppression, spare a thought for the many forms of unfreedom that Indigenous people live with" (2022).

Such incisive critiques of the very different modalities through which the settler state responds to white-coded protest as opposed to Indigenous political action have been coupled with recurrent images of and evidence for settler police sympathy for the protests. There were multiple videos of individual police offers expressing their support for and even gratitude toward the convoy (e.g., Amato 2022; Epstein and Press-Reynolds 2022), and a video circulated widely on social media of RCMP officers seemingly hugging members of an allied convoy near the border between Alberta and the United States. The message that the convoy represented "white privilege in action," as Little Pine First Nation columnist Doug Cuthand (2022) put it, seemed crystal clear, echoing Joanne Barker's broader point that imperial-cum-colonial states typically "all but ignore" "white" protest, as it represents the violent vanguard of racialized empire rather than an actual challenge *to* empire (Barker 2021, 67).

The Freedom Convoy did not, however, proceed solely under the sign of whiteness. Instead, much like Lynn Beyak, it selectively appropriated the language of reconciliation-era Canada, positioned itself as having Indigenous support, and, on occasion, presented at least some of its membership as Indigenous and the convoy itself as an outgrowth of Indigenous political and spiritual practice. Antivaccine organizer Pat King, for instance, attempted to declare February 11, 2022, as "Orange Shirt Day," mimicking the September 30 holiday that was renamed Truth and Reconciliation Day in 2021, and encouraged convoy participants and their allies to explicitly invoke the language and iconography of truth and reconciliation in their attempts to fight for their "freedom": "'Every child matters, baby! Countrywide walkout. All schools. Protect your children. Wear orange tomorrow. Tomorrow's Orange Shirt Day,' King said on Facebook Live" (Zoledziowski 2022). King was no stranger to such strategies, having earlier released a video falsely suggesting that RCMP officers were forcing members of the Black Lake First Nation to receive vaccinations and pursuing those who did not comply into "the freezing wilderness." Both the Athabasca Health Authority and the chief and council of Black Lake have denounced King's narrative as completely invented (Lamoureux and Zoledziowski 2021).

While King attempted to refigure antivaccine activism as an articulation of anticolonial struggle, his peers in the convoy movement participated in direct and indirect appropriations of Indigenous ceremonialism, from falsely claiming that a 2018 video of a round dance in Frog Lake, Alberta, was an "Algonquin dance in support of truckers" (Reuters Fact Check 2022) to constructing a "teepee" and conducting their own "pipe ceremony" and building a "sacred fire" in Ottawa's confederation park (Zoledziowski 2022). These latter appropriations were roundly condemned and even mocked by Indigenous participants on social media (Ede 2022), and became so egregious that the leaders of multiple Algonquin Nations released a joint statement on February 2 making clear that they and their Nations did not give permission and would not consent to these mimicries of Indigenous ceremonial form, noting that they "could cause more harm to who we are as First Nations/Algonquin people" (Algonquins of Pikwanagan, Algonquin Anishinaabeg Tribal Council, and Kitigan Zibi Anishinaabeg 2022).

As absurd as these race-shifting gestures were on the surface, they demonstrated something very serious indeed. For the convoy organizer Pat King, indigeneity was not simply available for appropriation; it was a necessary dimension of his articulations of white supremacist politics. The convoy's organizers positioned Indigenous communities in opposition to a figure of Canadian politics that is akin to the "deep state," that phantasmagoric configuration of different far-right and white supremacist conspiracy theories that is imagined as responsible for limiting white "freedom."[9] But, of course, Indigenous actors do not need to invent fantastic scenarios as Pat King did in order to convey the possibility of state violence against "innocent" protest. Rather, that possibility is a simple and ever-present reality for Indigenous Peoples. "Some of us," Green and Starblanket write,

> still remember the 1990 Oka Crisis, when Quebec Premier Robert Bourassa called the army in to engage Kanesetake land protectors and assert Quebec jurisdiction over the disputed territory known as The Pines; the 1995 dispute over Secwepemc territory that led to 400 RCMP with helicopters and armoured personnel carriers engaging a handful

of Indigenous occupiers at Gustafson Lake; the 2006 Caledonia incident, when activists from the Mohawks of the Six Nations of the Grand River occupied a disputed piece of land in Caledonia, resulting in a violent OPP engagement and a still unresolved land dispute. In 2020, Wet'suwet'en land defenders blocked Coastal Gas Link pipeline work through their traditional territory, a matter that is ongoing and has been an object of RCMP punitive action against Wet'suwet'en and against journalists. We could go on. (2022)

What the convoy's organizers enact with their appropriations is not solidarity. It is erasure. It represents yet another means through which Indigenous sovereignty is made illegible, replaced and co-opted by the concerns of what is, at worst, a deviant whiteness. Deviant whiteness—just like bad faith conduct—might require discipline, but such disciplinary measures do not fundamentally displace such deviants from the settler political community of Canada. The convoy was often described as a "fringe" movement, as a "small minority" of Canadians (Reuters Fact Check 2022). While at least some of the convoy participants rejected this label, it seems to me that it is an accurate one, if not, perhaps, in the ways in which it is commonly understood. The fringe of a piece of fabric marks its edge, its border. But a fringe still forms part of the broader fabric. The messages of support and gratitude from RCMP and police officers to the convoy participants reminded the protestors themselves and the rest of Canada that white demonstrations in the nation's capital could be accepted and construed as legitimate by the forces of state power. They could be encompassed within a shared political framework. By signaling that this shared political community can be articulated through the language of reconciliation, of a falsified indigeneity, actual articulations of Indigenous sovereignty that refuse the state are both elided from within and fixed without the political community of settler Canada.

## "At Least He Isn't Surfing"

On September 30, 2021, then–Prime Minister Justin Trudeau and his family took a brief holiday, visiting the beaches of Tofino, British Columbia. As readers might recall from earlier in this chapter, September 30 also marked the first National Day for Truth and Reconciliation in Canada. Perhaps recognizing the problematic timing for the prime minister's vacation, Trudeau's public itinerary for the day initially listed him as in "private meetings" in Ottawa, before being rapidly changed once the prime minister's presence in

Tofino was discovered and photographed. Criticism of Trudeau's choice was rapid, centering on the perceived disrespect of Trudeau using a holiday intended to engage the public with the legacy of Canadian colonialism as a chance to rest and relax. Articles were published such as one in *MacLean's* on October 1 entitled "Trudeau Hits the Beach in Tofino. At Least He Isn't Surfing." One of said article's most pronounced points, repeated in the article at multiple points, was that "symbols matter," and that Trudeau's seeming disregard for the National Day for Truth and Reconciliation was the wrong kind of symbolism for the federal government to be sending to Indigenous Peoples (Fraiman 2021).

I would suggest, by contrast, that Trudeau's badly timed beach vacation is precisely the right kind of symbol for settler reconciliation in Canada. Reconciliation as articulated in settler discourses is made into an empty signifier. It is evacuated of concrete relations to real and ongoing Indigenous politics, made instead to encompass many different meanings, some contradictory to each other. In so doing, settler discourses of reconciliation constitute a particular kind of political community. This political community, as I have argued throughout this chapter, is in turn fundamentally *opposed* to the very Indigenous Nations it claims to include, at least in so far as those nations engage in the critical articulation of their own sovereignties. It is crucial here that in all the media reporting on Trudeau's vacation, very little attention was given to the fact that Tofino, like the vast majority of British Columbia, lies on unceded Indigenous territory—in that case, the ancestral, sovereign lands of the ƛaʔuukʷiʔatḥ (Tla-o-qui-aht First Nation).

What could be a better representation for this semiotic emptiness than Trudeau on the beach on Truth and Reconciliation Day? Reconciliation does not mean anything in particular; reconciliation is thus everything that a settler politician engaged in reconciliation does. In going to the beach, Trudeau banalizes the holiday, metonymically reiterating the vicious, intentional banality of settler reconciliation. In the process, he also takes for granted his freedom of movement and holiday on Indigenous territory. Here we see the closed loop of reconciliation in microcosm—an authorizing gesture on the part of settler society to further legitimize its own ongoing possession of the lands and waters it claims and continues to occupy. And there's little reason to expect otherwise.

CHAPTER FOUR

# Our Drums Are (Not) Silenced

## *Refusing the Ruse of Liberal Fairness in the Commission of Inquiry*

### "Today Is a Sad Day"

On June 13, 2012, the panel commissioners for the Enbridge Joint Review Panel (JRP) refused permission for the HIGaagilda Youth Dance Group to perform at the Skidegate hearings for the JRP. They were told that the hearings on this date were intended solely for individual testimony, and that it would accordingly not be appropriate for them to perform the choreographed ocean story that they had prepared. While the first round of JRP hearings on the islands of Haida Gwaii had been open to dance and other forms of group expression, this second and final set of hearings was reserved for individuals who had registered to testify months in advance of the hearing, and who had agreed to speak for a maximum of ten minutes and avoid remarks intended to "inflame" the crowd. Effectively, the HIGaagilda dancers were told that the time for dancing was over. In response, the group's leader, Jenny Cross, told the panel's commissioners that "today is a sad day. . . . Our drums are silenced. We are heartbroken and very disappointed that we have been deterred to present our strong opposition to the proposed pipeline by the JRP's strict rules and guidelines" (Joint Review Panel 2012c, para. 6508–10).

In silencing the drums of the HIGaagilda Dancers, the commissioners demonstrated that one of the most important powers displayed by contemporary commissions of inquiry is precisely the power to refuse to "hear," to regulate the forms of testimony that may be presented before them and reject those that do not conform to their "rules and guidelines." That is, effectively, to silence. Such rules are necessary, the panel's chair, Sheila Legett, told her audience repeatedly, so that the JRP can "*be fair to everyone who we're hearing* and to make sure that we've got the time to hear from everybody who's registered to speak with us" (Joint Review Panel 2012a, para. 4863, emphasis mine). For Cross and her dancers, however, this application of "the rules" was "strict" as opposed to fair, a hurtful and disappointing refusal of their attempts to speak to the commission and its audience in the way they wished. More, in her emphasis on the commission's silencing of "our drums," indexical icons par excellence of Haida culture and traditional expression, Cross situates the commission's decision in a long history of Canadian attempts at "regulating" Indigenous expression (and existence) through prohibitions on their practices, ceremonies, and speech.[1] In other words, the question of *who* has the right to determine what is fair and what is not is hardly an insignificant one for Cross, and for the many who like her who go before commissions of inquiry such as the JRP.

The Enbridge Northern Gateway Pipelines Project, first proposed in the mid-2000s, sought to construct two pipelines to transport crude oil and condensate from northern Alberta to Kitimat on the coast of British Columbia. The oil would then be transported via "supertanker" from the coast, through the Hecate Straight that passes between the west coast and the islands of Haida Gwaii before being exported to other nations (particularly China). The Enbridge Joint Review Panel was constituted in order to solicit testimony from the communities that would be most impacted by the proposed project—a demographic that was primarily Indigenous and almost exclusively "rural" in so far as the category is understood by mainstream settler society (Government of Canada 2014). The hearings were held between 2012 and 2013, in a political moment immediately prior to the victory of Justin Trudeau's Liberal Party and its attempts to recode the relationships of settler colonial governance to Indigenous Nations via the language of reconciliation. While it was ultimately rejected by Trudeau's Liberal government in 2016, at the time of the Joint Review Panel the Northern Gateway Project loomed over the coast as an imminent and catastrophic future, one that seemed all but certain given the immense support it received from the Conservative government that was then in power federally (Weiss 2018). Indeed, corporate initiatives such as the Northern Gateway Project shadow the era of reconciliation, undergirding settler discourses of collaboration and respect with the consistent demands for extraction and the exploitation of the lands and waters that constitute Indigenous territories.

The Enbridge JRP is a modal figure for the rapacious appetites for extraction that the era of reconciliation at once attempts to satisfy and, simultaneously, to disavow. Its distinctive melding of the logics of liberal proceduralism and predetermined colonial outcome, I argue in this chapter, acts itself as a kind of empty signifier, offering the appearance of engaging with Indigenous perspectives while in fact dismissing them as having any substantial importance. In figuring Indigenous voices as already "heard" even as they are silenced, the Enbridge JRP mobilizes a procedural logic of fairness that at once authorizes the commissioners as arbiters of legitimate political speech and compels Indigenous Peoples to either conform to the rules of the commission (and, by extension, colonial corporate and state power) or to be made to appear delinquent in relation to those rules (and that rule).

This has something to do with the nature of commissions of inquiry themselves. After all, as Adam Ashforth (1990) has argued, such commissions are not simply neutral organs for the recording of information or the production of data. Rather, they act as theaters of legitimation for states, performing the capacity of the state to record and control information and, thus, its authority over knowledge itself. In settler colonies such as Canada, moreover, these theaters take on particular significance because they act as venues in which the settler state can stage what Audra Simpson (2017) has termed the "ruse of consent"; that is, the presumption that Indigenous Peoples have in some sense given their consent to the expropriation of their own sovereign territories because they have participated (or been forced to participate) in ostensibly fair processes such as treaty negotiations.

Engaging in these processes in bad faith and under false pretences, colonial actors secure their own authority *as if* it is legitimate, even as they always-already know they need not honor any agreements thereby made. Indigenous actors, by contrast, are made into criminals if they continue to resist colonial domination, as by their very participation (willing or coerced) they are taken to have accepted the authority of the settler state. "This," Simpson writes, "is the ruse of consent, they did not consent to this fully, they know this, it is the liberal move again and again to pretend as if this ruse of consent signals freedom and the free will to consent to this" (2017, 29). Here again, as in chapter 3, we see how the settler state constitutes Indigenous sovereignty as criminalized opposition to the liberal good that is also, always, the power and authority of the colonial state.

Commissions such as the JRP help us see how empty signifiers are not mere discursive tricks; rather, they are instantiated via the legal and quasi-legal mechanisms of colonial state and corporate authorities. They are theaters at which the ruse of consent is played out, each one acting as a metonymic enactment of the ongoing legitimacy of colonial governance and its commitment to the "fairness" of liberal proceduralism. They form part of the "spectacle of reconciliation," as per Michelle Daigle (2019), reiterated across the many different hearings held by the Truth and Reconciliation Commission of Canada itself (likewise critiqued for its strict proceduralism and limited scope, even as it promised to "hear the truths" of Indigenous survivors) and by so many smaller commissions such as the JRP that share its procedural structure. These commissions represent a deliberate and vicious colonial irony; that is, they are technologies of erasure that enact their work of silencing through the ruse of listening. In turn, they enable the kinds of discursive positions that we saw Lynn Beyak and the antivaccine convoy wield in chapter 3.

Indigenous actors such as Jenny Cross, however, do not *allow* themselves to be silenced by such theaters of colonial disavowal. Not only do they continue to speak, but they do so in ways that point to the very acts of power and erasure that are made possible through the proceduralist structure of commissions of inquiry. This too is metonymic, one space among many in which Indigenous Peoples refuse to be erased by the very forms of liberal proceduralism that claim to be ensuring "equity" for all Canadians. Cross used her ten minutes of individual testimony to summarize the performance the HIGaagilda Dancers had intended to present, continuously marking their exclusion by the JRP. She told the commission that her dancers' "power of statement is in their Haida dancing and they just want to ensure that our precious culture and the many sea creatures, birds and animals of which we hold in very high regard had a voice too through traditional Haida dance" (Joint Review Panel 2012c, para. 6509). In so doing, she linked the refusal by the commission to hear her dancers with a refusal of the voices of the animals of Haida Gwaii and Haida culture as such, all of which she also presented as being under threat by the proposed Enbridge pipelines. Rather than embracing the "fairness" of the commission, Cross instead discursively joined its attempts at regulation with the very threat she and her dancers sought to oppose and to inspire their fellow islanders to oppose even as she acceded to its authority in order to testify herself (para. 6522).

Such refusals are not isolated; instead, they are social, and they are generative. Here, for instance, is Michelle Brown's, which began, "I'm here to let you know that I'm opposed to the Northern Pipeline Project. I feel that the government has already made up their mind and they're—I don't even know why they're bothering with this because I don't think they're listening to us. But I thought I'd take a chance and speak anyways" (Joint Review Panel 2012b, para. 5686). Brown was one of a number of Haida speakers who suggested that testifying to the JRP would be a futile gesture, either because the commission itself was unequipped to fairly consider their testimony or because the government had already made its decision and the commission was a sham, but then emphasized that they felt they needed to testify regardless. If Indigenous actors recognize the hollowness of the commission form in a settler colonial context, then, we might ask, why bother testifying before them at all?

One answer, I argue in this chapter, is that in the very act of testifying, Indigenous people expose the erasure that lies at the heart of the commission form (and, by extension, Canada's liberal narrative of reconciliation) and, even as they know their testimony likely will not be "heard" by the commissions in question, nonetheless chart out paths for possible political and social futures between Indigenous Nations and settler society that do not rely on the ruse of Indigenous consent to domination (cf. Weiss 2018). This might be seen as a form of what anthropologist Justin Richland has termed "cooperation without submission" in the context of the engagements of Hopi leaders with US settler governance. Richland characterizes cooperation without submission as "acts of official Native-US engagement that insist on a kind of stunning noise (Byrd 2011), interruption (A. Simpson 2014), ironic inversion, or mark of assent that does not connote agreement but, first and foremost, an enduring indigenous *insistence*" (2021, 13, emphasis original).

Engaging with the tribunal, for Haida speakers such as Cross and Brown, is not *consenting* to the Enbridge Pipeline Project or the dominion of settler corporate and state governance over Haida lands or waters. Rather, it is an opportunity to remind Canada that Haida people will not accept and do not approve of this plan, and that they will act accordingly. They mark the emptiness of the commission form and sketch out better ways of proceeding and better futures; indeed, they insist on them, to echo Richland's language. They are engaged at once in refusal and in world-building, incarnating a moment of Indigenous blockading (L. Simpson 2021) in every act of testimony. In so doing, they offer an alternative not just to the discursive violence of the commission form, but to the empty promises of reconciliation itself.

This chapter next proceeds by situating these processes of erasure and refusal historically, contextualizing the JRP as part of a longer history of commissions in British Columbia. There are strong parallels in the ways in which the Native land commissions of the late nineteenth and early twentieth century exerted authority over Aboriginal subjects and those attempted by the JRP. My interest here in particular is in tracing the historical continuities in the ways in which commissions of inquiry regulate what can be received as "legitimate" forms of Aboriginal speech before a representative of Canadian settler authority. In so doing, I suggest, these commissions attempt to fashion Indigenous Peoples as particular kinds of docile subjects, willing to accept Canadian control of the terms of appropriate political discourse and, thereby, of their own sociopolitical (and territorial) realities. However, then just as now, Indigenous actors have consistently refused the framework of docility, questioning instead the very right of commissioners to determine what should take place on their lands and how their lives should be lived. I then return to the JRP itself, showing how those same dynamics unfold despite Canada's seeming shift from an overt embrace of colonial mastery to a framework that emphasizes liberal fairness and equity as articulations of the era of reconciliation.

## "We Are Here to Examine the Indians"

The banning of the HIGaagilda Dancers echoes a long history of silencing in British Columbia between commissions of inquiry into Aboriginal issues and the peoples testifying before them.[2] Such exchanges were almost commonplace a century before the Enbridge hearings, when from 1912 to 1916 the McKenna-McBride Commission toured British Columbia in order to determine reserve land allocation and thereby "resolve" the "Indian land question." Consider, for example, the attempts of one Dan Pierre to hold this commission to account at its Enderby sessions:

> *Pierre* [In response to a question about acres cultivated on his reserve]: I will ask you a question first. What do you intend to do with the land that is already under cultivation. If you will tell me your purpose, I will explain it all.
>
> *Commission Chairman Wetmore*: I can't say anything about that until we find out what the character of the reserve is like.
>
> *Pierre*: I am in the same fix, and would like to know what is going to be done with the land that is already under cultivation.
>
> *Wetmore*: We are not here to be examined by the Indians. We are here to examine the Indians, and if we cannot find out what we want here we will find it out elsewhere. Do you know that we could place you in prison for not answering our questions? (excerpted in C. Harris 2002, 231–32)

The historical commissions, operating under (and thus reinstantiating) colonial assumptions of settler superiority bolstered with the ever-imminent threat of military violence, performatively enacted their ability to allow (and thus compel) certain forms of speech and reject others as a simple given of their interactions with Native Peoples. Of course, as Dan Pierre made clear, "the Indians" did not consent to that right, and used the commissions as an opportunity to directly interrogate the commissioners as to the goals and intentions of the settler society they represented.

But let us move back a bit more first. As I have engaged with in more detail in chapter 1, when British Columbia entered Canadian Confederation in 1871, the young province faced a seemingly intractable problem. Its rapidly growing settler population demanded an ever-increasing land base for settlements and agriculture. However, the vast majority of the province was already occupied by the area's First Nations, who moved over quite large territories as they fished, gathered, and hunted seasonally. Making treaties with these First Nations would be expensive, and, perhaps even more significantly, it would mean acknowledging that they had some form of title to or legitimate jurisdiction over the territories on which they lived. Colonial officials in the late nineteenth century refused to acknowledge any such forms of Indigenous sovereignty or jurisdiction, despite the fact that the Royal Proclamation of 1763 recognized that Indigenous nations had legitimate rights over their lands that would need to be extinguished prior to colonial occupation (C. Harris 2002, 3–16). And yet Indigenous presence could also not be ignored entirely. In one sense, this was a material dilemma, as Indigenous bodies continued to occupy territory desired by settler Canadians. At another scale, the potential for an Aboriginal coalition to develop in opposition to colonial encroachment was of great concern to officials in Victoria and Ottawa, particularly the possibility of a full-on Native uprising. While Canada and the province differed on their interpretations of how best to resolve these dilemmas, both required their resolution so that British Columbia could "develop" as a province (C. Harris 2002; D. Harris 2008).

In 1876, Canada and the province launched the Joint Indian Reserve Commission. Its purpose was to apportion reserves for the Indigenous Nations whose territories the colonial government was appropriating while reassuring those nations that the Crown and the province were keenly committed to their well-being (C. Harris 2002, 100–101). In assuming the authority to designate reserves, the commission asserted Crown possession of British Columbia as if it was already a fait accompli. This, to reiterate, disavowed not only the existence of any kind of Indigenous sovereignty or territorial jurisdiction, but also the demands of British common law itself, given the requirements stipulated by the Royal Proclamation (cf. Bhandar 2018). More, it was an authority to which Indigenous Nations were forced to present themselves, with the threat of military violence hovering perpetually in the background—thus leading to the euphemistic phrase "gunboat diplomacy" (Gough 1984). The commission likewise disavowed this ongoing threat, attempting to fashion a reality in which BC's Indigenous Peoples were subject to settler authority as an articulation of legitimate colonial legal jurisdiction rather than as the forceful actions of an invading power.

Here is Cole Harris's description of a typical commission session:

> At Musqueam, and at each stop thereafter, the party made camp and held an initial meeting with the Natives (in several places they were received by the inhabitants with flags flying). At this meeting the Dominion commissioner (Anderson) made a speech explaining his government's views about the Indians and its "earnest desire . . . to promote their welfare," and the provincial commissioner (McKinlay) did the same for his government. . . . *The chiefs then spoke, and the commissioners listened politely to them*. Then, accompanied by a group of Indians, they visited the area, particularly examining all the sites they were asked to see—if possible after [census taker George] Blenkinsop . . . had completed a census. Then they returned to camp, talked matters around, revisited the land as often as they needed, consulted with settlers, sought out relevant records if they could be had, and eventually decided on the reserves. The surveyor marked them out roughly, usually with tree blazes. *At the end of the stay there was a meeting at which commissioners explained their decisions and invited the chiefs to respond*. Some adjustments might be made. *Then there were final speeches all round*. . . . Depending on circumstances the process might take a day or two, or as much as several weeks. (2002, 105–6, emphasis mine)

Consider how brief the actual moments of interaction between commissioners and Aboriginal peoples are in this entire process, or to what extent actual discussion *between* parties is absent. What we see instead is a series of audiences in which Native voices are "listened to," but kept entirely removed from the decision-making process. Both moments are performative, figuring Natives as subjects with the right to be heard, and thus acknowledged *as* subjects of the Crown, but not as independent political communities with the ability or the authority to govern themselves.

Underlying the orderly veneer of these commission sessions was the ever-present threat of colonial military power. When the commissioners arrived at Chemainus on Vancouver Island, for instance, they found that land claimed by settlers had been fenced by the local Aboriginal population. In response, they called on the assistance of the gunboat HMS *Rocket*, which anchored nearby as a reminder to the "offending" First Nations of the consequences of violating the commission's rule(s). The fences were quickly removed. "White military power," as Cole Harris puts it, "was tangible and potentially lethal, as both commissioners and Natives well knew, and it was in the background whenever commissioners and Natives spoke to each other" (2002,

107). The commission's performance of "civilized" authority rested on a foundational capacity for violence. This made its acts of regulation through protocol as difficult to challenge for the province's Aboriginal Peoples as its ultimate decisions regarding reserve allocation. Simultaneously, as we will see again regarding the Enbridge JRP itself, it suggests how instable the commission's authority really was. What appeared to be the "bringing into order" of First Nations through European-style discursive practice in fact could only be achieved through the ever-present threat of violence.

While the 1876 commission's performance of order in relation to Indigenous Peoples worked to transform the basically violent nature of colonial occupation into an already established relationship of dominance and subordination, the commission's proceedings spoke to a quite different insecurity when considered as performances for the province's settler population. Responding to tensions between federal and provincial governments in a space in which it was not fully clear which parties had jurisdictions over which issues in the newly minted province, the 1876 commission was also a performance of discussion across disjuncture, a demonstration of how representatives from the province and federal Canada could arrive at decisions together on issues of great public import. That the commission fell apart after little more than a year because of this disjuncture suggests the tremendous anxiety and ultimate inefficacity of its performance of unity. As it had neither finished allocating reserve territories in the province nor "resolved" the question of Aboriginal title, the work of the 1876 commission was left to a series of individual Indian commissioners, who continued the mapping of British Columbia's reserve geography in tension between the demands of Dominion and provincial officials (C. Harris 2002, 136–219). Eventually, in 1912, another joint commission was attempted between Canada and the province, charged once again with "finding a final solution to the Indian land question" (218).

The McKenna-McBride Commission, as it became known, was in many ways similar to its predecessor. Like the 1876 Joint Commission, the McKenna-McBride Commission was a joint commission between Canada and British Columbia, mandated with arriving at the "final adjustment" of Aboriginal territory in the province based on an extensive tour of the province's reserve geography. Also like its predecessor, the McKenna-McBride Commission was not authorized to decide on the existence of Aboriginal title for BC's First Nations. Rather, it acted as if the territory was already vested in the Crown in order to defer (and disavow) this question (C. Harris 2002, 219). Similar, as well, finally, were the McKenna-McBride Commission's elaborate rituals of authority and official legitimacy. The commissioners sat in dark suits behind a table prominently displaying the commission document bearing the governor general's seal, the witnesses and their translators were sworn in with all solemnity, and the entire proceedings were recorded by stenographers (231).

This new commission's performance of authority was anxious in many of the same ways as that of its precursor. Moreover, it encountered an Indigenous population that had no intention of becoming passive objects of colonial subjugation. The exchange between Dan Pierre and the commissioners quoted earlier shows one instance in which the right of the commission to interrogate without being interrogated was being overtly challenged by its Native respondents. Others, following the advice of the Indian Rights Association, refused to testify entirely as long as Aboriginal title itself was not under discussion (Tennant 1990, 97). Still others in their testimonies called attention to how promises made to them about land rights had been broken, criticized the actions of white settlers that seemed to violate the laws the commission ostensibly represented, or even attacked the self-serving ways in which whites seemed to be making laws in the first instance (e.g., C. Harris 2002, 237–40). On Haida Gwaii, Haida chief Alfred Adams told the McKenna-McBride commissioners that Haida "had been in sole possession of the island, with our houses scattered at the mouths of every river and stream." Fellow Haida leader James Sterling commented in response to the commission's effort to establish and demarcate reserve boundaries on the islands that "we tried to make ourselves believe we were in our own country, but we are more and more reminded that what we supposed was ours, is said on [*sic*] many cases to belong to men who never saw these islands" (quoted in Krmpotich 2014, 29).[3]

Most of this criticism was erased in the commission's final report, though Harris argues the commissioners did believe they were "satisfying" the needs of the province's Aboriginal Peoples as well as they were able to, given the more significant "need" to prioritize settler interests and not encroach too greatly on the province's rights or authority (C. Harris 2002, 246). In their final report, they allocated 87,286 new acres of land to various First Nations and eliminated 47,085 acres of previously reserved land (247). However, as a Union of BC Indian Chiefs narrative points out, this new land was valued at about one-third of the value of the land cut off, and the commission only honoured 45 percent of Native land applications, whole or in part (Union of BC Indian Chiefs n.d.). The key point, in any case, is that once again these decisions were made as if the First Nations being "given" land were passive participants in the process, entitled to give their opinion, but not to take part in decision making. Their concerns over their rights to title, their questions over the legitimacy of Canadian lawmaking, and their fears that settlers would continue to erode their land base and make it impossible for them to survive were all ignored or considered resolved by the land-allocation process. Instead, Canada and British Columbia performed their "respect" for the province's First Nations by "examining" their opinions even as that performance made it clear and public that Aboriginal Peoples had no say in the final decisions that directly affected their material, even their existential, well-being. At the same time, the commissions undertaking this work were a theater of Canadian civilized authority, ordered and rule governed, contrasting implicitly with perceptions of Native savageness and the nation-state's own foundational violence and internal disarray.

We see here just how much deception is embedded within the ruse of consent. The ruse attempts to deceive not only Indigenous Peoples, who are made to seem as if they have consented to domination, but settlers themselves, whose embrace of the procedural equity of the commission forms disavows the violence that lies at the heart of colonial domination and the fundamental instability of settler colonial legitimacy. The contemporary Enbridge Joint Review Panel inherited this anxious performance, an empty signifier of respectful attention that erases the very voices to which it purports to give attention. There is also direct continuity with the present in the complex ways in which Indigenous actors critically navigated these early land commissions, using them as spaces in which alternative ways of acting politically and socially could be articulated, even as they acknowledged that their efforts were not likely to be heeded by settler authorities.

## The Enbridge Joint Review Panel

The Enbridge Northern Gateway Pipelines Project was extremely controversial. While it enjoyed enthusiastic support from Canada's then-Conservative government, there was a wide coalition of different groups and individuals who objected to the project, often vociferously. The project was severely criticized by Aboriginal groups and environmentalists (Mickleburgh 2012) for the potentially shattering ecological damage that would be caused by a pipeline or tanker spill, and even British Columbia's then-premier, Christy Clark, expressed strong reservations about the risk posed by the Pipelines Project to the province compared to the relative economic gains that it offered (Fowlie and Hoekstra 2012).[4] All of these concerns were shared by the residents of the communities of Old Massett and Masset on Haida Gwaii's north end, as they made clear to the Joint Review Panel. As community members repeatedly asserted in their testimonies, an oil spill would devastate the islands' marine population, potentially spreading contamination to the coastline, the forests, and the fauna that feed on the islands' fish and plants. In turn, this would cripple both subsistence and commercial fishing, destroying livelihoods and removing a major food source, particularly for lower-income community members. Plant and berry gathering would become impossible, eliminating another food source and most of the traditional materials for Haida weaving and carving.

In short, opposition to the pipeline in the Massetts was, as one witness put it, "an existential issue" (Joint Review Panel 2012b, para. 5206)—this in terms of not only lives of individual community members and their families, but also, for many, Haida culture understood as such. Here, for instance, is a representative excerpt from 2004's Haida Land Use Vision, *Haida Gwaii Yah'guudang*: "Our physical and spiritual relationships with the lands and waters of Haida Gwaii, our history of co-existence with all living things over many thousands of years is what makes up Haida culture" (Council of the Haida Nation 2004, 3). Disrupting these relationships would shatter that co-existence and the relational systems that, in this framing, constitute Haida culture as such.

The official purpose of the Enbridge Joint Review Panel was to give hearing to concerns such as these. Formed in 2009 by Canada's minister of the environment and its National Energy Board, the JRP was tasked with assessing the Northern Gateway Pipelines Project. This assessment was to be based both on direct evaluation of the potential environmental effects of the pipelines and on consideration of testimony from Canadian citizens, particularly the Aboriginal Peoples whose territory lay along the proposed pipeline route (Government of Canada 2014). The JRP was composed of three commissioners, two of whom were National Energy Board Members. In pursuit of this mandate, the JRP held hearings in First Nations communities throughout northern Alberta and British Columbia, ultimately holding 180 days of hearings along the path of the proposed pipelines (National Energy Board 2013).

On Haida Gwaii, these hearings took place in two phases. The first sessions focused on "oral evidence," defined as "oral traditional knowledge, such as that given by Aboriginal peoples, and "personal knowledge and experiences about the potential effects of the Project on you or your community" (cited in Crist 2012, 38). While the format of these sessions was somewhat less temporally restrictive than the hearings that followed, in her master's thesis focusing on responses to the Northern Gateway Project in Old Massett, Valine Crist notes that Sheila Legett, the JRP panel chair, frequently interrupted testimonies that she considered not to fit this definition, particularly those that made arguments against Enbridge rather than simply reported "knowledge" about its potential effects (38). By contrast, the second sessions were intended to gather "oral statements," defined as "a way for you to provide the Panel with your knowledge, views or concerns on the proposed Project during the community hearings" (cited in Crist 2012, 38).

While the distinctions between "oral evidence" and "oral statements" appear somewhat arbitrary (something we will return to shortly), the difference between the two for the JRP appeared to be that "oral evidence" hearings were meant to gather knowledge relevant for *the commission's* evaluation of the Pipelines Project, while the "oral statements" were focused on *individual* opinions about and arguments for or against the project. This distinction is what Commissioner Legett drew on when she intervened to silence what appeared to her to be explicit arguments against Enbridge in the "oral evidence" hearings, as such direct critiques were meant to be reserved for "oral statements." I now turn to a more detailed analysis of the JRP "oral statement" hearings that took place on June 1 and 2 in Old Massett, focusing in my next section on how the commission attempted to produce its own authority by controlling the terms for the discourse that it received and how, in turn, both the testifiers and the broader audience refused that authority. It is here that we can see both the attempt to empty the hearing of significance, rendering it a hollow performance of consent, and the ways in which Indigenous witnesses refused to allow the commission to be a mere vehicle for procedural silencing.

### *"Fairness" and the Authority to Organize*

The JRP's tight control over the "oral statements" that it received extended considerably before the hearing dates themselves. The registration cutoff date for providing an oral statement to the JRP was October 6, 2011, almost nine months before the hearing dates on Haida Gwaii. Those who had not registered were not permitted to offer testimony. These registered speakers were then organized into a schedule by the JRP in advance, with each speaker receiving a ten-minute period of time in which to make their testimony. Copies of the schedule were made available (and, therefore, visible) to all participants in the hearings and to the audience. Each speaker was "sworn-in" by the JRP's representatives before their testimony, confirming that the "content of [their] statement is accurate to the best of [their] knowledge" (cited in Crist 2012, 38). At this time speakers were also enjoined from making any "inflammatory" comments, a category whose terms were (implicitly) moderated by the JRP commissioners. Inflammatory speech could, of course, be stopped by the commissioners. Speakers then sat with the rest of the audience to await their turn. Before each day's hearings began and periodically during the sessions, the commissioners reminded the audience of the strict time limit of each oral statement, explaining in some detail how witnesses would be notified of the length of their statements: "*Commission Chair Legett*: The timeframe for oral statements is 10 minutes. And we have a black instrument here that will make an audible sound and noise at seven minutes, and then at 10 minutes it will make another sound and the red light will go on. *And we do this to be fair to everyone who we're hearing* and to make sure that we've got the time to hear from everybody who's registered to speak with us" (Joint Review Panel 2012a, para. 4863, emphasis mine).

Taken together, these rules for testimony enacted a strict regimen of JRP control over the statements they received. Now consider this structural rigidity alongside the ambiguity of the commission's definitions of "oral evidence" *vs.* "oral statements." There is an incoherence here, but one that I would suggest produces a very distinctive social effect. On the one hand, the JRP commissioners have performatively enacted the commission's regulatory power and its quasi-legal status via the act of "swearing in" the panel's witnesses. On the other, the actual rules that *govern* that testimony were not fully clear, particularly whether a given witness's testimony fit within the boundaries of an "oral statement" or whether it could be considered "inflammatory." This decision rested ultimately and exclusively with the commissioners themselves. This had the effect of making the commission's decisive authority appear to exceed the legibility of its own rules, positioning the JRP as a kind of pseudosovereign within the space of its hearings, its commissioners able to determine what did and did not fit within the apparently strict boundaries of its sessions without its logics necessarily being made clear to speakers or the wider audience.

This too is part of the ruse of colonial liberalism, metonymically reiterating an authority that is bound by rules that are presented as fairly applied to all and yet, simultaneously, acts as the sole determinant *of* those rules. This is incoherent in the sense famously argued by political philosopher Carl Schmitt (1988), but as Brenna Bhandar (2018) has pointed out, the very incoherence of settler legal and political formations is itself a kind of colonial strategy, demanding that Indigenous Peoples negotiate constantly shifting rules and laws that are rarely internally consistent but are always forcefully applied as if they are. Here, in other words, is the trick of procedural fairness. The JRP, we were told, needed its regulations in order to be "fair" to every speaker, to give them equal chance to speak, and to make sure that all those who wished to testify (or, more precisely, wished to testify nine months ago) were given the opportunity.

It is not my contention that Commissioner Legett or her fellow JRP members were deliberately dissimulating here. Quite the opposite, I would submit that it is in this constitution of "fairness" that some of the most potent disciplinary work of the commission form is achieved. By framing the commission's strict regulations as being "for the benefit" of speakers, the logic of fairness makes it appear as if both the commission's rules and its authority to impose them are *necessary* for speech, that they are the only way to create a space in which the commission can be addressed that would be "fair" to all speakers. In short, it constitutes the commission's regulatory authority as enabling speech itself—and, crucially, it disavows the possibility that these regulations can in fact have the opposite effect, silencing the voices of protest and resistance to a project that was, at the time, understood to be all but inevitable by settler corporate and state interests. What we are left with is a microcosm for a state that is just, fair, and attentive to the wishes of its people without any need to consider their perspectives in their own terms, and a citizenry compelled to speak in the terms of that state. Anything that lies outside of this circle of fairness is rendered literally "unhearable," unable to be engaged with as politically "real" speech (cf. Rancière 1998). Nothing could be easier to disavow—indeed, here liberal proceduralism attempts to realize itself as a closed circle, excluding anything that could offer an alternative perspective to the "equity" that liberalism presents itself as ensuring.

The deliberately contradictory logic of fair speech attained through silencing continued into the commissioner's management of the testimony itself. Let us take, as a representative example, the commissioner's handling of audience applause during witness Peter Reynolds's testimony:

> *Reynolds*: So—but people—the people proposing this project consider that reasonable when they talk about risk but it's not reasonable because they're not risking anything. All this is happening in someone else's home. Other—
>
> *(Audience Applauds)*
>
> *Commissioner Legett*: Excuse me. It's been our experience that people who have prepared oral statements have taken a lot of time and effort to prepare them, and they are in a—in a 10-minute time window. So *I would*

*ask the audience please respect the oral statement speakers and—and let them proceed with their statements within their timeframe.*

Thank you.

*Reynolds*: *It makes me feel good when people clap* anyway, but I'll continue quickly (Joint Review Panel 2012b, paras. 5404–7, emphasis mine).

In this exchange, Mr. Reynolds points explicitly to the incoherence of Commissioner Legett's "defense" of his own right to speak in saying the applause "makes me feel good." Rather than interrupting his speech and impeding it, Reynolds interprets the applause as being an expression of support for his position and solidarity from his fellow community members. To Reynolds, the applause is precisely a way of *showing* respect for his views. But this mode of respect cannot appear as such in Legett's framing, as it interrupts the commission's regulatory monopoly on speech—which, recall, is what is guaranteeing fairness in the commission's proceedings. It transforms the space from theater of authority to dialogue, rendering the ruse of consent that the commission maintains unsustainable. We can see this play out in the response from Legett that purports to affirm Reynolds's right to speak "uninterrupted," attempting to reframe community solidarity as disruption to the (liberal) right of the individual to speak—and, ironically, in so doing actually taking precious time away from Reynolds's own speech.

What's more, the risk the applause poses goes deeper than the disruption of the commission's timetable. In that moment of sudden applause, the JRP's Old Massett audience threatens to reveal the unstable foundations of the JRP's claims to decisive authority. Just as did the land commissions of British Columbia's past, the JRP operates *as if* the social reality it seeks to bring out already existed. In this case, that social reality is one in which the government of Canada has the ultimate (and exclusive) right to decide whether or not the Enbridge Pipelines Project is approved. Taken at face value, this authority might seem obvious. After all, it is the Canadian government that would ultimately approve or disapprove Enbridge's Project Proposal. The possibility that our inconvenient applause indexes, however, is that this legal Canadian authority might not in fact be total; that it might, rather, be itself a performative lamination of order upon a landscape of colonial fragmentation that has never in fact been reconciled. The audience thereby refuses to be reconciled to the terms of the hearing as laid out by the commissioners, pointing to the ways in which the JRP is being actively understood and framed as an agent of domination and asserting their own right to speak in their own terms. These "cacophonous" speech acts, as Richland, drawing on Jodi Byrd, terms them, "point to and comment on, often ironically, the specific historical and political contexts in which they emerge and to which they contribute" (2021, 12), with an intended audience that goes well beyond the representatives of the colonial order themselves. They thereby turn the commission's hollow performance on its head, rendering the hearings, instead, into vital, social meeting points at which Indigenous sovereignty and the refusal of colonial domination can be asserted. These refuse to take the hearings as empty.

The JRP hearings in Old Massett were not, after all, held in a "neutral" Canadian space (if such a thing even exists); instead, they took place on unceded Haida territory, in a community with a history of political life that goes back well before Canadian "settlement." It is also a community that only a few decades before had successfully resisted the logging of Athlii Gwaii (Moresby Island) through a sustained blockade, one that saw many Haida arrested before an agreement was reached (Weiss 2018, chap. 6). This means not only that the possibility of outright resistance on the part of Haida and non-Haida loomed over the proceedings—echoes here, once again, of the figure of the "Indigenous terrorist," as per Joanne Barker (2021)—but that the very right of the Canadian government to make decisions about waters (and land, should a spill occur) the Haida Nation has claimed as its own was not at all certain. In applauding out of turn, the audience asserted to the commissioners that it should be they, not the JRP or its government sponsors, who should be setting the terms for this conversation and, moreover, that to them a decision refusing the Enbridge project had already been made. All these ideas were also expressed in individual testimonies, and through their applause the audience also indicated a particularly unsettling capacity to disrupt the commission's regulatory authority. There is no such thing as a closed circle in a settler colonial context. Those asserting domination over others cannot erase their own action, because Indigenous Peoples refuse this erasure, and they refuse to allow it to be left unspoken.

### *Consent and Consultation*

In 2004, just under a decade before the Enbridge JRP, the Supreme Court of Canada released its decision in the case of Haida Nation v British Columbia (Minister of Forests), which turned on the question of whether the provincial government could issue tree farm licenses (which in turn would grant logging rights) in areas to which the Haida Nation claimed title as its traditional and sovereign territory. The court's response was that the Crown had a "duty to consult" with the Haida Nation, even in such areas where its title had not been proven (under the terms of colonial law, at least):

> The government's duty to consult with Aboriginal peoples and accommodate their interests is grounded in the principle of the honour of the Crown, which must be understood generously. While the asserted but unproven Aboriginal rights and title are insufficiently specific for the honour of the Crown to mandate that the Crown act as a fiduciary, the Crown, acting honourably, cannot cavalierly run roughshod over Aboriginal interests where claims affecting these interests are being seriously pursued in the process of treaty negotiation and proof. *The duty to consult and accommodate is part of a process of fair dealing and reconciliation that begins with the assertion of sovereignty and continues beyond formal claims resolution*. The foundation of the duty in the Crown's honour and the goal of reconciliation suggest that the duty arises when the Crown has knowledge, real or constructive, of the potential existence of the Aboriginal right or title and contemplates conduct that might adversely affect it. (Haida Nation v. British Columbia 2004, 512)

This decision would be revised and expanded in 2014 in Tsilhqot'in Nation v British Columbia. The case, which was heard roughly contemporaneously with the JRP, once again queried the extent of "meaningful consultation" with Indigenous Nations in regard to logging, and concluded, building on *Haida*, that consultation had to take place to a particular set of specifications in order to allow the Crown to proceed with its proposed resource extraction activities. As both cases made clear, however, Indigenous *consent* to resource extraction was not, in fact, legally necessary, as long as consultation had taken place to a degree that settler authorities deemed appropriate. Settler reconciliation, in a microcosm, is a duty to consult that performs a ruse of consent while, in fact, maintaining colonial authority over the lands, waters, and lives of Indigenous communities.

The Haida speakers and audience members at the JRP *knew* this, to echo Audra Simpson here again. In their testimony and their responses, they consistently and reiteratively refused the ruse of consent, making clear they were not "appealing" to the Canadian government as its subjects but, rather, articulating their own sovereign authority and expectations, even as they knew this would only be "acknowledged" rather than genuinely respected by the commissioners. Allow me to offer another illustrative vignette. At the beginning of the Friday JRP sessions, Chief Sgaann 7iw7waans, Allan Wilson, was asked to speak by the JRP commissioners as a gesture of respect to the Hereditary Chiefs of Haida Gwaii:

> *Chief Sgaann 7iw7waans*: As noted, we have the Hereditary Chiefs Council standing here before you. And at this time, we respectfully ask that we be stood down and given a time at a later date to speak.
>
> We, as Chiefs, would like to listen to all the citizens of Haida Gwaii speak first and then we would like to make a final statement. Not even necessarily at the end of tonight or end of tomorrow, but quite possibly in Skidegate or at a time later that would be—that would suit your timeslot. (Joint Review Panel 2012a, paras. 4503–4)

Commissioner Legett appeared surprised by his request, and responded, with slight hesitation:

> *Commission Chair Legett*: Chief Wilson, we have a slate of people who've registered to speak, of which I understand five are Chiefs who were going to speak initially. We can adjust the timing within each hearing session so that you could speak at a different point this afternoon or, if we've got time—my concern is that we have a full slot of speakers for every single session that we're here.
>
> So I don't know if we can make some adjustments within the timeslot that each individual registered to speak, but if we start moving the slots in different ways we may not be able to listen to everybody who's registered to speak. (paras. 4505–6)

The negotiation between Chief Sgaann 7iw7waans and Commissioner Legett continued for another few minutes, in which it became clear that Chief Sgaann 7iw7waans meant for the chief's "final statement" to come at the very end of the Haida Gwaii JRP sessions. Commissioner Leggett's response attempted to divert Chief Sgaann 7iw7waans's intentions without appearing to be an overt refusal: "*Commission Chair Legett*: I'm not—*I don't know* what our schedule is for Skidegate; so I can't speak to that. So let's—because we take each hearing one session at a time. So *let's plan on wrap-up comments* here because *we know* we can accommodate that" (para. 4512, emphasis mine). Note the ways in which Legett deploys certainty and uncertainty in her statement. The reason Chief Sgaann 7iw7waans's request cannot be granted is because the commission does not possess the knowledge to *guarantee* he and his fellow chiefs will be able to give statements at the conclusion of the Skidegate sessions. Legett attempts to move Chief Sgaann 7iw7waans to a place where the commission does possess certainty—the schedule of the Old

Massett sessions—while figuring him together with the commission itself by using the phrase "let's plan," indexing a consensus between the commission and the chiefs that she is in fact attempting to enact. But this is a consensus whose terms remain tightly controlled by the commission itself—shades here of many different iterations of Aboriginal-settler "alliance" throughout Canadian colonial history.

Chief Sgaann 7iw7waans responded immediately after the commissioner finished speaking: "*Chief Sgaann 7iw7waans: I know* we can accommodate it in Skidegate also *because our fellow Chiefs from Skidegate are present here today*" (Joint Review Panel 2012a, para. 4513, emphasis mine). Here, Chief Sgaann 7iw7waans inverts both the commission's monopoly on knowledge and the grounding of that monopoly in Canadian state power. In other words, Chief Sgaann 7iw7waans can know that his request will be accommodated even when the commission itself does not because it is not the commission that has final decision-making power over events on island. Rather, in his rendering, it is the Hereditary Chiefs of Haida Gwaii. Note that Chief Sgaann 7iw7waans's response is not an outright *rejection* of the commission or its right to adjudicate testimony related to Enbridge. Rather, he implicitly reframes Commissioner Legett's attempt at folding the interests of the chiefs together with those of the commission by reminding the commissioners that, from his perspective, they are essentially guests on Haida land. As guests, therefore, the commissioners are subject to the authority of the chiefs in whom are vested rights to their clans' territories. By this logic, it is not significant whether the commission "knows" its schedule for future events, because it is the Skidegate Chiefs who ultimately have the right to determine what takes place at an event on their territory, whoever may be "organizing" it. This is a generative refusal par excellence; it is an invitation to proper relationality, an articulation of proper protocol to which the JRP *could* have acceded. It is world-building activity (L. Simpson 2021).

Commissioner Legett partially refused this interpretation, reiterating that because she "just [wasn't] privy to the schedule of Skidegate," they would have to "proceed with being in Masset first," and "then tackle Skidegate when we get there" (Joint Review Panel 2012a, para. 4514). And yet, by deferring the decision, Legett leaves the question of ultimate authority unresolved. This is significant. Despite the fact that Commissioner Legett appears to control the JRP proceedings, she chose not to reject outright Chief Sgaann 7iw7waans's request. It seems telling that immediately after this exchange, Legett thanked the community's "honoured Chiefs, distinguished elders, and ladies held in high esteem" for "welcoming [the commission] back into your community. Haaw'a [*sic*]" (para. 4518). Thanking the elders and using the Haida word for "thank you," *haa.wa*, seems rather clearly to be intended by the commissioners to show respect for the Haida community, its language, and its culture.

This gesture of acknowledgment, of recognition, figures a larger (ostensible) Canadian commitment to Aboriginal culture. Its proximity to Legett's disagreement with Chief Sgaann 7iw7waans, in turn, reveals the limits of that respect, as it cannot tolerate Aboriginal attempts to take control of structures of organization or governance in ways that contravene perceived Canadian state interests (cf. Blackburn 2009; Mackey 2002; Nadasdy 2003). Legett's position, then, appears as a precarious one. She must perform Canadian respect for Aboriginal Peoples and cultivate a sense of First Nations "common cause" with Canadian institutions while simultaneously maintaining an absolute Canadian monopoly on the power to determine, in both the political and the epistemological sense. That these two projects are contradictory positions the JRP as inherently ambivalent, attempting to perform a Canadian authority that it cannot realize for intrinsic *and* extrinsic reasons. Or, put another way, the JRP's instability comes as much from its own inability to mediate between contradictory Canadian colonial positions as it does from the impossibility of maintaining a performative absolute control over either Indigenous Peoples or the contexts in which their positions are formed and maintained.

Moreover, Chief Sgaann 7iw7waans was absolutely correct. He was indeed the last speaker at the Skidegate JRP sessions, something that was achieved, I was later told by another hereditary chief, by a well-placed phone call from the Hereditary Chiefs Council to the local Skidegate organizers of that community's hearings. The chiefs, in short, were able to effectively ignore the JRP Commissioners by working through their own relational networks of influence, demonstrating rather potently the limits of the JRP's own authority in relation to their own on Haida Gwaii. Moreover, in his closing statement, Chief Sgaann 7iw7waans accomplished one last inversion, informing the commissioners and the hearing's audience that, "just so the JRP knows, and their faithful timer, I have my own stopwatch" (Joint Review Panel 2012d., para. 7567). Though meant playfully, I suspect, one can read Chief Sgaann 7iw7waans's reference to his stopwatch as being itself suffused with a certain ambivalence. On the one hand, he was again demonstrating how the JRP hearings were an event that he could subject to his own control, timing himself rather than accepting the use of the JRP's timer. At the same time, Chief Sgaann 7iw7waans was acquiescing to the basic format of the JRP hearings by accepting that his speech would need to be timed, something that violates what is often described to me as the basic Haida value of "letting everyone have their say."

Chief Sgaann 7iw7waans did not publicly question the right of the JRP to conduct its hearings, though he certainly condemned the proposed Enbridge project. Rather, Chief Sgaann 7iw7waans reiterated the terms of the JRP's authority even as he subverted them. Or, more precisely, he *allowed* the panel to maintain authority in this instance, even as he also instructed them in how they should behave more properly as guests on Haida territory. Chief Sgaann 7iw7waans maintained a sovereign Haida position in his critique, one that allowed for the existence of settler institutions in so far as they were able to exist respectfully in relation to the Haida Nation and other Indigenous Peoples. The JRP's inability to either fully accept or reject Chief Sgaann 7iw-7waans's framing makes clear that liberal proceduralism can never, in fact, close itself off from critique even as it cannot properly respond *to* those critiques. This is a paradox of settler colonialism, one that disavowal cannot make disappear (Kauanui 2018a; Bruyneel 2021).

## Resignifying the Emptiness of the Colonial Commission

It is precisely this critical power that helps us to understand why Indigenous actors choose to testify before commissions such as the JRP even when they do not believe them to be effective. Many residents of Haida Gwaii did not consider the JRP to be an especially credible entity. In particular, recent changes in Canadian environmental policy that retroactively streamlined the approval process for projects like the Enbridge pipelines had convinced many on island that Prime Minister Harper's Conservative government had no intention of honoring the already highly restricted JRP process. To them, the JRP was hollow, a false theater masking state disregard with an empty performance of recognition. While some who held this opinion choose not to testify, or ignored the JRP entirely, others did not. Rather, they brought forward their uncertainty about the JRP into their testimonies before the commission itself. Recall Michelle Brown informing the commission that "I feel that the government has already made up their mind and they're—I don't even know why they're bothering with this because I don't think they're listening to us" (Joint Review Panel 2012b, para. 5686). Jaalen Edenshaw told the commission he "didn't have much faith in what was happening" (para. 5624), while Sophie Harrison, a non-Haida, stated that she believed that the commission was "just going through the motions of democracy" (para. 5550).

Valine Crist questioned "why I have to validate my life" before the commission (para. 5189).

Nevertheless, each speaker followed their critiques by emphasizing that their speech before the commission must *still* have some form of efficacy. Michelle Brown: "But I thought I'd take a chance and speak anyways" (para. 5686). Jaalen Edenshaw: "And I know that it has to be getting through to you guys, you know to—you know, I know it's a tough decision ahead, but I know that you guys are hearing it" (para. 5625). Sophie Harrison: "However, I do feel that it is important to go on the record saying that this proposal in its current iteration is not in the interest of Canadians" (para. 5551). Valine Crist: "Being here today is not a choice for me. It's my democratic right and responsibility" (para. 5205). The efficacy in question for each witness is different. Jaalen Edenshaw suggests that the impassioned appeals of his fellow islanders "must" have a convincing effect on the commissioners as people (marked by the repeated refrain of "you guys"), even if the larger structures enabling the commission are unworthy of trust. Both Sophie Harrison and Valine Crist index elements of their understanding of democracy. For Harrison, testifying is important because it "go[es] on the record," implying that even "going through the motions of democracy" produces a public record, and this is significant in itself. Crist frames her entire testimony as a democratic "responsibility," something she *has* to do as a citizen of Canada (and of Haida Gwaii) rather than something she has chosen. In so doing, she leverages her status as both Indigenous *and* Canadian, taking advantage of the same language of liberal equity that is so integral to the ruse of consent itself. Michelle Brown, finally, does not offer a concrete reason why she believes her testimony is necessary; rather, she is "tak[ing] a chance," expressing the hope that despite her own critical feelings her testimony, and those like hers, might still accomplish something "anyways."

Each of these responses offers insight into why individuals chose to testify before the JRP, and perhaps more generally why they might go before commissions of inquiry when not compelled to do so. Harrison and Crist point us to how significant imaginaries of public action are in democratic contexts, to what extent democracy is envisioned by its citizens as being constituted by their participation in public forums and law-making processes: echoes here of a very classical vision of democracy, perhaps, but also one that is indicated primarily through its absence. Put another way, both Sophie Harrison and Valine Crist suggest they would *like* to belong to a democratic nation that takes them seriously as citizens, but feel that they do not. Instead, they bring it to life performatively through their own acts of (purportedly futile) testimony. Of course, left implicit here is the fact that such a nation need not, necessarily, be Canada (or, indeed, any settler colony). Here again, the *insistence* in speaking anyway, speaking to everyone in the room, Haida and settler, is also a mode of world-building, one that can bridge settler and Haida worlds on Indigenous terms.

Edenshaw also points us toward a particular vision of affect, a claim as to the power of shared feeling in the creation of solidarities across significant social and structural distance. For him, "getting through" to the commissioners is an achievable end through the very act of communication and, as he notes elsewhere in his testimony, through the influence of simply "being on Haida Gwaii" on the commissioners. For Edenshaw, testifying is at once a performance of his own solidarity with the different communities on Haida Gwaii who oppose Enbridge alongside him and an invitation to the commissioners to join this solidarity mediated by shared affect.

In her testimony, finally, Michelle Brown indicates both the significance and the ambivalence of aspiration, of hope, to the choice made by many witnesses in testifying before the JRP. Brown suspects very strongly that the JRP is meaningless, that the government's decision on (and for) Enbridge is already de facto made. But the fact remains that officially, at least, that decision is still pending. In the space between her doubt and its confirmation, there exists for Brown the possibility that her testimony *could* matter, and like Crist and Harrison, she chooses to perform that possibility, to attempt to bring into existence a social world in which the government *does* listen to its citizens. And, perhaps, to mark her outrage at the fact that the government does not, she believes, care to consider her opinions or the opinions of those like her. Hope is here a kind of imaginative resource (see Miyazaki 2004), but it is not to be confused with optimism.

Brown is not affirming a conviction that her testimony *will* (despite everything) make a change; instead, she testifies because there exists a possibility, however small, that it could, and it is thus worthwhile for her to "take a chance" on her testimony. In so doing, she marks the commission as inefficacious and figures herself as someone who makes the attempt "anyways," combining public critique and self-performance in a single gesture. And, as with her fellow witnesses, her audience for this work is not just the commissioners themselves, but the other people in the room, both Haida and settler, with whom solidarity can be generated even as the content of individual testimonies might be foreclosed. Recall Peter Reynolds: "It makes me feel good when people clap."

Each of these sketches illustrates a reason why individuals choose to testify before the JRP, and, more broadly, why Indigenous Peoples in Canada still choose to engage with institutions that promise "equity" or "reconciliation" even when they understand these promises to be hollow. We should not forget, in addition, that there is a long history of Haida oratory on Haida Gwaii, one in which, many Haida assert, "everyone was allowed to have their say" (see Umeek 2011, 45–46, for a Nuu-chah-nulth parallel). But what I would like to emphasize here in particular is the simple fact that all of these different forms of social work were *able* to be brought together in the context of the JRP hearings. In other words, the JRP and other commissions of inquiry create a space in which political imaginaries and critiques, aspirations, and powerful affective forces can be publicly deployed in ways that are not reducible to the simple reproduction of state power or its subversion. Though these commissions might attempt to effect themselves as purely authoritative performances, empty in so far as they might actually take up the perspectives of the Indigenous actors who testify before them, they cannot maintain this ruse in the face of the many different ways that these same Indigenous actors take up the space of the commission to their own ends.

Put another way, when considered purely from the vantage point of political rhetoric and settler policymaking, the empty signifiers of the era of reconciliation—of reconciliation itself—might appear to erode any possibility for any alternative political frameworks. The ways in which both the settler state itself and corporate representatives take on the mantle of the good, the fair, and the just might make it seem as if there is no space for Indigenous sovereignty outside the frameworks of delinquency, criminality, and, most broadly, the refusal of the good, frameworks that, in turn, justify military and police violence against Indigenous communities that dare to resist or refuse the terms and demands of settler state and corporate bodies. But as the Enbridge JRP shows, such efforts at totalizing are fragile. They fail on the ground, as Indigenous people not only refuse their terms, but resignify them toward their own ends, toward generative refusals that build social and political worlds that are not already overdetermined by colonial power.

# PART III | Colonial Generosity

CHAPTER FIVE

# Objects with Invalid Title

## *Myths, Fantasies, and Other Liberal Fictions of Legitimate Museum Acquisition*

Settler colonialism lives in the fine print. Consider the repatriation policies of three major museums in Canada: the Canadian Museum of History (CMH), the Royal British Columbia Museum (RBCM), and the Royal Ontario Museum (ROM). Each lays out specific criteria under which artifacts can be considered eligible for repatriation, with the CMH's and ROM's policies in particular focusing primarily on ancestral remains, associated "burial objects," and "sacred objects," in the rather blunt language of the ROM's policy (Royal Ontario Museum 2018, 2). Much has been written, led by Indigenous scholars, on the problematics of these modes of categorization, which maintain the colonial authority over defining what is and is not "sacred" and apply often-inappropriate settler ontological categories to other-than-human beings that have existed and continue to exist in long-standing relationships with Indigenous Peoples (see, for instance, Gray 2015 and Bell, Collison and Neel 2019).

What I am interested in this chapter, however, is something else that recurs across all three policies. Alongside their more explicit typologies of categories *of* artifacts that might be eligible for repatriation, each policy also includes an even more vaguely defined category, one that we might refer to as the "illegitimate" or "illegal" museum acquisitions. Here, from the Canadian Museum of History's policy: "6.3 Objects will be repatriated only to an Aboriginal Government, except where the following conditions are met: i) or the requestor is an individual or group of individuals with an undisputed historical relationship to the objects and the objects are demonstrated to have been acquired under conditions which were illegal at that time" (Canadian Museum of History 2011, 4). The analogous passage in the ROM's policy: "The ROM recognizes that some objects may have been acquired in circumstances which render the ROM's title invalid. Based upon legal advice, objects with invalid title will be returned to the appropriate party" (Royal Ontario Museum 2018, 1).

The RBCM's policy is most distinctive here. Alongside eschewing references to "sacred objects" or objects associated with "traditional curers" as the other policies do, the RBCM lays out a temporally limited period in which museum acquisitions can be understood as illegitimate: "The Museum acknowledges that many cultural materials were alienated from Indigenous peoples during the period when the potlatch and other Indigenous cultural practices were illegal under the *Indian Act*. Therefore, the Museum considers cultural materials that were taken from Indigenous communities between 1884 and 1951 to be eligible for repatriation, on a case-by-case basis" (Royal British Columbia Museum 2018, 5).

The RBCM's policies go considerably further than those of either the CMH or the ROM, defining an entire period of colonial acquisition as effectively illegitimate due to the legal apparatus of the settler state. But what all three share is an implicit category of *legitimate* acquisition, a nonspecified field in which all acquisitions can be seen as valid unless either they can be proven to be illegal under colonial laws, as per the CMH, or they fall within an already-given period of "bad" colonial law. Or, put another way, the unmarked category in every repatriation policy is the nonrepatriable artifact, the object that the museum simply has the right to retain, and, outside of 1884 to 1951 at the Royal British Columbia Museum, the burden of proof lies on the Indigenous actor, organization, or nation to show otherwise. And, unlike, for instance, the Native American Graves, Protection and Repatriation Act (NAGPRA) in the United States, there is no unified Canadian legislation that would specify certain categories within museum collections that are universally eligible for repatriation. These policies, and the complex negotiations they engender between individual Indigenous Nations and museums, are the primary stage upon which the logics of repatriation in Canada are negotiated.

In this chapter, I seek to excavate and problematize this unmarked category of legitimate acquisition. I begin here from the by now well-understood contention that museums are imperial formations that legitimate and articulate logics of domination through the work of collecting, archiving, and exhibiting. While they are not exclusively settler colonial in their character, museums play a particular role in the structures of settler colonialism, authoritatively reproducing colonial representations of Indigenous Peoples as premodern, and at the same time figuring Indigenous material culture as the natural inheritance of the colonial state (Lonetree 2012; Wakehom 2008). While I have argued elsewhere (2021) that there is an urgent need for a transformation in how Canadian museums engage Indigenous sovereign authority, my focus here is not on museum policy as such but, rather, its ongoing conditions of possibility. The fact that there even exists a de facto category of legitimate museum acquisition, I argue, works to conceal the violent conditions of *all* settler colonial appropriation.

Theft is foundational to settler colonialism. The appropriation of Indigenous territories is the crux of the settler project, and the attempt to render that appropriation into something that is legitimate and legal is among the most central ideological goals of the colonial state. Previous chapters have shown how these acts of theft are disavowed through legal and quasi-legal strategies, through discursive games and political rhetoric, and through the attempt to manufacture a coerced consent that would render Indigenous Peoples complicit in their own dispossession. This chapter turns to the recursive theft within thefts of museum acquisition, showing how the myth that most museum acquisitions were legitimate and consensual reiterates and reinforces broader logics of settler colonial disavowal. This myth characterizes the historical landscape as one in which there existed a norm in which Indigenous actors entered freely into contract-like agreements with settlers in order to sell or give away their belongings. In so doing, the myth of legitimate acquisition laminates the figure of a putatively liberal Indigenous entrepreneur onto the complex conditions of appropriation, exploitation, loss, and survival that characterize Indigenous experiences of colonial domination. It is a means of erasing the "duress" that characterizes the lives of colonial subjects, as Ann Laura Stoler might put it (2016), presenting instead the idea that Indigenous people and Peoples were fully and equitably participating in a market economy of their own volition.

This fantasy of legitimate acquisition resonates with the long history of colonial privatization, embodied particularly in allotment policies in the United States, Canada, and elsewhere.[1] "Privatization," as Daniel Heath Justice and Jean M. O'Brien have put it, "painted a civilized veneer of mutual consent over processes that were almost entirely violent and coercive" (2021, xiii). Through privatization, exploitation and theft are reframed as simple market exchanges, on the one hand; on the other, the rendering of Indigenous people as market actors achieves a "civilizational" end, justifying settler actions by suggesting they are elevating Indigenous communities toward proper modes of economic and social behavior as embodied by and embedded in common-law property rules (Bhandar 2018). Museum acquisitions through purchase are thus doubly, or perhaps even triply, legitimating: first, because they are the products of legal transactions; second, because that process allows Indigenous people *to* behave as proper economic actors within an ostensibly free market, thus aiding in their "civilization"; third, and most insidiously, because the sale of Indigenous artifacts to museums also removes these artifacts from Indigenous communities, further encouraging their assimilation into mainstream settler society.

Left unspoken are the conditions that might have *compelled* Indigenous actors to sell their belongings in the first place, which, as with allotment itself, devolve ultimately onto the violence that constitutes and maintains settler colonialism. Justice and O'Brien are concise and potent here: "For all that allotment was trumpeted by its advocates as an inevitability for benighted savages to aspire to an appropriate level of Christian civilization, the rhetoric of benevolent uplift was always backed up by threats of state, social, and religious violence. That violence—whether from everyday settler subjects, from church and state, legal orders, military, business interests, the tourism industry, or a combination of them all—undergirds all privatization schemes: allotment and its counterparts are mobilized by a constellation of violent settler structures" (2021, xxii).

Contemporary ethnological museum collections can no more be separated from these ongoing structures of violence than can land appropriation or projects of resource extraction. And yet, the fantasy—or, perhaps, "ruse," following from Audra Simpson (2017)'s usage—of mutual consent, of legitimate purchase, allows settlers to experience museum collections *as if* violence is no longer part of the story, just as they can experience the geography of the colonial nation-state as if a tiny patchwork of reserves in a sea of private ownership and federal lands is somehow normal, or even natural.

What, then, are the conditions of possibility for such a fantasy—or, perhaps more accurately, such a disavowal grounded in fantasy? How, in other words, have we arrived at a space in which we can take as given the idea that a museum's collection is legitimate unless proven otherwise? In order to begin to answer these questions, this chapter proceeds genealogically, moving from these contemporary policies to a few significant historical moments in their conceptual architecture. The first is the paradigmatic "good" repatriation in Canada, the return by the Canadian Museum of History of confiscated potlatch goods to multiple Kwakw*aka*'wakw Nations in the 1970s. My goal is not to criticize that repatriation per se, but rather to suggest that it established a framework for what repatriation *should* look like in Canada, limiting it in particular to a relatively narrowly defined field of "illegitimate" acquisitions. I then continue moving backwards, putting Victoria's turn-of-the-twentieth-century community of pawnbrokers-cum–Indigenous curio dealers into conversation with analyses of colonial property laws and norms in order to explore the conditions of colonial violence that produce seemingly "legitimate" acquisitions for Canadian museums. Finally, I consider by way of conclusion the seemingly thorny question of Indigenous agency in all this, arguing that to assert the "right" of Indigenous people to sell is always-already a mode of colonial erasure, naturalizing the very liberal subjecthood that colonizers have always attempted to impose on Indigenous Peoples as a means of eroding their sovereignty.

## The Good Repatriation

### *"It Is a Mistaken Idea that the Indians Will Forget This Affair"*

"Disregarding the sentiments of the Indian owners is dishonorable to all of us and certainly will jeopardize the image of the museum and our relations with the Indians throughout Canada. It is a mistaken idea that the Indians will forget this affair; particularly along the west coast where the detailed transmission of oral traditions still is unbelievably strong. The collection under concern is of but very limited use to us: we cannot exhibit it nor publish pictures of related information under these circumstances" (quoted in Knight 2017, 39).

The quote above comes from Ted Brasser, who was in 1971 the plains ethnologist at what was at the time the Museum of Man (eventually to be renamed the Canadian Museum of History). Brasser was reporting to his superiors on the discussions that took place that year at the National Conference on Native Cultures in Kamloops and, in particular, the account of a Kwakw*aka*'wakw woman named Mabel Stanley. Mrs. Stanley had described a 1922 RCMP raid into her community to arrest leaders and elders who were believed to have engaged in "the" potlatch, illegal at the time under the colonial ban on potlatching and other forms of Indigenous spiritual, cultural, social and political ritual.[2] Mrs. Stanley's account clearly affected Brasser. He compared the RCMP's actions to "the all-pervading terror during a German razzia, in which my father and many other men were arrested and sent off to a concentration camp" (quoted in Knight 2017, 39). His superiors seemed to concur. One noted that it was "correct that we do pay more attention to justice and less attention to the legalities of the case" (40), though his remark was in fact somewhat at odds with Brasser's earlier characterization of the RCMP's actions as having "no justification whatsoever to confiscate the ceremonial paraphernalia," despite their legal right to arrest ceremonial practitioners. Such internal ambiguities might suggest a certain tension or ambivalence on the part of museum employees reconciling colonial law with their own sense of what was right and just, one no doubt charged by the personal comparison Brasser drew for his superiors with the experiences of his own family under the Nazi regime. And regardless of what any officer of the museum believed, Brasser was firm in his declaration that "the Kwakiutl delegates could not but regard this affair as outright robbery" (39).

Given the clear and affectively resonant manner in which Brasser condemned the RCMP's confiscation of Kwakw*aka*'wakw belongings, one might be surprised to find that, in 1978, he was quoted in the *Washington Post* firmly stating that Indigenous Peoples cannot be trusted with the preservation of their own treasures: "Our conception of native arts and crafts would have been extremely hazy without the wide-ranging interests of European collectors," according to Brasser. It is doubtful that "they would have survived all their years in Indian hands. Take, for example, the large-scale destruction of medicine bags by the Ojibwa and other followers of the prophet Tenskwatawa in 1809, or the widespread custom of burying the deceased with their most cherished possessions" (L. Tuck 1978).

This is only a contradiction, however, if we read Brasser's earlier report as a condemnation of ethnological collection as a whole. But note that nowhere in Brasser's discussion quoted here or in the wider archive analyzed by museum scholar Emma Knight does he critique the act of collection as such. Rather, his fundamental concern seems to be with the *manner* in which Kwakw*aka*'wakw belongings were taken. The "all-pervading terror" of the raid and the questionable legality of its circumstances are at issue, certainly. This is an "unjust" acquisition, a "robbery," at least, Brasser speculated, from an Indigenous perspective. Yet he is also careful to note that "the Indians" will not "forget this affair," and that "the collection under concern is of but very limited use." After all, Brasser reminds his superiors, they cannot exhibit or publish photos of the collection "under these circumstances."

In other words, the question here is not about museum practice in general terms, but of a specific "bad" collection that cannot, in any case, be put to use museologically. Under those circumstances, one can infer, it makes no sense *but* to repatriate the potlatch goods. In other cases, in the context of collecting practices that are unmarked but assumed as "normal," Brasser's writing suggests not only that there is no issue but that, at a fundamental level, museum collection offers a social good in "preserving" Indigenous artifacts for the good of all, or, at the least, the all that is suggested in the similarly unmarked plural of "our conception." It is not challenging, given Brasser's audience in the *Washington Post*, to read this as settler society.

The space between Brasser's two texts limns repatriation in Canada: on the one hand, the presentation of a problematic instance that can be corrected through a selective and strategic repatriation—after, notably, the belongings in question have already become functionally useless to the museum. On the other, the normal field of collection as social good, as an act of preservation, of appreciation; that is, of *curation* in the strictest sense, a mode of caring that ultimately benefits everyone. After all, Brasser warns dramatically, if left in Indigenous hands, these artifacts might even have been destroyed! The ontological premise here, of course, is that a Euro-Western worldview that values preservation above all else is naturally (or, rather, naturalized as) correct, and any Indigenous perspectives that suggest otherwise are simply wrong, or, at best, childishly naive. Preservation can thus be read as a (colonial) good for everyone, including Indigenous Peoples who simply do not know better but precisely because of this can be legitimately acted upon (cf. A. Simpson 2014, 1).[3] In this way, repatriation becomes oriented toward the exceptional case, which is always-already recognized *by* settler society as exceptional. The norm, the space of ongoing colonial legality, remains fundamentally untouched. Such assumptions should feel familiar by this point in this book. Here again we see the presumption of a fundamental Canadian legitimacy that enables the disavowal of historical and ongoing modes of violence and domination in the settler colony. Repatriation is thereby transformed into a colonial technology of erasure in the very moment it purports to "restore" Indigenous ancestors and treasures to their homes and home communities, sustained by a pernicious combination of colonial unknowing and the fetishization of Canadian property law *as if* this law was universally applicable and always-already accepted by Indigenous Peoples. As we will see, however, this is resolutely not the case.

### *The Landmark Case*

In his recent analysis of the history of representation of Kwakw*aka*'wakw ceremonialism, anthropologist Aaron Glass refers, almost in passing, to the repatriation of what had become known as "the Potlatch Collection" as a "landmark case in Indigenous repatriation efforts" (2021, 330). Glass does not cite the claim, though he does provide extensive citations for his later reference that the case has been "well documented and analyzed," indicating texts from both Kwakw*aka*'wakw and settler scholars (330; see also 424n4). Glass's ability to pass so quickly over the significance of the repatriation is not a sign of any scholarly lapse on his part; rather, it indicates how ubiquitous the repatriation of the Potlatch Collection has become for both settler scholarly and Indigenous audiences—though, as we shall see, both the representation of the collection and the idea that it has been repatriated in its entirety are misleading. And yet, it is not at all clear that settler scholars and museum professionals share the same understandings of what the repatriation of the Potlatch Collection in fact represents as do the Kwakw*a*k*a*'wakw Peoples who fought for their treasures to be returned home. What, this is to say, is the landmark in this landmark case?

It is useful, at this juncture, to sketch out a brief review of the relevant history here, particularly involving the 1921 RCMP raid whose description so impacted Brasser and the eventual repatriation of *some* of the Potlatch Collection from the Museum of Man to the 'Namgis and We Wai Kai Nations. On Christmas Day in 1921, Dan Cranmer, a member of the 'Na̱mgis Nation from Alert Bay, held a potlatch in the nearby community of 'Mimkwa̱mlis (Village Island). While the ceremony itself was not disturbed, it came to the attention of William Halliday, then the Indian agent at Alert Bay. Convinced he could use the event as an excuse to strike a decisive blow against Kwakw*a*k*a*'wakw resistance to colonial assimilation, he had forty-five Kwakw*a*k*a*'wakw people arrested and charged, including, per Kwakw*a*k*a*'wakw scholar Gloria Cranmer Webster, "the highest ranking chiefs and their wives" (1992, 33). The arrested were humiliated.[4]

Halliday's goals went beyond brutalizing these individuals, however; in addition, the raid was an opportunity to appropriate a vast amount of Kwakw*a*k*a*'wakw regalia, which, Halliday imagined, would mean the end of the potlatch itself: "As part of the 1922 trials, an illegal agreement had been made. Those who were charged under the potlatch law did not have to serve their gaol sentences if their entire villages agreed to give up their ceremonial gear, including masks, rattles, whistles and coppers. The federal government paid the owners a total of $1,450.50 for several hundred objects, which were crated and shipped to Ottawa" (Webster 1992, 34–35). The final destinations for these Kwakw*a*k*a*'wakw regalia were the museum that would eventually become the Museum of Man and, then, the Canadian Museum of History, and the Royal Ontario Museum—though Halliday could not, it seems, resist some museological profiteering of his own, putting some of the "confiscated" belongings on display at the Anglican Parish Hall at Alert Bay, charging admission to curious settlers, and even selling thirty-three items to the American collector George Heye (U'mista Cultural Centre n.d.).

It is thus not difficult to see why this incident in particular would come to be understood as "the largest skeleton" in the "ethnological closet" of the Museum of Man, as one of Brasser's superiors noted (Knight 2017, 40), and, more broadly, as a signal example of the violence and cruelty of the ban on the potlatch and the individual excesses of Indian agents such as Halliday. Halliday's efforts to suppress and ultimately eliminate Kwakw*a*k*a*'wakw ceremonial and cultural practices seemed, by most accounts, to be virtually an obsession for the Indian agent, and the arrests after the 1921 ceremony represented a particularly dramatic instance of a broader pattern that Daisy (My-yah-nelth) Sewid-Smith (1979) refers to as "Halliday terrorism" (79). Equally, the quasi legality of Halliday's plea bargains—Webster names them explicitly as illegal and they were clearly tantamount to extortion—made the acquisition of these Kwakw*aka*'wakw belongings by Canadian and foreign museums suspect even within the bounds of colonial legality, a point that Kwakw*aka*'wakw activists and leaders highlighted recurrently in their subsequent efforts to bring them home (Webster 1992, 35). By the time of Brasser's report in the early 1970s, the Potlatch Collection had become a kind of scarlet letter for Canadian museums, in large part because of this Kwakw*aka*'wakw campaign, as Brasser himself notes. His superiors concurred, one of whom noting that the collection "would provide the museum with continual bad publicity" as long as it was not returned (Knight 2017, 40).

From a colonial museum administrator's perspective, repatriation solves the immediate problem of the bad acquisition, removing a source of bad publicity from which the museum can glean no more value. This is not to imply that the Museum of Man's eventual repatriation of its share of the Potlatch Collection was, in fact, easy or simple. As Knight notes, Kwakw*aka*'wakw communities had to compromise considerably in order to finalize the repatriation, building museum facilities according to settler standards to house the collection and consenting to community repatriations of the belongings rather than their return to their individual families (2017, 40). Such complexities are typically elided in framings that position museum repatriations as working *against* the overt violence of a bad colonial past, shifting the narrative so that museums can appear, instead, as dialogic institutions working *with* Indigenous communities to return objects that were taken "illegitimately." This, then, is the Potlatch Collection as settler landmark, a vivid moment in which colonial dynamics in Canada shifted toward their more contemporary form as "reconciliation," with the museum as metonymy for the settler state's attempts to take responsibility for its "shameful" past (cf. Povinelli 2002, esp. chap. 4).

### *U'mista*

This framing appears vividly in the 1992 Task Force Report on Museums and First Peoples, which was jointly sponsored by the Assembly of First Nations and the Canadian Museums Association (and formed the basis for the CMH's later autonomous repatriation policy). In summarizing the taskforce's consultation process, for instance, the report states, "The consultations also demonstrated that museums and cultural institutions are well aware of the necessity and value of working as *equal partners* with First Peoples. There is a strong *consensus* that partnerships should be guided by moral, ethical and professional principles and not limited to areas of rights and interests specified *by law*. The many case studies of collaborative efforts indicate that partnerships have been underway for some time in many cultural institutions across the country" (Assembly of First Nations and Canadian Museums Association 1992, 14, emphasis added).

Note the emphasis here on the language of equality and partnership, which the report itself demonstrates as the product of a collaboration between the AFN and the CMA with task force members carefully specified in the report (13–14). Echoing a quote from former AFN chief George Erasmus, the report characterizes its recommendations as an "effort to turn that page and in the spirit of new partnerships" (16–17). And yet, consider the way law is framed here. The report makes a number of references to exceeding the boundaries of law and favoring repatriation "based on moral and ethical criteria" rather than "a strictly legalistic approach" (15).

But nowhere in the report is any mention made of the fact that it is law *itself* here that is colonially imposed. Rather, the legitimacy of colonial legality is simply assumed, leading, for instance, to the report's distinction between repatriating objects that "are judged by current legal standards to have been acquired illegally," which it characterizes as a process of "restitution," and "materials which have been obtained legally" but should still be considered as potentially eligible for repatriation "based on moral and ethical factors above and beyond legal considerations" (18). Colonial law is firm as the baseline in this discussion. Yet the notion that for Indigenous Nations it is their *laws*, not moral or ethical factors, that should be respected in relation to repatriation (or anything else) is not considered. Is this really what Chief Erasmus intended when he thanked the "many people" who "have dedicated their time, career, and their lives showing what they believe is the accurate picture of indigenous people [*sic*]," and then asserted, "but we want to turn the page." (16)?

The answer, for Gloria Cranmer Webster at least, is clearly no. From her perspective as a Kwakw*aka'*wakw curator and scholar, the repatriation of the Potlatch Collection was simply one task among many:

> We do not have a word for repatriation in the Kwak'wala language. The closest we come to it is the word *u'mista*, which describes the

> return of people taken captive in raids. It also means the return of something important. We are working towards the *u'mista* of much that was almost lost to us. The return of the potlatch collection is one *u'mista*. The renewed interest among younger people in learning about their cultural history is a kind of *u'mista*. The creation of new ceremonial gear to replace that held by museums is yet another *u'mista*. We are taking back, from many sources, information about our culture and our history, to help us rebuild our world which was almost shattered during the bad times. Our aim is the complete *u'mista* or repatriation of everything we lost when our world was turned upside down, as our old people say. The *u'mista* of our lands is part of our goal and there is some urgency to do it before the provincial government allows any more clear-cut logging, destroying salmon spawning streams which affect the livelihood of many of our people. (1992, 37)

Webster's rendering of u'mista is both explicitly political and by definition anticolonial. She does not limit the work of repatriation to what is "moral or ethical" in excess of settler laws; rather, she takes u'mista to be the repatriation "of everything we lost," including not just belongings, but language, ceremony, and, perhaps especially, land. Webster is clear in this regard that there is immediate urgency to the u'mista of Kwakw*aka*'wakw land, which is being excoriated by settler extraction projects that, much like museum collection itself, remain legal and legitimate under colonially imposed systems of law and enforcement. Published in 1992, Webster's insistence on protecting Kwakw*aka*'wakw land regardless of colonial law is shared thirty years later by Wet'suwet'en people protecting their land in the face of settler militarized and police violence, among so many other nations that are enacting blockades, in Leanne Betasamosake Simpson's (2021) sense.

Which is not to say that all blockades are identical in their character. Webster was not by definition opposed to the possibility of collaboration with settler museums. Indeed, she sat on the CHM's board of trustees for a period of time when the museum was still named the Canadian Museum of Civilization. Webster's work within the context of Canadian museology is not in contradiction with her fierce opposition to colonialism; rather, it speaks to the complexities of Indigenous action within settler spaces—both the modes of action that are available and the choices Indigenous Peoples make in relationship to those modes of action. For Webster, collaborations with museums and settler scholars could form part of what Aaron Glass refers to in reference to the vast library of anthropological engagement with

Kwakw*aka*'wakw Peoples as "a set of contested but open-ended and valuable resources for reckoning colonial histories and futures" (2021, 23; cf. Kisin 2024, 49).

In this sense, Webster's approach to engagement with settler institutions might differ from the message of "reconciliation is dead." But even despite such differences, each position is nonetheless firm in its assertion of the centrality of Indigenous law in the space of settler colonial claims to possession. U'mista, Webster makes clear, is not a question of ethics or morality in *excess* of colonial law. Rather, it precisely requires *asserting* Kwakw*aka*'wakw laws, even when the state declares those legal actions to be the work of "Indigenous terrorists" (Barker 2021). The repatriation of Indigenous treasures held in museum collections matters here as one form of u'mista, but seeking their repatriation does not entail accepting the legitimacy of the legal regime of the settler colonial nation-state, nor does it make Indigenous Nations "equal partners" in a performative fantasy of settler-determined equity. Quite the contrary, u'mista opposes the pretense of colonial jurisdiction whenever it attempts to limit or supersede Indigenous laws. It reminds us that beneath the surface veneer of Canada's "era of reconciliation" lie incommensurable legal systems and the always-ongoing settler project of attempting to hollow out Indigenous laws of their actual legal, political, and perhaps even ontological demands (cf. Moreton-Robinson 2021).

## Acquisition

### *Aporias in the Database*

Consider a particular mask, currently held by the Canadian Museum of History and searched on the museum's publicly available online database. Entitled simply "dance mask" in this database, it is identified under this simple name and a color photo by an "artifact number," in this case, VII-B-7–4. While this is not explained in the database, each of the three different components of this number indicates something different about the artifact in question (Canadian Museum of History n.d.-a). The "VII" is a regional code indicating that this artifact is part of the Northwest Coast collection at the museum, a system initially developed by Edward Sapir when he became head of the Anthropological Division of the Geological Survey of Canada, eventually to become the Canadian Museum of History, in 1910 (Canadian Museum of History n.d.-b). Within that VII region, there exist "cultural codes" intended to indicate the provenance of artifacts, which map similarly onto early-twentieth-century understandings of significant Indigenous "cultural groups" (not, note, Nations). In this case, "B" tells us the artifact is of Haida provenance. Finally, the "704" is a simple numerical indicator that tells us, roughly speaking, that this is the 704th artifact catalogued within the VII-B identification.

These codes are effectively shibboleths for a register of professional museum expertise (Agha 2006), acting as a shorthand that is only available to those who are already conversant with museum codes and thus marks their (exclusive) expertise. The presence of an esoteric code for this dance mask is not an insignificant issue given that *only* ethnological artifacts—that is to say, artifacts understood to have an Indigenous provenance—are marked using these geocultural codes at the CMH; all others are simply identified by their date of acquisition. There is thus already a layer of opacity that marks Indigenous belongings—and only Indigenous belongings—in the museum, a transformation of a belonging's name, purpose, and identity as understood by its community of origin, to use the museum's own term, into a coded identifier that renders the belonging legible only within the archival orders of the museum.

Though a handful of database entries are limited only to the geocultural code, for the most part they contain a bit more information for public perusal. The dance mask, for instance, is specified as "Affiliation: Haida (cultural)," a fairly direct translation of the code that, as if in passing, reiterates that the category of "Haida" is here understood not as a sovereign Nation but as a cultural affiliation. It then lists a series of dates: "Date made: Circa 1899; Earliest: 1894/01/01, Latest: 1904/12/31." The date at which the museum acquired the mask is not listed, though more contemporary artifacts in the museum's collection, even ethnological ones, will sometimes be given an accession number that begins with this date. One might assume that one could extrapolate the date of acquisition as being, at the very least, after the last day of 1904, but, as we will shortly see, this would be incorrect. The listing then gives a series of additional identifiers, materials, and the dimensions of the mask, before turning to a section entitled "Additional Information."

It is here, in additional information, that we at last discover a bit more information about how this dance mask came into the possession of the museum. After an initial sentence suggesting that the mask is a "secret society dance mask portraying a mosquito," the section states that the mask was purchased "from the A. Aaronson collection in 1899 but probably acquired earlier at Masset by James Deans." No further specification is given, and the section then moves on into a number of sentences describing Haida secret societies and their "disappearance" in the 1870s, all given in the past tense. A reader casually browsing the database will thus be left confused as to the identities of Aaronson and Deans, the precise nature of the Aaronson collection, and/or the identities of the individuals who purchased the mask from it in 1899. The 1899 date, in addition, makes it unclear just why the latest "date made" given in the database would be the final day of 1904. Most significantly, though, no information whatsoever is given regarding the identity of the person from whom either Deans or Aaronson initially acquired the mask (Canadian Museum of History n.d.-a).

If the curious reader then decides to search "Aaronson" in the CMH online database, they will discover an additional eighteen images alongside the dance mask, including a photo *of* said dance mask. These images, primarily of Haida argillite sculptures, each identify in their titles that the photo is of an artifact "collected by A. Aaronson," with dates varying between 1879 and 1899. But the artifacts themselves do not appear when the word Aaronson is searched. To give but one example, the entry for the panel pipe identified in one of these photos as having been collected by Aaronson in 1879 makes no mention of either Aaronson or the 1879 date (Canadian Museum of History n.d.-c). Instead, it includes only "1899 or earlier" as the "date made" and general information about Haida argillite carving in the "additional information" section, though the entry does give the place of origin of the pipe firmly as "The Queen Charlotte Islands" (Canadian Museum of History n.d.-c). These "additional information" sections, one should add, do not consistently appear at all and, even when they do, are not consistent between entries, lending the entire database a patina of confusion and incoherence.

The details of acquisitions, in other words, are neither completely hidden nor made visible in clear and internally consistent ways in the CMH's public database. Rather, they are a hodgepodge of seemingly disconnected data, offering little means of determining precisely how individual belongings came to be in the possession of the museum and few guidelines for how one should read or understand the information that is given. My point is not that more detailed information does not exist within the museum; indeed, there are both internal digital databases and archival materials within the museum that contain a far greater degree of information, though rarely, in my own experience as a former curator in the institution, all that one might wish to know.[5] Neither am I arguing here that the museum is deliberately concealing this information from interested parties. While the fact that it is not easily available maintains the authority of the institution to determine who has access to what kinds of knowledge regarding the museum's collection, it has been my experience that the CMH makes the full extent of its collections information available to First Nations both as part of formal negotiation processes and more broadly for the purposes of Indigenous community knowledge and research. That includes attempting to reconcile some of the inconsistencies in its own internal records in order to make this information more precise and more useful. The point, that is to say, is neither that the museum is incompetent nor that it is, necessarily, acting in bad faith.

Rather, my claim here is a more prosaic one. As one can glean from its own online database, the CMH is simply not concerned with systematically specifying the details of acquisitions for individual records that are available to the public. Provenance is clearly considered important, but the conditions of acquisition are not. Virtually every record made available from the Ethnological (read: Indigenous) collections makes provenance information known if it is known by the museum at all.[6] Similarly, material details and dimensions are common throughout the database records. Yet acquisition is not a standard category, and when it does appear it is given most frequently in the additional details, which, as we have already seen, are not a consistent or coherently organized field of information across (or even within) different records. The simple fact that it is possible for acquisition details to be left so ambiguous in the database suggests that, at least for those organizing its online elements, the details of acquisition are not considered important to clarify for public inquiry. The legitimacy of those acquisitions can safely be assumed without further specification; and, as we have already seen in the language of the repatriation policies and the 1992 taskforce report, any challenge to this assumption would be understood to proceed on a case-by-case basis. Acquisition *as such* is made legitimate by default precisely in its meaningful absence from the online database.

### *Fair Purchase*

The notion of purchase—and, in particular, *fair* purchase—is at the heart of the claim to colonial legitimacy in Canada and other settler colonial states. In her study of the intersections of colonial property law and the social production of race, *Colonial Lives of Property*, Brenna Bhandar argues that, over the course of British colonial history, "the English common law of property became the sine qua non of civilized life and society, an axiom sharpened at the expense of Indigenous peoples throughout the colonial world." The exclusive and individualistic rendering of property at the center of English common law was at once "a set of both techniques and mechanisms" that "structured colonial capitalist modes of accumulation" and "a central fixture in philosophical and political narratives of a developmental, teleological vision of modernization that set the standard for what can be considered civilized" (2018, 3). Bhandar is clear that this complex formation was not simply formed in the metropole and exported to the colony; rather, she suggests, the English common law of property was itself formed *out* of colonial encounters, offering an at-times retroactive means of justifying settler appropriations of Indigenous lands and resources. In this rendering, Indigenous peoples were paradigmatically uncivilized *because* they did not properly "understand" ownership or the capacity to appropriate, meaning they could not have meaningful legal rights to the lands they occupy or even their own belongings—even as these very laws were being developed *to* exclude Indigenous Nations from their territories and resources.

This closed circle of colonial legality also co-constituted and was co-constituted by emerging European theories of racial superiority and inferiority, but, as Bhandar makes clear, their intersection into "racial regimes of ownership" was most often a matter of violent and cynical opportunism on the part of settler actors moving strategically between different philosophical and legal registers: "Racial regimes of ownership make use of the plasticity inherent in both of its constitutive dimensions—race and property—and deploy rationalizations for the way these phenomena are articulated in conjunction with one another in a recombinant manner using both scientific and prescientific modes of thought as a matter of brutalizing convenience" (10). Bhandar's key insight here is, again, that neither racialized ideologies nor legal regimes preceded their enactment in the colony; rather, they were codified in the context *of* their deployment, with Indigenous dispossession as their already-predetermined endpoint.

Settler efforts to assert that Indigenous peoples did not truly "own" their land, nor could they understand what civilized ownership of private property entailed, were among the most paradigmatic and significant forms of this dispossession in colonial history, but they did not exhaust its logics.[7] Crucial to the civilizational elements of property ownership was the fact that, as Bhandar puts it, "property ownership was central to the formation of the proper legal subject in the political sphere" (4). This means both that Indigenous peoples were not considered legitimate legal agents because of their improper (and often improperly collective) relationships to their own lands and belongings but, just as importantly, that the path toward "civilization" for the Native lay in teaching them how to act as a proper property owner.

This is why, for instance, religious organizations such as the Friends of the Indian in the nineteenth-century United States advocated for allotment. "To these largely Calvinist and evangelical activists," Justice and O'Brien write, "there could be no Christian American civilization without individual ownership of that land. Private property in the mortal sphere was linked to salvation in the afterlife, the singular authority of God reflected in miniature. It was the distinguishing mark of civilization and individual achievement. And it was not enough to embrace these principles oneself; all of society had to conform to the worldview, by force if necessary" (2021, xv). Allotment policies in which reservation lands were converted into individual plots owned by Indigenous individuals or families thus (ostensibly at least) achieved a civilizing end, forming Native people as properly legal subjects who would then be able to shed away the limited understandings and improper values of that Nativeness.

As Justice and O'Brien make very clear, however, the end goal of these policies was not, in fact, Native people *owning* land, but, rather, parting with it through means that would appear legal and legitimate. They quote Carl Schulz, a prominent Friend of the Indian, who made this priority clear in 1881:

> When the Indians . . . have become individual property-owners, holding their farms by the same title under the law by which white men hold theirs, they will feel more readily inclined to part with such of their lands as they cannot themselves cultivate, and from which they can derive profit only if they sell them, either in lots or in bulk, for a fair equivalent in money or annuities. This done, the Indians will occupy no more ground than so many white people; the large reservations will gradually be opened to general settlement and enterprise, and the Indians, with their possessions, will cease to stand in the way of the "development of the country." (xvi)

The aim of alienating Indigenous peoples from what land they had remaining (albeit typically already in trust to the colonial state) was born out by the realities of the allotment process, which produced devastating land loss and poverty for Indigenous Peoples throughout the United States (and elsewhere, as Justice and O'Brien's volume demonstrates). Crucially, moreover, this is land loss that is *legitimate* under the terms of colonial law, a systematic dispossession that can be blamed on the financial mismanagement and civilizational immaturity of the Native. This not only obscures the fact that much of the allotted land was further appropriated through settler theft, exploitation, deception, and outright brutality, but retroactively purifies earlier forms of colonial appropriation from their own unsettlingly illegitimate foundations, similarly grounded in and enforced through colonial violence.

Which brings us back to the paradox of fair purchase in the colonial museum. In Canada, just as in the United States, one of the primary objectives of colonial domination was to forcibly inculcate Indigenous Peoples into regimes of private property ownership in order to erase the political existence of Indigenous Nations and, thus, their actual and ongoing sovereignty over their territories, resources, and belongings. The properly entrepreneurial Native actor was thus both civilizational means and colonial end, justifying colonial domination even as it erased the object of that very domination. The absence of proper collections information in the CMH's public database is thus a remarkable colonial sleight of hand, *assuming* that entrepreneurial Indigenous actors freely parted with their belongings in order to form the basis for the museum's collection. Even the absence of full records from the earliest collections of the museum is itself a similar trick, leaving empty the details of acquisition so they can be filled in with an assumed-to-be consenting Indigenous subject. After all, why would such consent not be assumed, when private sale and purchase are taken as transparent indexes of proper legal, civilized subjectivity? Pace this archival disavowal, however, the Indigenous entrepreneur actor could not, in fact, be assumed. Rather, it had to be *produced*, historically and into the present. And this in two senses. On the one hand, the Indigenous entrepreneur had to be constituted and maintained as a fiction of colonial legitimacy, as Bhandar argues. On the other, Indigenous people had to be forced into positions in which they engaged in the "sale" of their belongings to begin with.

### *The "Johnson Street Gang"*

This brings us back to A. Aaronson, seller of the so-far enigmatic Aaronson collection in the CMH's database. It also brings me back to an ongoing conversation with my friend and colleague, Haida artist, writer, and historian Jaalen Edenshaw. It was from Jaalen that I first learned about the predominantly Jewish community of curio dealers who operated in the late nineteenth and early twentieth centuries in Victoria, the then–recently designated provincial capital of British Columbia. Informally known as the "Johnson Street Gang" for the locations of their stores, this community, of which Aaronson was a prominent (and, as we will see, rather dramatic) member, was essential to the Indigenous art trade of the turn of the twentieth century, supplying "valuable artifacts" and Native contacts to museums and scholars. They also bolstered settler tourism to the area, "often providing the only avenue for purchase [of Indigenous art] to the casual private collector and the souvenir seeking tourists" (Hawker 1989, 10). It was also through my conversations with Jaalen that I began to understand the profound aporias within the relatively scant histories of this community, which focused overwhelmingly on the collectors themselves (and sometimes their relationship to Victoria's broader Jewish community), but rarely if ever offered any details on their transactions with Indigenous Peoples or the specific artifacts they acquired and sold. The analysis that follows does not fill in those aporias—indeed, it relies primarily on scholarly material that Jaalen himself collected and shared with me—but it does attempt to better understand why those gaps in the archive might exist in the first instance (cf. Trouillot 1995).

In 1886, Andrew Alfred Aaronson attended a Colonial and Indian Exhibition in England "dressed in a buckskin suit and a wide sombrero," per art historian Ronald Hawker. Appropriating elements of the performative reputation of figures such as Buffalo Bill and Wild Bill Hickock, Aaronson informed the British press that he was also known as "Wild Dick" and that, while his role at the exhibition was to be "in charge of BC Indian curios" at the exhibition, in British Columbia he was "employed to hunt the recalcitrant Indian to his forest retreat." When these reports reached Victoria, Hawker notes, the local press found the idea of Aaronson "hunting Indians" to be ridiculous (1989, 11). Even if his attempts to refashion himself in the then-contemporary vernacular of the Wild West show failed in the eyes of Victorian settlers, however, Aaronson's performance in England tells us something significant about the nature of the curio trade and the kind of relationships of exploitation it engendered between settler traders and Indigenous people.

Unlike his "Wild West" models, Aaronson was born in London, in 1856, immigrating to North America at the age of twenty-one and eventually settling in Victoria in 1877. His work as a pawnbroker involved "collecting old jewelry and Indian curios," as Sarah Tobe, a local historian of the Jewish community in Victoria, put it (1999, 15). Aaronson had this background in common with many of his peers in the Johnson Street Gang. In 1887, for instance, Frederick Landsburg and his partner Samuel Kirshberg expanded their clothing business into a pawn brokerage, described by Tobe as follows: "With all the Indians trading and frequenting their shop, the business became a combination loan office and curio boutique in 1890. Landsberg learned to communicate with his Native customers and before long was selling their handicrafts. Honorable in his dealings, their relationship evolved into trading for artifacts" (12).

Left unexamined by Tobe in her account of these "honorable dealings" is why Native people would have needed to engage with a pawnbroker and loan office in the first instance. Nor were all the dealers so honorable, at least in the colonial sense of the word; John J. Hart established his business by trading liquor illegally to Tsimshian and Haida people in exchange for furs and gold and silver work before beginning his own curio shop in Victoria in 1880 (Koffman 2012, 180). The "hunt" for the "recalcitrant Indian" about which Aaronson bragged might not have been a literal one, then, but it is nonetheless quite apparent that these early transactions between Indigenous sellers and settler purchasing agents were taking place in the context of loans and pawnshops—that is to say, of an inculcation into debt and other mechanisms through which settler capitalism obligated Native people to part with their possessions in the context of ongoing colonial domination.

This was not limited to Victoria. Rather, as Jewish historian David Koffman has suggested, the immigrant Jewish community of the latter half of the nineteenth century played a distinct and important role in spreading American (and Canadian) capitalism to the "frontier" through their role as a "merchant minority," incorporating Indigenous peoples into settler capitalist networks and, in particular, "creating new markets for a new commodity, curios, objects that originally had little to no concrete value outside of their Native American communities." In "inventing this new market," Koffman further argues, "Jewish merchants played active parts in the expansion of not just American capitalism but American colonial expansion" (2021, 170).

Koffman describes this process as "a kind of missionizing for capital," a means through which Jewish immigrants could gain important social as well as material capital by teaching "Native Americans to be better capitalists and therefore better Americans" (180). While Koffman is sympathetic to the ways in which this enabled that generation of Jews to combat long-standing antisemitic tropes in settler society, he is nonetheless clear that the condition of possibility for their business was the ongoing dispossession of Indigenous Peoples: "Native Americans had been either forcibly encouraged to become agriculturalists by the Dawes Act of 1887, designed to produce "surplus land" upon which further settlement and commerce could take place, or forced onto reservations with limited opportunities for acquiring capital. Part of the process of frontier conquest involved commodifying and monetizing the land itself. Along with many other whites, Jews gained from the broad commercial transformation of colonized territory, which had been supported by capital, law, and military, and which dislocated native populations to make living room for European and American settlers" (179–80).

We should not forget this process of "frontier conquest" was also taking place in British Columbia during the period of the Johnson Street Gang's operation. Indeed, the consistent threat of military violence—and the frequent resort to it—characterized the early interactions between Indigenous Nations and settler forces over the course of the nineteenth century, as British Columbia transitioned from a British colony to a province of the newly confederated Canada (C. Harris 2002). These modes of what one naval historian has referred to, euphemistically, as "gunboat diplomacy" (Gough 1984) aimed to remove Indigenous Peoples from territories that newly arriving settlers found appealing throughout BC, typically preceding the establishment of formal reserves as determined by a series of colonial commissions. Military violence also undergirded the spread of smallpox to Native communities; as Penelope Edmonds chronicles, the recurrent expulsions of Indigenous residents from Victoria in the latter half of the nineteenth century were supervised by gunboats and led to the spread of illness throughout the coast (2010, 14). With their access to both land and water sharply curtailed[8] and facing decimation from disease and the constant threat of settler violence, it would be difficult to claim that Indigenous communities in British Columbia were in any sense "free" to transact with settlers on their own terms.[9]

We should not ignore, likewise, the fact that many of the "curios" that were being sold in the Johnson Street shops had been targeted by colonial laws banning every mode of Indigenous ceremonialism that had been conflated into "the" potlatch. Between 1883 and 1885, the federal cabinet amended the Indian Act—the blanket legislation that determined (and continues to determine) Indian law in Canada—to make engaging in both "the" potlatch and "the tamanawas dance" a misdemeanor offense (Cole and Chaikin 1990, 14). The fact that these categories were not further defined, as Christopher Bracken (1997) has argued, enabled colonial authorities to effectively target any Indigenous practice they found problematic or objectionable, meaning that, in effect, Indigenous ceremonialism itself had been banned. Though the law did not in itself target Indigenous belongings, because any artifact could be defined as being in some sense "connected" to the potlatch, the ban offered a useful excuse to confiscate Indigenous treasures for museum consumption and without question led to some communities hiding, destroying, or selling their treasures for fear of prosecution alongside coercive missionary pressures. Here we see the legal background for the arrests at Alert Bay discussed earlier, but the impacts were felt throughout the province from the advent of the law until its formal end in 1951. It is no coincidence, in other words, that so many Indigenous artifacts were collected between the mid-1880s and the end of the law; likewise, as Jaalen Edenshaw has incisively pointed out to me, it should not be seen as innocent that one of the law's primary supporters, Israel Powell, was both superintendent of Indian affairs in British Columbia between 1871 and 1889 and a well-known collector of Indigenous artifacts himself (cf. Cole and Chaikin 1990, 14–18).

This is the context through which we must understand Sarah Tobe's characterization of the Johnson Street Gang's purchases. "Victoria's curio dealers," Tobe writes, "did not appropriate or plunder the items that were included in the various collections, they acquired them through normal commercial transactions which occurred in their trading relationships" (1999, 10). Tobe thus sharply differentiates the purchases of the Johnson Street Gang from the explicit illegality of colonial agents such as William Halliday. It does not follow thereby that such purchases were made under the conditions of mutual freedom that liberalism imagines for capitalist markets. The point is precisely that these transactions *were* normal; to return to the language of the repatriation policies with which this chapter began, they were entirely legal under the colonial laws of the time. But that legality was not neutral or impartial, however much both museum policies and sympathetic historical accounts might cling to the fiction of the law as impartial arbiter. Rather, it was imposed as part of the process of settler colonization, undergirded by explicit and implicit violence and without any cessation of Aboriginal title, much less Indigenous consent.

The normalcy of the transaction, furthermore, was not an a priori property of free exchange, but a normative system of property ownership that operated simultaneously to justify colonial dispossession and forcefully inculcate Indigenous subjects into capitalist sensibilities as a mark of their own "civilization" (Bhandar 2018). A normal transaction, in short, is itself an extension of colonial domination that produces a veneer of consent, allowing it to appear as if Indigenous people are fully and freely participating in their own dispossessions as opposed to navigating within the "strangulating" conditions, to borrow a phrase from Audra Simpson (2014), of settler colonialism. This same "normalcy" also conceals Indigenous regimes of property, ownership, hereditary prerogative, and other forms of possession (and, indeed, title), that existed prior to contact and continued under the conditions of colonial domination, even if strangulated.[10]

This, then, is the absence in the public archive. The impetus here is *not* to know the details of the individual transactions that filled the collections of Canadian museums. These aporias are forms of what Manu Vimalessery, Juliana Hu Pegues, and Alyosha Goldstein have called "colonial unknowing," acts of ignorance that are "aggressively made and reproduced, affectively invested and effectively distributed in ways that conform the social relations and economies of the here and now" (2016, 1). What such gaps hide are not the "bad" acquisitions, the acts of "plunder" represented by figures such as William Halliday against which Tobe indemnifies Aaronson and his fellow collectors. Rather, they conceal the ongoing conditions of settler colonialism itself, the ways in which Indigenous subjects were (and are) compelled to engage with colonial capitalism for survival and survivance. This elision of detail holds open space for fantasies of colonial equity, of liberal Indigenous subjects civilized by enacting property law, of possessions freely sold absent both direct *and* indirect conditions of coercion. The records of individual transactions with the Johnson Street Gang are partial because the "veneer of mutual consent" offered by commercial transactions was assumed to be enough by all parties, and I think it is unlikely that Aaronson or his peers would have considered individual Indigenous sellers important enough to record in detail. The details are absent—even when known—from the CMH's digital archive because the fantasy of fair purchase is assumed to be enough for contemporary settler Canadians; indeed, too much information might prove unsettling.

## On the False Premise of Agency

A common response I have encountered in discussions of the limits of repatriation is the importance of not erasing Indigenous agency in relationship to the legitimate commercial transactions—as Tobe might put it—that filled the ethnological collections of Canadian settler museums. After all, this discourse goes, does assuming that Native sellers were not making rational, adult decisions in regard to their belongings not reduce Indigenous people to the status of mere victims or, even worse, the very irrational actors that infantilizing colonial agents imagined them to be? I would, however, suggest that this very question is already accepting a set of fundamentally colonial premises. As we have seen throughout this chapter, the production of the Indigenous subject as agentive entrepreneur, cognizant of the significance and necessity of private ownership and able to freely purchase and, especially, *sell* their possessions, was a cornerstone of nineteenth-century settler colonialism in both Canada and the United States. The properly civilized Native was precisely a capitalist agent, and the inculcation of that agent into private property was understood as the process by which that Native would leave behind their atavistic cultural ways and become a proper citizen of the settler nation-state. Both the allotment policies of the nineteenth-century United States and the legal commercial transactions on Victoria's Johnson Street form part of a structure of domination that erases itself by centering the concept of individual agency and eliding the conditions of ongoing violence that compel these forms of dispossession.

This does not mean that the choices made by Indigenous people within the constraints of colonial domination do not matter. We might consider them, like the x-marks on treaties that Scott Lyons (2010) has analyzed, as "contaminated and coerced sign[s] of consent made under conditions that are not of one's making." But, as Lyons also reminds us, a "decision one makes when something has already been decided for you . . . is still a decision" (3). Indigenous people were not passive objects of colonial imaginaries; they engaged (and continue to engage) settler society with a vast diversity of intentions, strategies, goals, desires, and aspirations. In this light, we might note anthropologist Eugenia Kisin's analysis of an "aesthetics of repair" within contemporary Northwest Coast Indigenous art, which aims to "hold in tension trauma, resilience, crises, critiques, and new locations of the contemporary avant-garde *without* turning to ontological incommensurability" (2024, 14). Art and engagement with museum worlds, Kisin suggests, hold open spaces for Indigenous artists both to critically intervene within the conditions of settler society and to imagine alternative futures for shared world-making that are not already overdetermined by settler imaginaries. Collaboration and contamination shade together here, and it is neither easy nor necessarily appropriate for settler scholars to make the determination of what should be emphasized in these complexities.[11]

My goal is not to erase the significance of those contaminated and coerced decisions that are nonetheless still decisions. I am firm, however, in asserting that these decisions cannot be made into the grounds for the ongoing legitimacy of an imposed colonial legal order. The violent extortion enacted by William Halliday in Kwakw*aka'*wakw territory is not an exception to the proper functioning of settler colonialism; it is its very essence, the continuing maintenance of conditions of threat and terror designed to compel Indigenous Peoples to "consent" to ongoing domination and dispossession because there is no choice otherwise. The museum is metonymy here, at once a material archive of both legitimate *and* illegitimate looting (cf. Leathem 2025) and a symbolic repository of the logics that naturalize dispossession as being a requirement for the Native subject to arrive at the level of proper civilization. Repatriation, as we will see in chapter 6, need not accept the restrictions, erasures, and disavowals of such fantasies of colonial legitimacy. Indigenous Peoples do not and need not accept either the naturalization of settler theft or the violent concealment embedded within acts of return that are imagined as gifts given by the colonial state as part of the era of reconciliation.

CHAPTER SIX

# Giving Back the Name with Respect

## *Repatriation and Refusal Between Canada and the Haida Nation*

> It wasn't the province giving our name Haida Gwaii back to us. We were giving the Queen Charlotte Islands name back to them and having ours formally recognized, and all within the spirit of respect and reconciliation.
>
> —GWALIGA HART

On June 3, 2010, the provincial government of British Columbia passed Bill 18, the Haida Gwaii Restoration Act, legally restoring the name "Haida Gwaii" to the island archipelago that forms the ancestral home and sovereign territory of the Haida Nation. Two weeks later, on June 17, a ceremony entitled Aajii kyee gan saa guudang aas.uu sahlgaan dang ga t'alang isdaang—Yahguudang dangad kiigaay dang gwii t'alang sdiihlda (Giving Back the Name with Respect) was held in Gaw (Old Massett), a Haida community at the north end of Haida Gwaii's largest island. At this ceremony, representatives from the Haida Nation formally returned the islands' colonially imposed name, the "Queen Charlotte Islands," to the provincial government of British Columbia and the federal government of Canada. The returned name was symbolically given to the Crown through BC's then-premier Gordon Campbell in a bentwood box (Government of British Columbia and Council of the Haida Nation 2010), which was eventually taken by the Duke and Duchess of Cambridge to Britain in 2016.

As is made clear by the name chosen for the ceremony and Haida artist Gwaliga Hart's retrospective comments about the event (quoted in RBC 2013, 5), the return of Haida Gwaii's colonial name was not intended as a mere acknowledgment of the province's legal restoration of the indigenous name of the islands. Rather, it was framed as an act of respect and reciprocity, the return of something the Haida Nation had never asked for and never needed. If we follow Hart's argument, the ceremony did more than simply give back the "Queen Charlotte Islands"; it took control over the power to name, and to give, in the first instance. "It wasn't the province giving our name Haida

Gwaii back to us," contends Hart. "We were giving the Queen Charlotte Islands name back to them."

In so doing, Hart positions settler governance within a broader regime of property and relationality, one in which the right *to* give is as important, if not far more so, than the content of the gift itself. In this mode of reckoning property and possession—immaterial as well as material—Haida people are preeminent, cognizant of the rules according to which names can be given or received, recognized as legitimate or rejected as the opposite. The ceremony marks a distinct and, in Hart's reading, quite deliberate break with a prior colonial regime of imposition, where Indigenous perspectives, practices, values, and names were ignored, attacked, or outright erased by settler colonial actors and policies, replaced without consultation or consent. Instead, in the "spirit of respect and reconciliation"—both politically charged expressions—the "Giving Back the Name with Respect" ceremony compels past and present settler governance into a network of relations and reciprocal obligations that extends from time immemorial into the present and cannot be ignored. It refuses the "gift" of a colonial return and the erasure that comes with it, asserting instead the simple fact that Haida Gwaii was never given up by Haida people as the name of their home and sovereign territory.

In this chapter, I explore the return of the "Queen Charlotte Islands" to the Crown as a process through which the Haida Nation can incorporate settler governance into a regime of respectful relations that functions on Haida terms. In constituting the return of the settler name as both the rejection of an unacceptable imposition and a respectful act of relationality in its own right, I argue, the Haida Nation simultaneously offered a searing critique of colonial domination and invited settler powers into an alternative modality of relationship based in mutual understanding and respect. Less obviously, perhaps, but no less importantly, I suggest that in returning the islands' colonially imposed name, the Haida Nation constitutes itself as a particular kind of political entity with clear traditional antecedents and essentially equal—if not superior—relationships with foreign governing powers.

The "Giving Back the Name with Respect" ceremony is thus generative on multiple scales, at once refusal of colonial domination and world-building activity. The ceremony explicitly refuses the notion that settler governance is in a position to give gifts to Haida people; indeed, it makes clear that this false sense of equity exists in order to make the ongoing ways through which the Crown attempts to maintain dominion over Indigenous lands to which it has no legitimate claim. Coupled with this, as we shall see, is an invitation to proper relationality, a map for how respectful relations *could* exist between settler governments and Indigenous Nations. And finally, the ceremony acts as a space in which *Haida* political worlds are reconstituted, reminding us that Indigenous political actions are never solely determined by their referents to settler worlds, however much they may press down upon Native lives and livelihoods.

This is significant in itself; in addition, we can understand it as an alternative to the liberal model of repatriation critiqued in chapter 5. What is "giving back the name," after all, but a repatriation? And one *from* an Indigenous Nation to the colonial power that is so typically understood as the entity that presides over repatriation. Here, instead of the focus on discontinuous "gifts" from colonial power and debates over equity that center the liberal individual, the ceremony frames repatriation as social action, already embedded in relations of power that must be recognized and addressed by all the parties involved in ongoing relations with each other. This chapter thus provides an answer to the previous one, offering a Haida model for Indigenous-led repatriation that does not reiterate either the violence of theft itself or the erasure of that violence under the guise of a colonially determined equity.

In order to situate this complex critical and cultural work that is being done by the "Giving Back the Name with Respect" ceremony, I begin with a double history of names and naming on Haida Gwaii. If the colonial imposition of names on Haida Gwaii is a mode of settler erasure of Indigenous presence, then it is important to understand the stakes of naming *for* Haida people. Names, in a Haida sense, are a mode of immaterial property, whose proper attribution ties individuals to broader social, political, and cosmological relations in the present and stretching back to time immemorial. An improperly given name voids the very relationality that makes naming possible. Understanding these two histories together gives purchase on contemporary Haida social action, which speaks to crucial questions of sovereign power, of repatriation, and of political possibility in Indigenous contexts. These questions help us understand the stakes of what the Haida Nation is doing beyond the islands of Haida Gwaii. With all this in place, I turn to the "Giving Back the Name with Respect" ceremony itself, drawing on participant reflections and Gwaliga Hart's recent documentary to sketch out the different forms of political and social work at play during and following from the event, paying particular attention to the break between the discourses of the ceremony and the metacommentary on these discourses offered by Haida participants.

## Islands of the People

### *Island Names*

The name "Haida Gwaii" derives from the Haida language and means "Islands of the People." For my friends and colleagues in Gaw, Haida Gwaii has always been the name of the archipelago that is the ancestral homeland and sovereign territory of the Haida Nation. But that "always" is worth nuancing. Like many such ethnonyms throughout the Indigenous world, the word "Haida," or, rather, *xaada*, is a Haida term meaning "people." As such, the name Haida Gwaii did not refer to a single, politically unified nation in the manner of a Westphalian nation-state. Rather, the lands and waters of the islands of Haida Gwaii were (and continue to be) divided among different matrilineal clans, each affiliated with either the Raven or Eagle "side" (moiety, in a more technical anthropological parlance). Each clan held particular territorial rights and resource prerogatives, including fishing grounds, berry picking areas, and access to house sites (Bell 2016; cf. Boelscher 1988, 36).[1] Significantly, this means that "Haida Gwaii" was not the name of a single, monolithic polity. The islands were where people lived; thus, they were the "Islands of the People."

These Haida people were not consulted by any of the European explorers who began surveying the islands near the end of the eighteenth century. While there is some debate whether or not Juan Perez's 1774 expedition marked the first contact between Europeans and Haida (White 2006), Perez's voyage marked a sustained period of "discovery" for the islands of Haida Gwaii, as different European voyageurs began to claim discovery, and thus naming rights, to the archipelago, without consideration for the rights or perspectives of its inhabitants. Here is a short inventory: In 1786, the early fur trader James Hanna sailed briefly around the shores of the islands and named them "Nova Hibernia." The next year, on August 3, 1787, Captain George Dixon navigated the islands, confirming that they represented an archipelago (a fact that Perez had not understood) and naming them the "Queen Charlotte Islands" after his ship, the *Queen Charlotte*, itself named for the wife of George III. While it was eventually adopted as the "official" name of the islands, Dixon's choice of name was not immediately authoritative. Instead, the islands were named "The Great Islands" in 1788 by one "John Meares of Nootka," another trader, who was either unaware of or unconcerned with Dixon's prior act of naming. In 1789, the American sloop captain Robert Gray also named the islands, christening them "Washington's Isle" after *his* vessel, the *Lady Washington*. Finally, at around the same time a Spanish map drawn by Spanish navigator Esteban Jose Martinez identified the islands as "Isla Infante Don Fernando," though Martinez's mapmaker corrupted the name to "Elefante" (Dalzell 1973, 13–15).

In her 1973 history of place names on Haida Gwaii, Kathleen Dalzell suggests that the polyphonic burst of naming that marked the islands' early encounters with Europeans set something of a pattern, even as the Queen Charlotte Islands became the accepted name for the islands by the coast's British and, eventually, Canadian settlers by the early nineteenth century. "THE QUEEN CHARLOTTE ISLANDS," Dalzell writes (capitals original), "have been known by many names—from the old Haida reference of *Islands-of-the-People* to the modern day MISTY ISLES often affectionately bestowed on them" (13). Dalzell does not, however, problematize this consistent, colonially-imposed pattern of renaming. Quite the opposite, for Dalzell, writing from the perspective of her own status as a long-time island resident and daughter of a settler family, the fluidity in name marks a broader social and political truth about the islands. The "old Haida reference[s]" are still present but they are part of a broader contemporary synthesis between Haida and settler communities:

> Today a new Queen Charlotte Islands' culture is evolving and may prove to be as satisfactory as any previous one. Creed, colour or sex are unimportant—so is wealth of the monetary type. The prime bond is a desire to guard and retain all the unique physical factors of these Islands. . . . For although human values change, the Islands themselves remain constant and create, in those who achieve rapport, a sense of personal involvement infinitely fulfilling. The Charlottes do not morally *belong* to anyone, be it a nation—a government—or profit-hungry corporations. They are the *Islands-of-the-people* . . . all people. . . . And are in trust. (14–15)

In Dalzell's rendering, "Islands-of-the-people" becomes an explicitly general referent, naming a social, political, and physical space that cannot "morally" belong to any individual nation, any governing body, or any one individual. No one name could encompass such diversity. In the process she erases the specificities of Haida sovereignty, of the particular rights and relationships that have tied Haida people to their islands since time immemorial.

### *Naming and Power 1: Erasure and Sovereignty*

Dalzell's assertion of a diverse and accepting island community unified by its commitment to the protection of the islands still had strong resonances more than forty years later, as island residents continued to work together regardless of "creed, colour or sex" to protest possible oil and natural gas pipeline and tanker projects. Blue "UNITED" signs were dotted all over the island communities in 2015, indexing unified island opposition to the proposed Enbridge Northern Gateway Pipelines Project (Weiss 2018, 181). At the same time, however, Dalzell's presentation of an "islands of the people" that encompasses any and all without differentiation is radically different from either a historical or contemporary Haida perspective. As noted above, the islands of Haida Gwaii have been divided into traditional territories, the rights over which are held by individual matrilineal clans; it has never been a nondifferentiated commonweal, even for Haida, much less the newly arrived settlers. Dalzell's notion of an "island for all people" erases those historical and ongoing rights, positioning Haida as just one of many communities living on island. In a relational context in which Haida sovereign rights had not been acknowledged, much less honored, Dalzell's seemingly celebratory invocation of the "islands of *all* people" appears as colonial imposition.

Names have power in such processes of erasure. As Dalzell herself reports elsewhere in her text, even the current name of the Village of Masset, next door to the Haida community of Gaw, is the result of a colonial act of eponymic appropriation. In 1907, when the site for the future village was first surveyed, the town site was given the name "Graham City." However, when the city planners discovered that the postmaster for the Haida community then called Masset was leaving, they applied for a post office in *their* townsite and claimed its name was "Masset." Effectively, the city planners had stolen both the post office and the name "Masset" from their soon-to-be neighbors (Dalzell 1973, 381), leading to the settler community carrying the name of "New Masset" and the Haida reserve community becoming "Old Massett." This story, I should add, is well remembered by the Haida community, and I was told a number of variations on it during my time in Gaw, Old Massett. While some details varied, the key point—that the settlers made possible their acquisition of a post office through the theft of the name "Masset"—remained consistent (Weiss 2018, 101). Note here too the extent to which colonial imposition of language is felt not just in the need to "rename" Masset, but in the use of an Anglicized name for the community itself.

As this account makes clear, to name and to have the right *to* name should not be understood as neutral (or naive) in the context of settler colonialism. The city planners who appropriated the name "Masset" were able to do so because they better understood the particular means of navigating the early Canadian bureaucratic apparatus. This same apparatus was already engaged in multiple acts of (re)naming all over the northwest coast as part of the process of the "allocation" of reserves in British Columbia, reconstituting complex fields of Indigenous social and political organization into individually labeled administrative units with legal English names derived from frequently inaccurate settler understandings of Indigenous naming practices, groupings, and even pronunciation (C. Harris 2002). Naming was (and is) a crucial tool of colonizing power, a way to simultaneously erase the presence of Indigenous Peoples from their land and assert the right of settler governance to define and administer those same peoples. And this happened over multiple generations, as Indigenous names were taken at best to be "old references," colorful origins for contemporary place names without any necessary legal or political connotations. As we will see, the restoration of the name Haida Gwaii is a distinct sovereign refusal of forms of settler colonial erasure, emblematizing the contemporary political authority of the Haida Nation and indexing its unceded history by the assertion of Haida Gwaii as the *real* name of the islands.

### *Naming and Power 2: Haida Names*

The "Giving Back the Name with Respect" ceremony represents a potent political intervention by the Haida Nation into a colonial history that both encompasses and exceeds Haida Gwaii; it is also an intervention framed through a distinctly Haida logic. In their article "Gam tluu tllgaay aa kii*xa* Gang ga, There Is No Land Strange," *K*ii'iljus, Barbara J. Wilson, and Luu Gaahlandaay, Kevin J. Borserio, discuss the Skidegate Haida Immersion Program's collaboration with the Gwaii Haanas National Park Reserve, National Marine Conservation Reserve, and Haida Heritage Site to document Haida place names in the Skidegate dialect. They note that that the acknowledgment of the islands' "original name in its commonly used form, Haida Gwaii," is "but a first step in the long process of fully reintegrating all Haida with their traditional ways, lands, waters, and traditional knowledge" (2011, 188).

Haida place names, as *K*ii'iljus and Luu Gaahlandaay make clear, are more than just convenient geographic identifiers; they index social and cosmological history (though drawing a sharp distinction between these two is rarely appropriate in Haida oral histories), strategies for navigation, and even the availability of particular food and resources. "Over thousands of years of living on this island," *K*ii'iljus and Luu Gaahlandaay write, "our Ancestors *named* every mountain, stream, point, body of water, current and area. These names are regional in some cases, meaning direction was part of the naming—where the ancestors sat on the land was important. . . . Many prominent mountains, points or islands carry the names of the Supernatural beings that live beneath them, and when the Ancestors spoke of a particular place they would refer to it as the home of a specific Supernatural. Other names signify places where food or medicine was gathered. . . . Other names contain a physical description of a place" (190, emphasis added). To study Haida place names is not just to learn words, but to come to understand the specific history of the lands and waters *as* Haida places, as landmarks, homes of Supernaturals, and spaces of resource gathering, among other roles, all entailed by their Haida names (cf. Basso 1997).

The rights to the places and resources indexed by Haida place names were and continue to be held by and vested in individual Haida clans. The right to name a given place is not politically neutral, nor has it been, on Haida Gwaii since time immemorial. In order to have a sense of the stakes of names and naming for Haida people, a quick sketch of practices concerning Haida personal names will prove useful to foreground the political and cultural significance of names as particular forms of immaterial property. "Everyone and everything of importance had meaningful names," writes Haida linguist Lucy Bell, Sdaahl *K'*awaas. "People, houses, canoes, and even feast dishes were once named" (2016, 123).

The significance of Haida naming, Sdaahl *K'*awaas, argues, continues well into the present. Marianne Boelscher likewise characterizes Haida names as being "of prime importance in expressing the social and political order, and in linking the social order to both the supernatural and the material world" (1988, 152). Unlike names in the Western European tradition, Haida names are owned by the different Haida clans and only held by individuals, conferred over time to multiple inheritors at that clan's discretion and within a ceremonial context (L. Bell 2016, 124). As the symbolic property of their clan, the names "an individual receives provide a social record of his inherited as well as acquired social status," linking the current holder of a name with those who have held the name in the past, with their lineage and the territory owned by that lineage as expressed in the stories of the name's origin, and with the Supernaturals from whom many names originate (Boelscher 1989, 152). An individual, concomitantly, can hold multiple Haida names over the course of their life, reflecting their own connections to their family, their development, and potential acquisition of chiefly or other high-ranking positions within their clans.

Sdaahl *K'*awaas and Boelscher both emphasize the extent to which the act of naming is foregrounded by this proprietary system of Haida names. Even the word for "name" in the Gaw dialect of the Haida language, *kyaa*, is used primarily as a verbal stem, inextricably associating the possession of a name with the acts of naming and of having been named, which are in turn "expressions of the *rights* of the name given conferred upon the name receiver" (Boelscher 1989, 152–53, emphasis in original).[2] In order for a name to be properly conferred, it must be validated within a ceremonial context through the giving away of an amount of property adequate to the stature of the name (152). Haida names are only really names, only social facts, if they are properly given, and they stand by their very nature as both evidence for and reiteration of this course of social action. When Kii'iljus and Luu Gaahlandaay specify that the Ancestors *named* individual places on the islands, they are not describing a haphazard or incidental process. They are speaking to an essentially right-full set of social actions through which Haida Gwaii came to exist as a social-cum-cosmological landscape of clan territories, prerogatives, and responsibilities that cannot be separated from the system of ceremonial practices through which the material and immaterial property of clans are asserted, articulated, and evaluated.

## Repatriation and Refusal

> Contorting oneself in a fundamental space of misrecognition is not just about subject formation: it is about historical formation. And by refusing to agree to those terms and be eliminated, Mohawks are asserting actual histories, and thus legislating interpretive possibilities in contestation . . . not only individual selves.
>
> —AUDRA SIMPSON, *Mohawk Interruptus*

When Gwaliga Hart asserts that the state was not returning the name Haida Gwaii to the Haida Nation, he refers to this history of appropriation on the one hand, and to these right-laden acts of naming on the other. The provincial government could not return something that it never had the right to take away in the first instance. But Hart's refusal—and the refusal of the "Giving Back the Name with Respect" ceremony as a whole—go beyond a simple rejection of the legitimacy of colonial appropriation. In positioning the settler state as *able* to accept a gift, Hart and the Haida Nation were also refusing to hold the settler state exempt from their protocol, from their regimes of rights and obligations. They reframed colonialism's agents as subject to Haida social, political, and legal systems, implicitly positioning colonizers from Juan Perez on as historical delinquents, ignoring a set of laws, practices, and names to which they should have been, and still can be, held to account. At the same time, they invited these same colonial agents into a better mode of relationality, one framed through the "spirit of respect and reconciliation," but on Haida terms.

Alongside other Indigenous Nations all along the Northwest Coast (and well beyond it), the Haida Nation is engaging in a politics of what Ts'msyen and Mikisew Cree anthropologist Robin Gray (T'uu'tk) refers to as "reclamation." "Settler colonialism," Gray writes, "is a claims-making process—we are sovereign, you are not; we want what you have; what is yours should be ours; we know you better than you know yourself; we know what is best for you" (2015, 1). These pernicious modes of colonial knowing, stealing, and claiming erase Indigenous rights and knowledge, and aim to obliterate Indigenous existence as such (e.g., 14). Yet the converse, as Gray explores in her elegant dissertation, is that acts of Ts'msyen ceremony, singing, dancing, feasting, recounting, and reaffirming Ts'msyen laws and histories are radical acts in the face of the expectation of Indigenous "in/visibility," the consequences, as Gray puts it, "of being rendered visible as static objects but invisible as active agents within and across settler societies" (14). Reclaiming and making present what it means to be Ts'msyen in its full political *and* cultural dimensions work to wrest the terms of visibility themselves from Canadian colonial authority.

Gray has recently pushed these ideas still further in more explicit discussions of what she terms "rematriation," referencing the central role of matriarchs and matrilineality in Ts'msyen social and political life. Thinking with different instances in which Coastal Indigenous Nations have repatriated material and immaterial property to *each other* rather than in relation to the settler state, Gray shows how repatriation—or rematriation, rather—in First Nations contexts is never distinct from broader worlds of ongoing relationality. Quite the opposite, to rematriate is to engage productively in relationship-building between communities, guided by protocols that are at once long-standing and emergently reiterated through ceremony and mutual acts of respect (2022).

So too with the Haida Nation. By reclaiming the name of their territories while rejecting the idea that colonial power could ever have legitimately stolen it in the first place, the Haida actors hosting the "Giving Back the Name with Respect" ceremony—just as their Ts'msyen neighbors do—sketch out the possibility of an inversion of the colonial overdetermination of Indigenous political possibility. Such Indigenous acts of reclamation respond to the problem first framed in anthropology by Elizabeth Povinelli in *The Cunning of Recognition*. While Povinelli is concerned with the "creative engagement of indigenous subjects with the impasses that liberal diasporas present to them" (2002, 31), her account emphasizes the dominating capacity of the settler state, which "purifies" itself of the violence of its own history through its selective recognition of Aboriginal difference, always and only "up to a point." The state holds the power to determine the bounds of acceptable difference—and, more immediately in our context, to define what can (and what cannot) be heard, counted, and recognized as legitimate political claims on the part of Indigenous Peoples. The studies that have followed from Povinelli or address similar contexts emphasize the power of the settler colonial state. Indigenous peoples are framed in these studies as living fundamentally *in response to* settler demands—"contorting" themselves to fit the "constraints" of settler domination (Povinelli 2016), reconfiguring their lifeways to conform to the "entailments of sovereignty" (Nadasdy 2017), or "negotiating" the boundaries of settler tolerance in order to enact culturally based laws and policies (Blackburn 2009), to give a few examples. In these renderings, the colonial state sets the terms, and Indigenous Peoples must in turn navigate the realities thereby engendered, often under conditions of profound ambivalence.

More recent work in anthropology and Indigenous studies has attempted to move past the monolithic emphasis on colonial state overdetermination. "The politics of recognition in its contemporary liberal form," contends Yellowknives Dene political theorist Glen Coulthard, "promises to reproduce the very configurations of colonialist, racist patriarchal state power that Indigenous peoples' demands for recognition have historically sought to transcend" (2014, 3). Almost as if echoing Povinelli's searing descriptions of the agony that her Aboriginal friends and colleagues in Australia feel when they "fail" in properly performing their culture as the settler state imagines it (2002), Coulthard argues that the reproduction of colonial domination "rests on the ability to entice Indigenous people to *identify*, either implicitly or explicitly, with the profoundly *asymmetrical* and *nonreciprocal* forms of recognition either imposed on or granted to them by the settler state and society" (2014, 25).

It is not enough to strategically engage with the politics of recognition, however sensitively rendered such strategies may be. As long as recognition politics are state driven and state determined, Coulthard argues, they will always effectively trap Indigenous Peoples inside simultaneously political and psychological traps, reifying settler control over Indigenous territory and organization and simultaneously constituting the Indigenous senses of inferiority and self-loathing that make such control possible, or even desirable.

In order to break free, Coulthard asserts the need to push "our struggles away from a politics that seeks to attain a conciliatory form of settler-state recognition for Indigenous nations toward a resurgent politics of recognition premised on self-actualization, direct action, and the resurgence of cultural practices that are attentive to the subjective and structural composition of settler-colonial power" (24). Coulthard's critique runs parallel to Mohawk anthropologist Audra Simpson's influential framing of Indigenous refusal. Refusal, for Simpson, is simultaneously forward and backward looking, a figuring of the past in which Mohawks have never simply acceded to the terms of Canadian colonialism, which, in turn, generates a future in which such refusals can form the basis of a vital, anticolonial, and ongoing Indigenous politics in Kahnawà:ke (2014).

Indigenous refusal is never simply negation. Instead, it shifts the terms of the debate and reclaims, in Gray's sense, the right of political and social definition (cf. Rancière 2004). While the "Giving Back the Name with Respect" ceremony is premised "on self-actualization, direct action, and the resurgence of cultural practices," its particular mode of refusal and the invitation it offers do more than just reject the terms of settler recognition. It is instead generative, akin to rematriation in Gray's analysis. Rather than engaging between Indigenous Nations, however, the "Giving Back the Name with Respect" ceremony sketches out a possible means through which genuinely respectful, mutual relationships *could* be formed between an Indigenous Nation and a settler state. In refusing the colonial "gift," the Council of the Haida Nation instead refigures the Canadian government as being in a junior, and ultimately deficient, relationship with that Haida Nation, just as it (re)constitutes itself as a particular kind of Indigenous governing entity. Canada is marked as a failure according to the terms of *Haida* recognition, just as the ceremony asserts that it is Haida—not settler—terms that matter when it comes to Canada's relationship with the Haida. Reconciliation, in this light, has teeth.

## Restoring Haida Gwaii, Returning the Queen Charlotte Islands

> Haida Gwaii is not only where we are, *this is who we are.*
>
> —GUUJAAW, President of the Council of the Haida Nation 2000–12

When the hereditary chiefs of Haida Gwaii; representatives of the Council of the Haida Nation, the Old Massett Village Council, and the Skidegate Band Council; and hundreds of Haida citizens came together to hold the Aajii kyee gan saa guudang aas.uu sahlgaan dang ga t'alang isdaang—Yahguudang dangad kiigaay dang gwii t'alang sdiihlda (Giving Back the Name with Respect) ceremony, they undertook different forms of social work. Most obvious was the assertion of uninterrupted Haida sovereign rights over the lands and waters of Haida Gwaii, symbolized by repeated invocations of Haida Gwaii as the "real name" of the islands, the name they have always truly held whether or not it has been acknowledged by settlers. The ceremony also resignified the name "Haida Gwaii," shifting it away from Haida Gwaii as a descriptor, the "Islands of the People" in a general sense. Instead, in the ceremony, Haida Gwaii acted as a proper name, designating the home and ancestral territory of a politically unified Haida Nation. Finally, the ceremony positioned the representatives of British Columbia (and, by extension, settler Canada) as participants in a set of formal, reciprocal relationships mediated by Haida ceremonial practices and essential in Haida control. In the next section I highlight a few ways in which interconnecting forms of social action unfolded over the course of the ceremony, with a particular eye to the framing of return of the Queen Charlotte Islands as a gift from the Haida Nation.

### *A Day to Remember 1: Entrances and Songs*

A newsletter from Old Massett's Chief Matthews School summarizes the events of the June 17 ceremony:

> June 17th, 2010, is a day to remember. It was the day we formally gave back the name Queen Charlotte Islands, and have now officially become known as Haida Gwaii to the rest of the world. The true identity of our islands ("islands of the people" as the name Haida Gwaii is translated), will finally be on the maps. Dancers were fully dressed up in all their regalia, as were the twenty hereditary chiefs. Both Masset and Skidegate dancers danced together for the ceremony. A girl from Masset and a boy from Skidegate presented Premier Gordon Campbell with two Haida boxes representing the name Queen Charlotte Islands. In return, he gave both George M. Dawson and Tahayghen Elementary School each, one of the *very first* globes that call our islands "Haida Gwaii." (Chief Matthews School 2010, emphasis original)

Note the care with which the newsletter marks Haida Gwaii as the "true identity of our islands," specifying that it will now become known to *the rest of the world* as Haida Gwaii, implying that it has always been known as such for Haida people. The "rest of the world" is positioned as audience to Haida Gwaii as distinctly Haida political and culture territory, itself a performative mode of sovereign intervention (cf. Rutherford 2012). The description emphasizes Haida unity in ways that might not be immediately apparent to those unfamiliar with the last century of Haida history. In brief, the Old Massett Village Council and the Skidegate Band Council were constituted at the turn of the twentieth century as the only two Haida bands in Canada through the reserve allocation process that claimed the vast majority of the lands and waters of Haida Gwaii as Crown land (C. Harris 2002). In the process, at least from a colonial perspective, the complex sociohistorical landscape of Haida clans was reshaped into two primary Haida communities, Gaw, or Old Massett, to the north, and Skidegate to the south, each with its own municipal governments and associated reserve land. The imposed division has, at times, led to tensions between the communities, exacerbated historically by local Indian agents encouraging their differences (Weiss 2018, chap. 2; cf. Van Den Brink 1974). However, the establishment of a joint Haida land title case for all of Haida Gwaii on behalf of all Haida citizens, the associated creation of the Council of the Haida Nation, and the ultimately successful blockade and protests against logging in what has now become the Gwaii Haanas region of the islands have all been spaces of intercommunity solidarity—acts of sovereignty framed as being from and for all Haida (see Gill 2010; Takeda 2015; Weiss 2018). It is particularly significant that a child from each of the two communities presented a box to Premier Campbell, acting as an indexical icon both of the broader unity of the Haida Nation in returning the settler name for the islands and, by their status as Haida children, of the ongoing futurity of the unity.

Solidarity was on immediate display from the beginning of the ceremony, which was initiated by the formal entrance into Gaw's community hall of the Haida hereditary chiefs, elected dignitaries, and representatives from the provincial government, including Campbell. Following the entrance, a large group of dancers and drummers performed the "Coming into the House Paddle Song." The song was a doubly significant choice, marking the formal entrance into the ceremony by the participants and commemorating the blockade at Lyell Island, with which the song has become associated as the "Lyell Island Song." It is no coincidence that the song was adopted shortly after the ceremony as the Haida National Anthem by the Council of the Haida Nation (*Haida Laas*, October 2010, 13). Through the song, the hall was marked as a Haida space in which the ceremonial and political spheres were essentially and necessarily conjoined. Seated alongside the Haida dignitaries at the "head table" of the hall, normally reserved for hereditary chiefs and important participants in community events, the premier and his colleagues were positioned respectfully as leaders, but defined as leaders within the terms of Haida social, political, and ceremonial practice. They were honored guests at an incontrovertibly Haida event, reiterating Haida sovereign existence and the expression of that sovereignty through distinctly Haida ceremonial means. Signifiers marked a distinctly unified Haida sovereignty, representing both bands and highlighting the history of Haida collective struggle *against* the appropriations of settler colonial governance, embodied in this instance by the premier and the political system he represented.

If the singing of the "Lyell Island Song" was meant to remind the Haida audience of their hard-earned but unified achievements as a sovereign nation and their non-Haida guests of their simultaneous social roles as guests on Haida lands and antagonists impeding the full recognition of Haida rights, the next song positioned the ceremony as a potent symbol of reconciliation *with* the Crown on the part of this Haida Nation. After a prayer, dancers in full regalia spread eagle down on the two bentwood boxes carried by the children representing Gaw and Skidegate and in the center of the hall, in front of the head table. The significance of eagle down in Haida ceremonialism is polyvalent; along with many coastal First Nations it is spread as a mark of peace, respect, and, at times, reconciliation (Mas Gak 1994, xi). By spreading eagle down on the boxes, the dancers marked them as symbols of peace, offered as a means of reconciling a conflict—but, nonetheless, reminders that a conflict had occurred, one that, as later speakers made clear, the Haida had not initiated. Note here the inversion of social power through ritual means, as the Haida participants in the ceremony positioned the imposition of a colonial name on Haida Gwaii as an inequity that they were authorized and able to remedy through simultaneously political and cultural means, inverting the initial imposition's attempted erasure of both of those spheres of Haida rights. So, too, note that the guests to whom the name was being returned, as non-Haida, would paradigmatically lack the ritual expertise necessary to fully understand and properly respond to the events unfolding around them, mirroring the legalized colonial processes of appropriation that led to Haida Gwaii being defined primarily as Crown land with an English (and royal, no less) name.

### *A Day to Remember 2: The Return*

Once the eagle down had been spread and the dance completed, Guujaaw, then-president of the Council of the Haida Nation, stepped into the center of the floor, drum in hand, and asked for help from the primarily Haida audience at the event: "I want you to help us put the name in this box here, and this box over here," gesturing to the two bentwood boxes held by the children from Gaw and Skidegate. Then, raising his voice, he asked, "The name we're giving back is?" At the raising of Guujaaw's drumstick, the audience responded, "The Queen Charlotte Islands." The hall, which can seat more than five hundred, was full for the event, and the audience's voices were clear and forceful. Guujaaw left a second for their response to be heard and silence in the hall to be reestablished before asking again, "Our real name?" After the tiniest of pauses, then he threw up his drumstick, markedly more forcefully than before, and shouted "Haida Gwaii!" which the audience picked up and echoed almost instantaneously. The applause was thunderous, accented by beats from the drums and additional collective shouts of "Haida Gwaii!" As the applause continued, the children presented Premier Campbell with the two boxes and participants unfurled large Council of the Haida Nation flags, including one held by children directly in front of Campbell and the head table. Finally, each hereditary chief attending the ceremony filed past the premier and shook his hand.

The symbolic placement of the names into the boxes through the Haida audience's ritualized responses to Guujaaw's questions has almost Durkheimian elements, binding the group together with a markedly effervescent energy to constitute central ceremonial objects as products of collective social action (Durkheim 1995). But this was also quite unlike Durkheimian paradigmatic rituals of collectivity, in which the symbols of group identity that generate and are in turn generated by collective effervescence are by definition *not* consciously understood *as* symbols of group identity by the group itself. Quite the opposite, as organizers of the event make clear in their interviews with Gwaliga Hart for his documentary, participants were meant to understand and experience the ceremony as a collective act of the Haida Nation, their voices blending together to form a single political and cultural collectivity united in its purpose (Hart 2017).

The deliberate quality has clear parallels with other large-scale Haida ceremonial forms, most of which have been glossed historically in anthropological literature and in contemporary reference as "potlatches" (Bracken 1999; Cole and Chaikin 1990). While early anthropological accounts of Haida potlatches characterize the ceremonies as being primarily concerned with elevating the status of Haida chiefs as part of a competitive display of material and immaterial wealth (e.g., Murdock 1934, Swanton 1905), more recent descriptions of potlatches in the Haida world emphasize the complex and multifaceted social roles that ceremonies of gift distribution play within the Haida community. In "Xaayda XaadaGa GiiahlGalang, Story of the Haida People," Jisgang, Nika Collison, asserts pointedly that "the potlatch is our legal system," a "vital part of our culture" and an "essential part of the social, economic, and political systems of all coastal First Nations." In particular, Jisgang writes, the potlatch is the ceremonial space in which "the fine points of who holds what rights, privileges, and territories and how they acquired them" are maintained, affirmed, reiterated, and, at times, potentially contested through the recounting of clan- and lineage-controlled narratives (Collison 2011, 17–18).[3] Potlatches in a Haida context are performative demonstrations of a lineage's rights to various forms of material and immaterial property. They are always deliberate in their sedimentation of certain modes of in-group solidarity and their definitions of who is to be a guest, who is to exist outside but in relationship with the ceremony's hosts. Names are of central importance within this process. In my own time in Gaw, I have heard the word "potlatch" used most frequently to characterize ceremonies at which new chiefs are inaugurated, taking on both the leadership of their clans and, just as importantly, a hereditary Haida name that represents that leadership (Weiss 2018, 23). Adoptions into clans are also frequent secondary events within these potlatches, ratified by the gift to new adoptees of Haida names, albeit most often ones newly created for this purpose rather than the high-status hereditary names carried by and conferred onto chiefs and other people of well-established high status within their clan.

The "Giving Back the Name with Respect" ceremony was not hosted by a particular clan, nor was it used as a space to conduct individual clan business such as adoptions or the conferring and validation of personal names. This was precisely the point. By drawing on some of the structural features of a chiefly potlatch, the ceremony positioned the Haida Nation as a whole as the host, giving away some of its property—the settler-imposed name for the islands—in the same moment as it ceremonially affirmed its possession of "Haida Gwaii" as the islands' "real" and only legitimate name. Just as guests at a potlatch would be, Premier Campbell and his staff were positioned as witnesses *to* the rightful property and status of the Haida Nations and recipients *of* its generosity. Constituting the ceremony in this way, as Jisgang's characterization of the Haida potlatch helps us understand, has profound legal and political significance in the Haida world. The ceremony validates (or, rather, reiterates) the unified Haida Nation that came together to give back the name as a socially real entity, one with its own rights, property, and ceremonial status. It figures settler government as a participant within a

Haida-defined legal, political, and ceremonial structure, fulfilling certain social roles and carrying a set of reciprocal obligations accordingly. Finally, the ceremony ratifies this relationship via the formal procession of Haida hereditary chiefs shaking hands with the premier. At the same time, the presence of the chiefs frames the ceremony as hosted in common by all Haida clans, and it is their joint authority that ratifies both Haida unity as such and the ways in which the Haida Nation presents itself *as* unified to the representatives of settler governance.

### *A Day to Remember 3: "That None of Us Ever Took Ownership of"*

After the formal presentation came speeches. I want to highlight below the twinned modalities of refusal and invitation that structure the speeches of the Council of the Haida Nation's representatives, working through both semantic messaging and pragmatic metamessaging to signal, on the one hand, that the Haida Nation as a whole is refusing the authority of the settler state and, on the other, that it is inviting the state into a different set of relationships. The speeches voice the political burden of reconciliation in a dual mode, sketching out new, relationally grounded futures for the Haida and settler communities while marking the tensions that condition and will continue to condition these relations under the conditions of settler colonialism.

The first, relatively short, speech came from the Haida Nation's master of ceremonies, future Council of the Haida Nation president Peter Lantin: "As you all know, today is a very symbolic day, and the ceremony that took place today is "Giving Back the Name with Respect," in Haida custom, to do with respect and give back the name that none of us ever took ownership of. [The crowd applauds and cheers.] Haida Gwaii is [inaudible] Haida Gwaii, and it has been forever!" (transcribed from Hart 2017). Loud cheers followed Lantin's short speech, which cued the assembled dancers to begin a song I've often heard referred to as the "Happy Song" (or "Tsinni Joe's Happy Dance"), a celebratory performance featuring Haida dancers dressed in full regalia and elaborate dance costumes. Here we see another moment of pointed effervescence, reiterating a unified Haida position on both the return of the colonial name and the underlying and unchanged reality of the islands' true name. Lantin's framing is worth noting because of his emphasis on the fact that the settler name for the islands being given back "in Haida custom" was a name that "none of us ever took ownership of."

Lantin's statement reiterates in microcosm the broader structure of the ceremony, figuring a unified Haida Nation asserting Haida Gwaii as the only true name of the islands and returning a settler-imposed name that the Haida community was never consulted about and had not chosen. Note that this is framed through a specifically proprietary language about Haida ownership. Lantin's emphasis is not on the *imposition* of the name the "Queen Charlotte Islands," but rather on the fact that this was a name of which no Haida ever took ownership. Recall, as noted earlier, the significance of the act of naming in the Haida language and in Haida ceremonial contexts—to have a Haida name is always an index of the clan that gave one this name and the particular social and political responsibilities and privileges that the name carries. When not properly given or properly received, a Haida name becomes, essentially, meaningless. Lantin's comments become even more pointed: The "Queen Charlotte Islands" could never have been a *real* name for Haida Gwaii because it was never given to the islands or accepted by the islands' rightful owners in the appropriate way. When considered from this perspective, the violence of settler-imposed naming becomes particularly palpable. Given that Haida names are meant to index the social, cosmological, and historical positionality of both the named individual and the naming lineage, a settler-imposed name's reference is only and exclusively to the fact of colonial settlement. Names like the "Queen Charlotte Islands" function as perpetual negations of the sovereignty and rights of the Indigenous Peoples whose lands have been claimed, and not just in the abstract but concretely, as interruptions of long-held and extremely socially significant systems of rights and laws that are embodied in and ratified through naming processes.

The language of ownership—and the ownership of language—is critically important for Lantin and his audience. Having never acknowledged the "Queen Charlotte Islands" as a true name for the islands, the Haida Nation has no responsibilities to keep the name or even to acknowledge it as ever having been socially real in any sense but as a colonial imposition. It doesn't "own it" in any meaningful sense, per Haida protocol. At the same time, the audience *does* lay claim to the name precisely as a gift that they are free to give, a symbolic rejection of Canadian settler domination that is at the same time an act of generosity to the offending colonial government. The "Queen Charlotte Islands" is thus transformed from an act of violence forced unwillingly on the Haida people to an attempt at giving the Haida Nation a name that it has chosen not to accept and, instead, has properly and formally returned to the offering party. Names in a Haida context, as Boelscher points out, are not mere descriptors, but are always forms of action, and "Giving Back the Name with Respect" retroactively redefines the "Queen Charlotte

Islands" as a perpetually failed action, an attempt at naming that could never successfully adhere by its very nature.

More speeches followed, including responses from Abbott and Campbell that tracked between echoing the "always was and always will be" reality of the name Haida Gwaii and Campbell's contrasting statement that Haida Gwaii will be the islands' only name "forevermore." Such discursive shifts reflect the complex position that the representatives of settler governance played at the ceremony, simultaneously participants in and objects of, honored guests whose role was nonetheless to be symbolically overcome, at least as dominators. Then again, as Guujaaw made clear in his speech following Campbell's, the goal of the ceremony from his perspective was to establish respectful and mutual relationships between the Haida Nation and the government of British Columbia, relationships premised on the idea of the different governments representing "two separate authorities." The Haida Nation will be, Guujaaw explained, "on our canoe, you'll have your ship and we're going to go along together." We have seen Guujaaw's framing of political autonomy here, readers will note, echo throughout the Haida political projects explored in this book, including, notably, the Kunst'aa Guu—Kunst'aayah Reconciliation Protocol discussed in the introduction.

As much as Guujaaw emphasized this vision of political mutuality, he made a number of discursive moves to indicate Canada's still-problematic status in the relations. He began his speech in Haida, switching to English only, he claimed, "for the sake of our guest." Guujaaw's joke relied on the shared audience awareness that relatively few Haida people in 2011 were fluent in Haida, and hence most Haida would also not have understood Guujaaw's speech. By singling out Campbell as the "guest" who could not understand Haida, he placed the premier outside the ceremonial-cultural system that all Haida participants were figured as sharing, even as the audience marked through laughter their awareness of the performative nature of the signs that were being used to index cultural solidarity in this context. Guujaaw followed with a second joke, suggesting that he should have spoken to the premier before Campbell's speech, as "I think he just torpedoed my political career by praising me in front of all my people." Much like the Apache jokes about "whitemen" described by Keith Basso, Guujaaw's comment and the laughter it engendered were able to highlight shared social understandings that it would not have been appropriate to voice explicitly (1979). The potential for an adversarial relationship with the Canadian settler governance—including Haida disagreement with continuing Canadian claims to sovereignty over the islands, whatever name they may carry—had not been ended by the recent shifts in the relationships between the Council of the Haida Nation, Canada, and the province,. Guujaaw's joke flags this ambivalence, affiliating himself with an implicitly majority Haida perspective—"my people"—regarding opposition to colonial governance and reminding Campbell and his colleagues that friendly relationships and mutual respect do not represent an end to this opposition.

The ceremony closed following the speeches with Premier Campbell's gift to two of the islands' schools of two of the first globes bearing the name Haida Gwaii, framed as a return gift for the boxes containing the islands' settler name. Campbell and the government he represented could be seen as recognizing their own role in a Haida ceremonial context that required reciprocal participation and exchange in order to sediment social relations. Yet, in a very real way the globes that were given by the premier were symbolic of something that Gwaliga Hart, among so many others, had marked explicitly as *not* a gift—the acknowledgment of the islands' name as having *always* been Haida Gwaii. In other words, at the "Giving Back the Name with Respect" ceremony, the Haida Nation gave back a name it has never owned and received in return an acknowledgment that categorically could not be a gift.

## Names, Territory, and Nation

The return of the settler name, coupled with refusal to acknowledge that the colonial government had the power to "return" Haida Gwaii's name or offer it as a gift, worked to close the sociopolitical distance between the governing bodies of the Haida Nation and the settler state through gifting (Sahlins 1974). The ceremony acted metonymically, both presupposing and entailing new and respectful relationships in place of the older ones and reconfiguring the social and moral order within which, on their respective canoe and ship, the governments and their people can work together. Crucial to this work were the actors' explicitly metadiscursive statements regarding the names as gifts and nongifts. Note the importance to the ceremony of the identification of ownership—or, rather, the rejection of ownership—of the "Queen Charlotte Islands" name, how often and how frequently during the event itself and in reflections afterwards Haida actors labeled the name as unwanted, imposed, and eligible for respectful return by the Haida. Likewise, it was marked as appropriate for the Haida Nation's respectful return of the settler name to be marked as such, as it reintroduced proper ceremonial and political protocols around naming into a relationship in which the other party had behaved improperly, to put it mildly. The provincial and federal governments, quite simply, had not yet entered into the kinds of respectful relationships with the Haida Nation that would make it *possible* for them to give it gifts. The (re)conciliatory tones of the ceremony did not quite align with the accompanying metacommentary, and this was precisely the point, enabling the ceremony's organizers to simultaneously build relationships with settler governance while maintaining Haida autonomy and their continued rejection of Crown sovereignty over the people, lands, and waters of Haida Gwaii. Refusal and invitation pointed to a possible future marked by a critical Haida awareness of continuing inequality and inequity, and continuing denial of their sovereign autonomy, as well as by the possibility of building a far more relational, perhaps even, as Jessica Cattelino might put it, an interdependent sovereignty (2008, 161).

I should reiterate that colonial governance was not the only object of the "Giving Back the Name with Respect" ceremony. As much as the ceremony was a means of establishing new, Haida-determined political relationships between nations and offering explicit and implicit critiques of colonial domination, it was also an act of making for the Haida Nation itself. Recall that the name "Haida Gwaii" was simply descriptive before the arrival of George Dixon and other European explorers and Euro-Canadian settlers. The islands (*gwaii*) were the islands of the people (*xaada*); thus they were Haida Gwaii. After the ceremony on June 17, 2010, "Haida Gwaii" was quite different, a name with a capital "N," so to speak, naming the ancestral, sovereign territory of a Haida Nation unified in its claim to political rights, to title over the islands' lands and waters, and to sovereign authority over those lands and waters and the people living thereupon.

The framing of the Council of the Haida Nation as leaders of this unified nation is not uncomplicated (see Weiss 2018, chap. 5), but, nonetheless, even as the Haida hosts of the ceremony were speaking in the durative case since time immemorial, they were engaged in political innovation, constituting themselves *qua* nation and Haida Gwaii *qua* national territory. Undergirding the language of reconciliation were two distinct acts of making: first, the (re)making of Haida relationships with the settler colonial state, beginning not from the imposition of unwanted regimes of naming and owning, but from Haida logics of right relationality; and, second, the reiteration of the Haida Nation itself in a politically and territorially unified form, ratified ceremonially. As Guujaaw put it in his speech at the ceremony, "We received our life and culture from Haida Gwaii. Over countless generations, our bodies are reclaimed by the lands we call Haida Gwaii. *Haida Gwaii is not only where we are, this is who we are*. While we cannot unwind history, we will leave colonialism behind us, as we have laid the foundation for a respectful relationship into the future" (quoted in Chief Matthews School 2010, emphasis original).

As we have seen throughout *Irreconcilable,* attempts by settler powers to figure themselves as generous, supportive allies to Indigenous Peoples mask the ongoing violence that maintains colonial domination. The promise of the colonial gift hides the realities of ongoing theft; the generous return conceals the power to determine what counts and does not count as falling within the settler-granted rights given to Indigenous people and Peoples within the settler colony. But these forms of erasure and disavowal are never totalizing, for the simple reason that Indigenous people refuse them. In the course of that refusal, political, social, and cultural worlds are made and remade, claimed and reclaimed. This means that the era of reconciliation is undoubtedly a productive one, but not, as is claimed by the federal government of Canada, because it represents a true transition in colonial attitudes toward Indigenous sovereignty. Rather, reconciliation brings with it deep—and deeply violent—historical continuities in both colonial violence and settler strategies for the disavowal of that violence. However, it also offers spaces for Indigenous forms of generative refusal, of anticolonial critique and analysis, and the capacity to take up the empty signifiers of reconciliation toward determinate ends that build new futures for Indigenous Nations and their citizens. This is, at least in part, what happened at the Aajii kyee gan saa guudang aas.uu sahlgaan dang ga t'alang isdaang—Yahguudang dangad kiigaay dang gwii t'alang sdiihlda (Giving Back the Name with Respect) ceremony; it is what has happened and will continue to happen throughout the Indigenous Nations that Canada still attempts to claim as its own.

# Outro

## *Irreconcilable Images, Irreconcilable Futures*

In the first letter of their collaborative volume *Rehearsals for Living*, Abolitionist scholar Robyn Maynard writes to Leanne Betasamosake Simpson describing a "virtual tour" she took, via Google Maps, of Toronto's Bay Street. Here, Maynard writes, can be found the headquarters of some of the more than one thousand mining companies based in Canada, a "direct line between capitalist accumulation and those racial subjects whose lands and labours are *being* accumulated and poisoned" (2022, 14). And yet, this is a "tour of invisible carnage," the systematic extractive violence of companies such as Copper One, Barrick Gold, or James Bay Resource Limited belied, at least ostensibly, by the banality of their outside appearance. James Bay is a "medium-rise grey building, flanked by two Starbucks cafés and underground parking;" Barrick Gold's headquarters "lack grandeur—the building is a sprawling high-rise with a face of green-tinted glass windows" (12); while a glitch means Maynard cannot properly see the exterior of Belo Sun, she suspects that it would not take "much imagination" to imagine that the building is "probably either grey or brownish or whiteish, probably tall, and it wouldn't take much time to take it in" (14). Looking at these bland grey buildings would give no indication either of their massive profits (Barrick Gold alone, Maynard notes, made a profit of $7.24 CAD billion in 2018) (approximately $5.2 billion USD), or the mass death and destruction their extractive efforts engender, both directly and indirectly, from Tanzania and Brazil to the traditional territory of the Algonquins of Barrière Lake.

But this is nothing new, as Maynard writes. "Toronto, like the Canadian society it encapsulates, keeps the violence on which it relies firmly out of view, a perfectly modern society that tidily keeps its atrocities out of plain sight" (15). Hidden perhaps, but no less real for the fact of their concealment. The future that this "perfectly modern society" promises, as Maynard makes clear, is deadly and deathly:

> I am acutely aware that it is our collective destruction as Black subjects, as Indigenous subjects, along with the rest of the global *wretched*

> *of the earth,* that is being drawn up in these boardrooms of global finance (and theirs and their grandchildren's too, though they are too arrogant to see this).
>
> The IPCC reports bring to light what is to come: previously unknown levels of fires, floods, droughts, famines, and shortages of all kinds. A planetary crisis on multiple frequencies, the state and corporate ruling classes working together to commit and recommit the planet, anew, to death and near-death. (16)

Distributed unevenly between Indigenous and Black subjects, who bear the brunt of the death-making projects of global and local extraction, and everyone else, but yet still ultimately inevitable for all of us, the future that settler colonialism offers, that it hides between those banal, grey buildings, is death.

In this book, I have attempted to echo Maynard's diagnosis of the settler colonial future and the at times stunningly banal strategies of concealment undertaken by the colonial state and its agents. Equally, I share with Maynard the conviction that this erased futurity of erasure is nothing new. After all, settler colonialism is itself premised on the extinction of Indigenous Peoples as peoples, a literally genocidal futurity. And as I have shown in these chapters, Canada's attempts to figure itself as a perfectly modern liberal society operate (and have always operated) by erasing the violence of that extinction. This is the central disavowal at the heart of the era of reconciliation. It might then come as little surprise that the futures such societies offer the world are futures of extinction that are concealed not only by the banality of the everyday operations of global capitalism, but by the arrogance and short-sightedness of their primary architects. But what I want to emphasize by way of an ending to this text is that this banality has to be *made,* socially produced, just as any other colonial technology of erasure must be produced and reproduced. In order to do that, I want to offer what I take to be an epitomizing image of contemporary Canadian colonialism and then, in response, a set of counterimages that return us, one last time, to the islands of Haida Gwaii. In so doing I want to emphasize that we who are settler subjects do not have to be taken in by erasure, by the sometimes dull, sometimes comforting veneers that make contemporary Canadian society seem so "perfect," in Maynard's words. Rather, we are all responsible for refusing colonial erasure, past, present, and future.

## Justin Trudeau's Haida Tattoo

On March 31, 2012, future Liberal prime minister of Canada Justin Trudeau fought Patrick Brazeau, a Kitigan Zibi Algonquin Senator affiliated with the Conservative Party, in a "celebrity" boxing match entitled the "Fight for the Cure." While the match was ostensibly intended to raise funds for cancer research, as its name suggests, its primary purpose was as a promotional vehicle for Trudeau, intended to counteract repeated Conservative messaging questioning Trudeau's masculinity (Anderson and Hokowhitu 2021, 146–49). The choice of an Indigenous opponent for Trudeau was no coincidence; rather, as Anderson and Hokowhitu suggest, it offered Trudeau a "less-evolved and self-restrained 'savage'" to fight, either demonstrating his more civilized virility should he win or, should he lose, an image of an "ignoble savage" that would further justify colonial control of the "potential" for Indigenous violence (158). Trudeau was surprisingly explicit on this point, telling *Rolling Stone* that he "wanted someone who would be a good foil, and we stumbled upon the scrappy tough-guy senator from an Indigenous community" (quoted in Anderson and Hokowhitu 2021, 148). He later apologized for these remarks, as they were not "in keeping with the Liberal party discourse of Indigenous-settler reconciliation" (148).

I do not think it will come as a surprise to readers at this juncture that I would suggest, by contrast, the identification of an Indigenous "foil" against which settler violence is legitimate is, in fact, precisely *within* the spirit (and discourse) of settler reconciliation; indeed, I have suggested (in chapter 3, in particular) that such figures of reconciliation in fact always and necessarily exclude any form of indigeneity that can be read as a threat to the settler state. In this sense, Trudeau's eventual victory over Brazeau can be seen as one of the definitive images *of* reconciliation in Canada, as a future leader of the settler state exerted his martial authority—the violence that always-already subtends colonial power—on an Indigenous actor with whom he disagreed politically.[1] There is one particular element within this image—a figure within a figure, so to speak—moreover, that I want to highlight here. Prominent within the photography of the event were images of a large tattoo on Trudeau's left arm, a tattoo that combined a sketch of the globe with a raven design derived from Haida artist Guud san glans, Robert Davidson, and his daughter Sara Davidson, *Raven Bringing Light into the World*. The "Thrill on the Hill," then, was not just a settler leader defeating an Indigenous opponent; it was a settler leader doing so while he himself displayed a

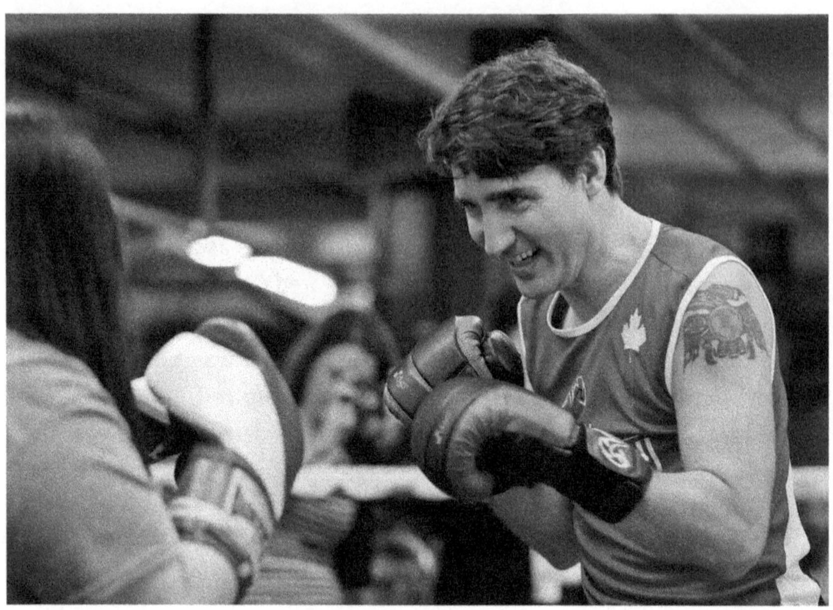

Trudeau's tattoo. © Reuters.

(modified) Indigenous design, quite literally tattooed onto his body.[2] Trudeau thus appeared as the perfect postcolonial Canadian, a harmonious union of settler and Indigenous able to combat those forms of indigeneity that did not fit, all legible within the world of settler political structures. What better image for the era of reconciliation could there be?

Trudeau's tattoo was completed in two stages. Its first element, the globe, was done when Trudeau was twenty-three. The second, the raven design taken from Guud san glans, was added by Trudeau when he was forty, encircling the initial tattoo of planet Earth (Ledbetter 2017). Trudeau did not ask permission from Guud san glans to place the artist's design on his arm, much less to modify it according to his own tastes. While Guud san glans was initially bemused by the discovery of Trudeau's tattoo, as time progressed and Trudeau's ongoing support for oil, natural gas, and other forms of extraction became increasingly apparent, Guud san glans offered the following formal statement on the tattoo:

> Traditionally in Haida culture—and even in modern pop culture—a tattoo is a statement of the values you stand for. Trudeau selected an image depicting one of the origin histories of the Haida Nation, where Raven brings light to the world. By selecting that image, he must uphold the responsibilities that come with that image. He must bring

> light to the world. That light cannot be only superficial—it must go beyond Trudeaumania and must have substance. It means protecting that which is the source of Indigenous cultures—the land and sea. It means choosing a new path forward from the path of big oil, big industry. Otherwise, it is cultural appropriation. (quoted in Prata 2016)

Taking on a Haida image, for Guud san glans, means taking on the responsibilities that that image represents. It is participating in a system of grounded normativity, in which one's obligations to lands, waters, and other-than-human beings take priority over one's own whims and impulses. Guud san glans calls on people who are behaving badly, who do not understand what it means to act properly, to act instead with yahguudang; which is to say, to act within a specifically located, relational network of protocols for respectful and appropriate behavior toward other beings.

That these protocols are specifically Haida is part of the point. As Glen Sean Coulthard and Leanne Betasamosake Simpson make clear in their discussion of grounded normativity, there is no one Indigenous way of engaging with the world ethically, no unified Indigenous positionality or unified Indigenous tradition that would cut across different territories or histories, nor *should* there be (Coulthard and L. Simpson 2016). Trudeau's choice of design engaged him at a corporeal level in a specific traditional of political, social, cultural, and artistic practice, which, as Guud san glans makes clear, renders him subject to an equally specific set of obligations and responsibilities, just as Trudeau's father's honorary adoption by Guud san glans's grandmother, Florence Edenshaw Davidson, obligated both the former prime minister and his family in specific and significant ways (see Macdonald 2016).

It is telling, in this regard, that Trudeau's tattoo is a modification of Guud san glans and his daughter's design, incorporating Trudeau's preexisting image of the globe whereas the original image represents the light stolen by Raven. In so doing, Trudeau erodes the design's specificity, incorporating instead a design that one is tempted to imagine not just as a generic globe, but as a representation of the generic global, the liberal aspiration toward surface-level international harmony subtended by globalized capitalism. Trudeau's tattoo can thus do double duty, robbing Guud san glans and his daughter's design of its full specificity in order to signify instead a quite literally surface-level appreciation of indigeneity (without respect for Indigenous rights to property or even consultation) in the same moment as it can speak to a liberal (and, for that matter, Liberal) vision of the globe. We can see these same assumptions of possession play out in Trudeau's ill-timed beach vacation, discussed in chapter 3. But in this instance, the (white) liberal possessive (Moreton-Robinson 2015) is specifically framed by spectacularized anti-Indigenous violence.

Trudeau the boxer thus appears much as those inconspicuous gray and glass walls do in Maynard's analysis: a safe, seemingly anodyne veneer under which the violence of colonial capitalism can proceed as it always has. His tattoo performs a "respect" for indigeneity without specificity, commitment, or substance, deforming Guud san glans and Sara Davidson's art into a resource for Trudeau's own consumption; it is a reconciliation enacted through appropriation and through violence, in which the actual voices of Indigenous actors are silenced even as their work is converted into a symbol of Canadian, liberal rapprochement. It is at once disavowal and empty signifier, an act of mock respect that in fact signifies the precise opposite. The future that this figure of settler reconciliation offers for Indigenous Peoples as such is to disappear, a mere ornament on the body of an ever-violent settler social and political order.

## Futures and Possibilities

This is not the only image possible, however, for the future of Indigenous (or settler) life in the territories currently claimed as Canada.

Consider the juxtaposition between two images of graffiti, painted within two meters of each other on the ruins of what was once Canadian Forces Station Masset, on Haida Gwaii. In the first, the most prominent word is YAKUUDANG, a variant spelling of the Haida word "yahguudang," a concept, loosely translated as "respect," that this book first engaged in its introduction. Right underneath, in bright red, is written "Stop LNG!," in reference to a proposed Canadian project to refine and transport liquified natural gas from the coast of British Columbia overseas for sale. The graffiti reminds us of the ubiquity of resource extraction across Indigenous landscapes, echoing not only Maynard's analysis, but also the sustained refusal of colonial domination currently taking place at the Unist'ot'en Camp and the similar steady and firm refusal of the Enbridge Northern Gateway Project we saw in chapter 4.

Yahguudang's twinning with "Stop LNG!" makes considerable sense. The proposed project is deeply unpopular on Haida Gwaii, particularly within the Haida community, and its environmental threat to the islands can be read both as an attack on Haida sovereignty—a violation of yahguudang between human communities—and, equally, as a violation of the rights of the islands'

“Yakuudang.” Photo by Hilary Morgan V. Leathem, July 2017.
Author’s collection.

“I’m glad you exist.” Photo by Hilary Morgan V. Leathem, July 2017.
Author’s collection.

other beings and thus precisely the opposite of "respecting Haida Gwaii." In short, these are mottos that can be read as deeply engaged with Haida rights, Haida politics, and the ways in which these things are fundamentally intertwined with Haida cultural practices and concepts.

At first glance, the second photo, with its slogans of "Hello, I'm glad you exist" and "Teach teens to be radical & love their bodies," seems to belong to a quite different world. And yet, we would suggest otherwise, drawing on Joanne Barker's (2005) formative (re)articulation of the concept of sovereignty for (and within) Indigenous polities. Surveying the then still-ongoing writing process for what would become the UN Declaration on the Rights of Indigenous Peoples, Barker writes, "Human rights for indigenous peoples, in other words, became translated to mean rights to a self-determination that was indelibly linked to sovereignty. So strong is this conceptualization that it is now virtually impossible to talk about what sovereignty means for indigenous peoples without invoking self-determination. As a consequence, sovereignty has been solidified within indigenous discourses as an inherent right that emanates from historically and politically resonant notions of cultural identity and community affiliation" (2005, 19–20).

Sovereignty, in this reading, is not just a political formation; rather, it is the assertion of an Indigenous right to exist *as such*, inextricably bound to both ongoing cultural histories and processes of community formation. Sovereignty thereby becomes read as a particular (broadly construed but *not* thereby underspecified) means of being human.[3] The graffiti that now adorns the ruined walls of the former CFS Masset can be read as sovereign in a similar sense: a means of expressing the complexities of what it means to be human, to be Haida or a neighbour of the Haida Nation, and to exist politically and personally without needing to draw firm distinctions between these categories.[4]

As first discussed in chapter 2, the buildings that made up the barracks, recreation center, and administrative facilities of Canadian Forces Station Masset stood in the center of the Village of Masset from the end of the 1960s to 2014, though the Base itself (as it was popularly known in the community) was decommissioned in 1997. The Haida community of Old Massett and the Village of Masset made the joint decision to maintain the recreation center—mostly in order to preserve its swimming pool—until this became cost prohibitive and the buildings were fully abandoned and then, ultimately, demolished in the fall of 2014. The squat brown buildings that had dominated the town were gone (though, of course, the military themselves were not, despite immediate appearances); all that was left (seemingly) were the outlines of concrete walls and a few old steps jutting out of the grass.

The ruins. Photo by Hilary Morgan V. Leathem, July 2017. Author's collection.

The graffiti that now festoons the ruins of the Base was painted by the Grade 11 and 12 students of Gudangaay Tlaats'gaa Naay Secondary School soon after the Base was demolished, between 2015 and 2016. The graffiti was painted under the supervision of a teacher, but beyond asking students to avoid sexually explicit images, the teenagers were given free rein simply to "express what they were feeling," as their instructor, "Sam," put it. Gudangaay Tlaats'gaa Naay is the only secondary school on the north side of Haida Gwaii, and its classes thus include both Haida and settler students. This means that in a certain, I think significant, sense, we can see the graffiti on the walls as being jointly authored by Haida and settler students, bringing together core ideas in Haida moral and philosophical life, politically engaged speech, and the work of affirmation in a settler colonial space that by definition must deny and denigrate Indigenous life in order to secure its own claims to legitimacy.

Graffiti pointing to Haida values, youthful political consciousness, and affirmation festoons the walls of the ruins. Other slogans include the two shown below, "HAIDA TITLE" and "in Haida we trust." Haida Title echoes the conflicts we saw discussed most extensively in chapter 1, as the province of British Columbia attempted to ground its theft of Indigenous lands and waters, including the islands of Haida Gwaii, in a fetishized colonial legal

"Haida Title." Photo by Hilary Morgan V. Leathem, July 2017. Author's collection.

"in Haida we trust." Photo by Hilary Morgan V. Leathem, July 2017. Author's collection.

Tableau. Photo by Hilary Morgan V. Leathem, July 2017.
Author's collection.

legitimacy despite the ongoing existence of Aboriginal Title throughout the territories claimed by, and as, British Columbia. Haida Title refuses those claims, historically and into the present, asserting, clearly and simply, that the only sovereign Title on Haida Gwaii belongs to Haida people and the Haida Nation. The slogan "in Haida we trust" cuts against the ongoing efforts of settler colonialism in Canada to undermine what it means to be Indigenous as both a political and cultural space of membership. From explicit state-sponsored projects of violent assimilation and erasure such as the residential school system to the banal everyday racism of settler Canada, over and over again, we see the agents of settler colonial domination—official and otherwise—attempt to erase Indigenous life as such, to render the very fact of being Indigenous an impossible space to live within and to occupy. The students of Gudangaay Tlaats'gaa Naay, instead, emphasize the importance of trusting in being Haida, in Haida governance, in Haida values, sharpening their critique still further by implicitly inverting the typically Christian formulation of "In God we trust" that was used to justify so much anti-Indigenous violence in the history of Canada and settler colonialism more broadly.

In this last image we see a tableau that runs alongside a full wall of the CFS Masset ruins. The full tableau includes affirmations, calls to "speak up," explicit references to Haida Gwaii and Haida youth, and assertions of unity, such as "We are one." One word, however, does not appear in this tableau nor, indeed, anywhere on the few remaining walls of what was once a Canadian armed forces military base. That word is "reconciliation." Instead, the graffiti consistently twins assertions of Haida rights and values with calls to work for peace and justice. To achieve the latter, the juxtaposition of these different ideas suggests, *means* fighting for the former. The tableau that CFS Masset has become situates unity and solidarity *within* the work of Indigenous sovereignty, centering Haida title rather than the hollow multiculturalism of the state (see Brown 2006; Povinelli 2002). It emphasizes love and critical thinking as opposed to fear, refusing the violence that the military base represented (if at times ambivalently) and transforming it instead into a particular understanding of possibility grounded *not* in the liberal promises of the colonial state but, rather, in the work of Indigenous youth and their neighbors under the sign of Haida sovereignty.

This is not to suggest that either fear or colonial domination is absent on Haida Gwaii or that the islands represent an unusually utopian space within settler colonial Canada. These issues most certainly exist on island—and, we would imagine, they bear down on the relationships between the different students of Gudangaay Tlaats'gaa Naay in many different ways. But this is not the point. The graffiti we focus on is performative social work, aimed at orienting both its authors and its audience to how the world *should* be. It sketches out a social world in which Haida and non-Haida are "one" in relationship to Haida rights, peace, and justice. Likewise, the graffiti positions self-care and cultural and personal affirmation as crucial elements in achieving these things. These messages do not form part of a single, coordinated platform, even though they can be read together; rather, they emerge organically, from young people being asked to "express their feelings." It matters tremendously that in this space we see no mention of Canada or the era of reconciliation. Call it, instead, a manifesto for a life-giving era of irreconcilability.

## Canada Is Irreconcilable

The graffiti on the ruins of CFS Masset offers us images for the future that affirm Indigenous sovereignty even as they oppose the endless extension of settler colonial militarism; that affirm Indigenous existence, culture, politics, and corporeality even as they recognize and contest the ongoing history of anti-Indigenous violence, racism, and white supremacy that constitute and maintain Canada and the nation-states like it. They meet the death-making projects of settler colonialism, in Leanne Betasamosake Simpson's (2022) evocative phrase, with the joy and celebration of Indigenous life. Like Justin Trudeau's Haida tattoo, these images represent a kind of synthesis of Indigenous and settler authorship. Unlike Trudeau's tattoo, they are not images taken without permission, modified at the whim at one of the most powerful settler subjects in Canada in order to offer a pantomime of Indigenous solidarity without substance, respect without relationships. Unlike Trudeau's tattoo, they are not a technology of erasure, meant to take possession of the signs of indigeneity under the control of the most direct authorities of the settler colonial state. Rather, the graffiti on the ruins represents the coming together of the next generation of Indigenous and settler youth who, together, foreground the importance of Haida Title, sovereignty, and life itself.

These graffitied slogans and designs offer a future that looks beyond the closures of the era of reconciliation. They refuse the capacity for Canadian settler colonialism to appropriate indigeneity as its own possession (cf. Moreton-Robinson 2015). Indeed, they do not even consider reconciliation worth mentioning. Instead, they unsettle the settler aspirations for a Canada that continues on colonial terms. They hold upon an Indigenous future, one that is for itself even as it carries the potential of including settlers on Indigenous terms. In arresting the dominant ideologies of Canadian colonial life in their own language, in their own ways, the youth of Haida Gwaii hold open the space of Haida sovereignty as generative, as productive, as life-giving. It is not something that can be reconciled within a framework of ongoing domination. It is not something that can be disavowed as not really real, something that can be reduced into nullity under the empty signifier of settler reconciliation. It is not something that can be repatriated to Haida people by the grace and generosity of the settler state, for, as the Council of the Haida Nation reminded the Crown in chapter 6, Haida people never gave up their sovereignty. They never gave up the right to determine their own futures.

Throughout the course of this book we have seen many different examples of settler colonial erasure. We have seen the disavowal of the violence of colonial domination. We have seen the attempt to render legal a colonial occupation that is illegal under its *own* laws (much less Indigenous laws), via the sleight of hand of Aboriginal title and colonial apology. We have seen the attempts to make military presence disappear, metonymic for the ongoing, never truly absent presence of the force of the state bearing down on Indigenous life and Indigenous sovereignty. We have seen the constitution of a

Canadian political community under the sign of reconciliation that renders into enemies, terrorists, and killable bodies the very Indigenous Peoples with whom the state is claiming to be "reconciling." We have seen different anxious theaters of Canadian legitimacy, from hearings of commissions of inquiry to museum repatriation policies, which attempt to reinscribe Canadian settler interests as always-already ethical and in relationships of respect with Indigenous Peoples, even as their policies silence Indigenous voices and erase the realities of their histories. These are just some of the distinctive technologies of the era of reconciliation.

None of these forms of erasure are natural, however, nor are they inescapable. They have to be made and remade, just as the banality of violence toward which Robyn Maynard points us must be. Canadian settler subjects are in the process of making and remaking these erasures—sometimes consciously, with deliberation and intention, at other times at the level of settler common sense, to borrow Mark Rifkin's term. Perhaps there might exist a future in which Canadian claims to dominion are not incommensurable with Indigenous sovereignty (though I remain unconvinced), but it is settler common sense to insist that this is obviously and transparently the only future that can come to pass, to fall back on the language of "harsh realities" that, in fact, only works to reproduce violence and domination as the only reality possible. As a Canadian settler scholar, I want to make very clear to my fellow settlers that *we need not do this*. We need *not* embrace a promise of reconciliation that is always-already "at the barrel of a gun," whether that gun is visible or concealed through the various liberal mechanisms of Canadian multicultural governance.

Instead, we can attend. Throughout this book, we have also seen, over and over again, how Indigenous people and Peoples have refused to reconcile with Canadian domination. They have refused reconciliation, arrested settler common sense, and interrupted colonial disavowal. Sometimes these refusals have been direct, epitomized by blockades halting colonial extraction projects and rejecting the assumption of Canadian Crown and corporate interests that they have the right to extract whatever they might wish from Indigenous lands and waters. Sometimes these refusals are manifested in the remarks of political leaders, the terms through which those leaders negotiate with Canadian federal and provincial authorities, or the critical analytical writing of Indigenous scholars. And sometimes Indigenous people ignore, contest, and ultimately surpass the violence of settler reconciliation simply by being themselves and living their lives. All these refusals are generative, creating spaces of Indigenous vitality, knowledge, sociality, tradition, and power. They exceed the terms of the colonial domination against which they operate, making and remaking spaces of Indigenous life against and beyond settler colonialism. They are more than simple opposition; rather, they sketch out ways of living that need not be limned by the assumption that colonial life can or must be reconciled.

I have titled this final part of *Irreconcilable* "Outro" because analytical writing will not bring an end to the ongoing violence of settler colonialism; neither will it bring an end to the efforts to conceal that very violence, to soften it with empty signifiers, hollow exclamations of shock, or aggressive assertions of colonial unknowing. But what the youth of Haida Gwaii are doing in their graffiti; what their parents and family members are doing in voicing protest, critiquing occupation, and affirming proper relations; what, indeed, Indigenous Peoples are doing throughout the lands currently occupied by settlers all over the contemporary colonial world is refusing the erasures of colonial domination, both overt and ideological. They forbid us the comforts of reconciliation, the fantasy that colonialism can be purified through speeches and holidays, spectacles and apologies, and settler good intentions. In rejecting the terms of settler reconciliation, Indigenous actors, scholars, activists, and scholars refuse to allow settlers or anyone else to square the circle of colonial legitimacy; they hold open colonial attempts at closure, sometimes subtly, sometimes forcefully, sometimes achingly, and they keep the colonial world irreconcilable.

# Coda
## *Rising Tide*

In April 2024, just as I was finishing an earlier draft of this book, I saw the announcement that the Council of the Haida Nation (CHN) had signed an agreement with the government of the province of British Columbia officially recognizing the Haida's Aboriginal Title to the entirety of the islands of Haida Gwaii. The agreement was the product of decades of work on the part of multiple generations of Haida elected and hereditary leaders and represented the first such colonial acknowledgment in the history of the settler state of Canada that an Indigenous Nation held title to the full 100 percent of its traditional territory. The agreement, entitled the Gaayhllxid/Gíhlagalgang "Rising Tide" Haida Title Lands Agreement, had been voted on and ratified by a huge majority of the voting citizens of the Haida Nation earlier that month. The CBC, Canada's national news service, quoted Tamara Davidson, one of the CHN's Vancouver regional representatives, emphasizing that the agreement did not represent the Canadian government "granting" anything to the Haida people: "This does not mean that the government is granting us anything. We have always held our inherent rights and title to our land" (Canadian Press 2024a). Davidson's comment marks an implicit distinction between the colonial legal construct of Aboriginal title, a subordinate title to the absolute title of the Canadian state, and her own sense of Haida title as inherent and not a grant from any colonial government (cf. Borrows 2015; Wood and Rossiter 2022).

Other news sources repeated a story I had heard many times during the years I had lived in Old Massett. During the proceedings that led to the landmark 2004 *Haida* court decision, the story goes, CHN's then president, Guujaaw, was offered a deal by the provincial government. The province would give the Haida control of a full 20 percent of their territory. In return, the Haida would drop their title case and acknowledge that the province and, ultimately, the Crown, had the legitimate right to sovereignty over the rest of the islands of Haida Gwaii. "Why," Guujaaw is said to have responded, "would we give up eighty percent of our land to get 20?" (Renner 2024). In other tellings of that story that I heard, the numbers are even more dramatic, with Guujaaw being offered a mere 5 percent of the Haida's own territory, though his refusal remains consistent across all narrations. Guujaaw, and his fellow Haida leaders, refused to be reconciled to a colonial compromise that seemed, to them, an absurdity: the demand to give up their own lands and waters simply so that a foreign power could claim that it had always had a right to them—and not just any right, but an absolute right.

The "Rising Tide" Agreement is being justly celebrated as a milestone in Indigenous-settler relations in Canada, though the fact that it represents only provincial recognition of Haida title and does not entail a federal commitment to the same is troubling (Onishi 2024). The agreement also follows from the Kunst'aa Guu—Kunst'aayah Reconciliation Protocol, and the ways in which that protocol and other, similar negotiations between the CHN, the Crown, and the province had already tacitly recognized the effective existence of Haida title, even if the settler parties to those agreements denied the existence of that title and the Indigenous sovereignty it represented as a matter of course (cf. Weiss 2018, chap. 6). As I noted in my introduction, the existence of the Reconciliation Protocol and other documents like it was a testament, precisely, to the refusal of the Haida to be reconciled to Canadian domination.

Likewise, the "Rising Tide" Agreement itself invokes reconciliation, noting in provision 8.8 that it is "not a treaty, but part of the reconciliation process," situating itself as the inheritor of previous reconciliation agreements (Gaayhllxid/Gíhlagalgang "Rising Tide" Haida Title Lands Agreement 2024, para. I) and, most strikingly, as representing an agreement to "advance reconciliation in good faith based on the principles of recognition of Haida Aboriginal Title, co-existence and collaboration that offers hope and opportunity for mutual respect, reparations, healing, renewal, and restoration of the lands" (para. K).

While it may seem as if the "Rising Tide" Agreement ends this book with a plot twist, the moment when, at last, reconciliation in Canada has been reached, I would invite the reader to instead take the "Rising Tide" Agreement as a problematic. The agreement does indeed represent a space in which we can see the ways in which both Indigenous and settler political actors have aimed to find common ground, but it also provides vivid evidence of the ways in which this common ground is still striated by erasure and the continuing colonial attempt to control the terms under which Indigenous politics can occur. Consider, in particular, the vicious irony of David Eby, current premier of British Columbia, stating that "we are moving beyond a place where the Haida Nation's rights were denied to a place where they are recognized and upheld" (Government of British Columbia 2024b), even as the provincial government continues to disavow the sovereignty of so many other First Nations whose territories the province continues to claim as its own, and even as the federal government of Canada continues to claim Haida Gwaii itself, along with the rest of the country, as falling under the sovereign jurisdiction of the Crown. Consider also Eby's attempts to continue to incorporate the Haida into the fabric of Canada as one more constituent whose rights can be "recognized and upheld," even as the agreement acknowledges that Haida political life precedes and exceeds the Canadian settler nation-state. Consider, finally, the gap between what it means to recognize Haida title as Aboriginal title, subordinate to the Crown and having no impact on fee simple ownership, and an articulation of Haida title as itself an absolute title, granted by no one else, subordinate to no other government. We have been here before.

And yet, what does most excite me about the "Rising Tide" Agreement is its capacity to act as a kind of "Trojan horse" for reconciliation, inverting the dominant order in which it is always Indigenous Nations that are expected to reconcile themselves to their own ongoing subordination, to the theft of their lands, the loss of their languages, and their forcible incorporation into Canadian settler society regardless of their own sovereign existences. In the "Rising Tide" Agreement we see, perhaps, a different path, in which it is colonial governments that are expected to conform *themselves* to the protocols and expectations of Indigenous legal orders. Here, it would be the settler state that must reconcile itself to Indigenous sovereignty. Such a path must begin, however, by unmasking the false promise that settler reconciliation initiatives will make the realities of colonialism simply go away. There is no pure and just Canada to be found, no matter how much we might wish one might emerge, distilled, as the end point of the era of reconciliation. Instead, there are other futures to be built that promise, not closure, but the opening up of different ways of being, existing, and living in futures that are not always, already foreclosed by settler colonial domination.

# Notes

## Introduction

1. Canada is a constitutional monarchy, ruled, as of 2024, by King Charles III. The state as a whole is thus formally referred to as "The Crown," similar to the use of "The People" to refer to the federal government of the United States. While the British sovereign is nominally Canada's head of state, represented by a governor general, in effect the country is a parliamentary democracy governed by elected members of parliament within the House of Commons, led by a prime minister. During much of the writing of this book, Canada's prime minister was Justin Trudeau, leader of the Liberal Party of Canada, first elected in 2015. The current prime minister and leader of the Liberal Party is, as of 2025, Mark Carney. Canada's legislature also includes a senate, whose members are appointed individually by the prime minister, but, like the governor general, the Senate is understood largely as an honorary body that does not substantively intervene in the making or passing of laws.

2. Particularly the Hudson's Bay Company, which was roundly criticized for the ways in which it has used the sale of orange shirts, a symbol of commemoration and respect for the victims and survivors of residential schools, in order to burnish its own image as a progressive company despite the Company's central role in the history of colonial expansion (e.g., Massie 2021).

3. Even a cursory Google search gives some idea of how common these workshops have become (e.g., Indigenous Relations Academy n.d.; Reconciliation Canada n.d.; Tribal Trade n.d.; cf. BC Gov News 2017).

4. There is one historical exception to this, the "Douglas Treaties" that were signed in the mid-nineteenth century between the earliest British settler colonists and fourteen Indigenous Nations in the southern areas of the island that the colonists had named Vancouver Island. These treaties were not honored, however, and remained largely ignored by (or unknown to) colonial officials after the initial "settlement" of Vancouver Island (C. Harris 2002).

5. It is worth noting here that, while it is certainly the case that Canada shares multiple axes of racism, particularly anti-Black racism, and white supremacy with other countries such as the United States, the country's racial logics are not necessarily identical to those in the United States or, for that matter, in other countries. For further, see Robin Maynard and Leanne Betasamosake Simpson's recent *Rehearsals for Living* (2022) for a sustained and generative dialogue about the relationships between anti-Black racism, indigeneity, and liberation in Canada.

6. I am sensitive here to Jodi Byrd's critique of this framework, which, as I read it, turns primarily on the commitment to normativity itself, which, as Byrd suggests, is a constrained and constraining commitment, particularly in its relationship to the possibilities presented by the intersections of queer and Indigenous theory (2020).

While I think this is an important intervention, I am not fully convinced that either Coulthard or Simpson takes normativity to be constraining in this sense. Rather, I see in this formulation a push for an ethics of relationality that is both accountable to other-than-human beings and firmly grounded in the assertion of Indigenous sovereignty as the necessary precondition for maintaining those relationships. This is normative, but it is not the normativity of settler cisheteropatriarchy, but rather a means of articulating the complex protocols between different communities of beings that make up Indigenous sovereign relationalities.

7. Yahguudang names, for instance, the Council of the Haida Nation's 2005 vision for land use, *Haida Gwaii Yah'guudang [Respecting Haida Gwaii]*.

8. Cree leader Harold Cardinal's 1969 book critiquing Trudeau's policies was, appropriately, entitled *The Unjust Society*.

## Chapter One

1. But see Weiss 2024 for a more detailed engagement with the psychoanalytic foundations of the concept of disavowal.

2. For a specific analysis of the intersections of white supremacy and settler colonialism in Australia, see Aileen Moreton-Robinson's *The White Possessive* (2015). Moreton-Robinson theorizes that the presumption of white superiority authorizes colonial domination as legitimate in the first instance.

3. The presentation of the Royal Proclamation at Niagara in 1794, Borrows makes clear, was effected through methods beyond and at times in contradiction to its written text, in particular including verbal guarantees of First Nations sovereignty that were not, in fact, included within the proclamation as written (1997, 161–62). Disavowal is here achieved not just through textual contradiction, but in the space between what was said and promised in discussions between colonial officials and Indigenous leaders and what was then ratified as colonial law.

4. European presence in the lands and waters that would eventually be claimed as British Columbia did not, of course, begin in 1846. British explorers, in particular, began laying claim to those territories before the turn of the nineteenth century, and white fur traders soon followed. These fur traders established small forts along the coast, some of which would become the basis for colonial towns and cities later in the nineteenth century (see Barman 2007).

5. The Oregon Treaty did not include the lands then claimed as Russian America (C. Harris 2002, 15), though these territories were later divided between the United States and Canada, forming parts of Alaska and northern British Columbia.

6. Significant cases in the interim between *Calder* and *Delgamuukw* included R v. Sparrow [1990], which held that Aboriginal rights that had not been extinguished in 1982 were protected by the Constitution of Canada, and R v. Van der Peet [1996], which further specified the legal status of Aboriginal rights. These cases did not, however, offer further substantive specification of the nature of Aboriginal title itself (see Wood and Rossiter 2022, 70–114)

7. Note especially Prime Minister Justin Trudeau's retrospective comment on the Tsilhqot'in case being a "pivotal moment" for the country.

8. For more details on both individual schools and the system as a whole, see the 2015 Final Report of the Truth and Reconciliation Commission of Canada, particularly both parts of volume 1. See also Milloy 1999.

9. With the words "potential unmarked graves" I follow the specific wording suggested by Supernant and Carlton (2022).

## Chapter Two

1. Gordillo opposes this way of thinking about rubble with more conventional heritage logics that prioritize the preservation of "ruins" as sacrosanct spaces (e.g., 2014, 6–11; cf.: Leathem 2022).

2. This chapter draws from the fieldwork I have been doing on Haida Gwaii since 2010, with a sustained period of full-time residence between 2012 and 2013, though most of the conversations I bring forward here took place over a number of summers between 2015 and 2019. All names in this chapter are pseudonymous unless they were quoted from a public context or identification was specifically requested. For a detailed discussion of my positionality as a settler scholar in general, please see the introduction to this volume. For a discussion of these dynamics specifically during my field research and, in particular, the ethical questions, demands, and requirements of this work, please see Weiss 2018, 21–25.

3. The Haida scholar Jisgang, Nika Collison, is explicit on this point, arguing that "the potlatch is our [Haida] legal system," a means through which territorial claims can be evaluated and verified (2011, 17).

4. There is also the impact of the so-called Davis plan on Indigenous fisheries on Haida Gwaii (and throughout British Columbia), which severely limited the ability for Indigenous fishers to participate even in relatively small-scale commercial fishing. See Newell 1993.

5. The language of "open-concept" was drawn directly from open-concept architecture, emphasizing notions of space and freedom in social and spatial design. The application of these values to military design is ironic, to say the least, especially given the ways that military presence fundamentally constrained Haida mobility on their own ancestral territories.

6. While many Haida worked for the Base in service positions, I am not aware of many individuals who joined the Canadian military themselves. This differentiates the social dynamics of Haida Gwaii from spaces such as Hawai'i, as Ty Kawika P. Tengan has explored, in which military service was a significant way through which Indigenous masculinity could be articulated under ongoing settler colonial conditions (e.g., Tengan 2008).

7. We might note, though, that during most of the twentieth century—and certainly during the period in which Armstrong was growing up—Haida women married to non-Haida men were stripped of their Indian Status and could no longer reside in Old Massett. Many chose to live in the Village of Masset with their spouses. The children of these marriages, likewise, did not have Indian Status until Bill C-31 brought substantial changes to Canadian Aboriginal law in the 1980s. (See Weiss 2018, 6ff, along with A. Simpson 2014 for a discussion of the impact of these changes

in a Mohawk context.) We might also consider Patrick Wolfe's suggestion that "binarism" itself might be a product of settler subjecthood (2013).

8. See Joanne Barker (2011) for a detailed discussion of the naturalization of colonial gendered norms in different US contexts, and Kauanui (2018a) for a discussion of similar issues in Hawaiʻi.

9. Indian status was "restored" to the wives of non-Indigenous men by Bill C-31 and, by extension, their children.

10. The funds were a combination of assets, financial reserves, and, perhaps most interestingly, a lump sum given to CMDC to manage or demolish the military's former buildings *in lieu of* their demolition by the Department of Defense. This arrangement was, in part, to preserve the rec center and, especially, the swimming pool. It was also at this point that the military sold the "private married quarters" to the Village of Masset, which in turn resold them as private real estate.

11. This is also true, and remains true, of officers deployed to Masset's RCMP Station.

12. This sense of military invisibility, I was recently told by a military officer, contrasts sharply with the military's own understanding of its continuing presence in Old Masset, which consists of a small crew who continue to operate the radio apparatus, now renamed CFS Leitrim Detachment Masset. And yet, the sense that the military was at best gone, at worst hiding, was almost ubiquitous in both Massetts during my time there. Here again the performative work of ruination and concealment works to disavow the social sense of an ongoing military presence.

13. Liddle is referring to the distinctive shape of the military radio station that remained operational in Masset, whose antennas form a ring that appears almost like a pen for a large animal. Thus, "elephant trap" is a local community nickname for the station.

14. It is not a coincidence, shifting briefly from one settler colony to another, that the United States Armed Forces still refers to enemy territory as "Indian country" (Lyons 2010, 17–18). Indeed, "The early US military," notes Catherine Lutz, "became entwined with the frontier project of removing Indians from the land and protecting colonists who settled there. In this sense, every Western fort—and there were 255 of them—was a foreign military base, established on native land during the Indian campaigns and the Mexican-American war." This formed an important precedent, Lutz argues, for American overseas expansion, which similarly operated through a dense network of territorializing US bases on foreign soil (2009, 10).

15. Even the "elephant trap" or "cage" itself seems to have lost at least some of its significance as a military facility for some of Masset's residents, as the marketing of a gourmet coffee by local non-Haida entrepreneurs under the brand Elephant Cage Coffee attests (Elephant Cage Coffee n.d.).

## Chapter Three

1. One of the eleven "Numbered Treaties" in Canada, Treaty 8 was signed in 1899 between the Crown and representatives of multiple First Nations, including the

Woodland Cree, Chipewyan, and Dane-zaa Peoples, covering 840,000 square kilometers of land including parts of the settler claimed provinces of British Columbia, Alberta, Saskatchewan, and the Northwest Territories. The city of Edmonton falls within Treaty 8 territory.

2. In 1911, for instance, Oliver championed an amendment to the Indian Act that would allow reserve lands to be expropriated for public works, announcing it by claiming that "Indian reserves would no longer be able to impede the economic development of the nation" (Donald 2004, 39).

3. One is reminded immediately of Aileen Moreton-Robinson's application of the notion of the "white possessive" to settler colonial Australia, a racialized colonial logic in which white subjects simply assume they have the right to possess Aboriginal lands and control Aboriginal bodies because of the innate racial superiority of whiteness (2015).

4. The particular tensions between "equivalence" and "difference" that play out differently within individual populist movements, Laclau suggests, can help us understand why some of these movements are more successful and durable than others (2005, 176–99).

5. Laclau himself distinguishes "empty" and "floating" signifiers on formal grounds in relation to how they relate to particular chains of equivalence and horizons of difference, but notes that, in practice, they operate in effectively the same way (2005, 135).

6. A note on terminology here. Barker's text does not explicitly name the formations to which she refers as settler colonial. Instead, Barker prefers "imperial," emphasizing the intersections between the interwoven forms of violence to which Indigenous, Black, and otherwise "marginalized" bodies are exposed as a normative aspect of the maintenance of state domination by both the United States and Canada (e.g., 2022, 21, 172). Barker is surely correct that these forms of violence intersect in myriad ideological and embodied ways, but I would nonetheless hesitate at eliding the specificities of settler colonialism (or, for that matter, anti-Black racism) in an analysis of state violence. I adapt Barker's argument to my own analytical vocabulary, accordingly.

7. Charles Taylor's 1994 *Multiculturalism and the "Politics of Recognition"* is something of a founding text for this perspective, particularly within Canada.

8. The Bay clarified that sales of the shirt would support a nonprofit focused on creating awareness of residential schools after facing sustained criticisms for appearing to profit off the Canadian colonial history of which the Bay formed such a significant part.

9. "Freedom" here acts very much as an empty signifier in and of itself, and it could be argued that what the convoy protestors represent is a much more traditional form of "populist movement" than the ways in which I've attempted in this chapter to think with Laclau about settler colonial Canada. I do not think the political communities of Canadian settler "reconciliation" and right-wing "freedom" are necessarily opposed, however. Quite the opposite, in fact, their mutual interpenetration is part of my point in this chapter.

## Chapter Four

1. Most notoriously on the Northwest Coast among these prohibitions is likely the ban from the late nineteenth to the mid-twentieth century on potlatches, complex public events with economic, ceremonial, social, and legal dimensions that were and continue to be practiced in various forms throughout the Nations of the coast (see Cole and Chaikin 1990; Bracken 1997; Masco 1995).

2. In the section that follows I draw heavily on Cole Harris's 2002 account of the reserve allocation process in British Columbia, *Making Native Space: Colonialism, Resistance, and Reserves in British Columbia*. For a more general history of the province, see Jean Barman's *The West Beyond the West: A History of British Columbia* (2007). For more detail on how the land reservation process was connected to the establishment of provincial fisheries and water regulations, see Douglas Harris's *Landing Native Fisheries: Indian Reserves and Fishing Rights in British Columbia, 1849–1925* (Harris). For a focus on indigenous political responses to these processes, see (among other texts) Paul Tennant's *Aboriginal Peoples and Politics: The Indian Land Question in British Columbia, 1849–1989* (1990).

3. I am grateful to Jaskwaan, Amanda Bedard, for pointing me to these exchanges.

4. According to a West Coast Environmental Law–compiled list, more than fifty individual band councils and First Nations opposed the proposed pipeline (West Coast Environmental Law 2012). Union of BC Indian Chiefs Grand Chief Stewart Philip claimed that BCs Aboriginal peoples were "prepared to go to the wall" against the Pipelines Project, citing its potential violation of the environmental integrity of the traditional territories along the pipeline and across the coast (Mickleburgh 2012). In January of 2012, then president of the Council of the Haida Nation Guujaaw went so far as to suggest that Enbridge's claims to have built relationships with various Haida government entities were "libelous" and risked bringing those organizations "into disrepute, not only with their own constituents, but also the many First Nations, organizations and people committed to the health of this planet" (Stoymenoff 2012).

## Chapter Five

1. Daniel Heath Justice and Jean O'Brien's recent edited volume, *Allotment Stories* (2021), offers a fulsome sense of the many different ways in which allotment logics were deployed (and continue to be deployed) as part of settler colonialism, linking together the "allotment era" in the United States with historical and ongoing allotment policies in British Columbia and the Canadian prairies, Palestine, Scandinavia, and elsewhere.

2. See Bracken 1997 on the conflation of many different ceremonies and practices across many different Indigenous Nations into "the" potlatch as a single discursive object against which settler law could operate in order to attack Indigenous social, political, and cultural life and arrest Indigenous people.

3. To the Indigenous communities from which they were taken, by contrast, many of the belongings held in museums have their own life cycles, including cycles of

transformation, decay, and even death. Indeed, some of these "artifacts" are in fact animate beings with their own modes of intentionality and existence that cannot be captured by settler museum logics that see all artifacts as, fundamentally, objects. This does not mean that "preservation" is always by definition inappropriate; the issue, rather, is the authority claimed by colonial museums over the possession, control, and condition of Indigenous belongings (see Weiss 2021).

4. In her 1979 text, *Prosecution or Persecution*, Kwakwaka'wakw scholar Daisy (My-yah-nelth) Sewid-Smith presents detailed narratives from some of the elders of their experiences while under arrest. I have not reproduced quotations from these here out of respect as a settler who has no right to tell these stories (much less to essentialize them as academic evidence), but I encourage readers to engage directly with Sewid-Smith's book.

5. I was curator of Western Ethnology at the Canadian Museum of History from July of 2016 to April of 2018. While this chapter does not directly summarize those experiences, it is certainly informed by them. None the less, it should not be taken to reflect the perspectives or ideas of any current or former employees of the museum besides, of course, myself.

6. The ongoing practice of determining provenance based on the place an artifact is known (or sometimes believed) to have been collected is itself a fraught one, eliding the complexities of relations that are "bundled," to borrow a term from Joshua Bell (2017), within given Indigenous belongings in museum collections. For a more thorough discussion of these issues, see Weiss 2021.

7. The ways in which these claims tracked between Lockean logics of agriculture as ownership and blanket claims of Indigenous territories as *terra nullius* in racialized and mutually entangled ways are well specified by Bhandar herself, but see also Aileen Moreton-Robinson's *The White Possessive* (2015) for a parallel analysis focusing on Australia and Cole Harris's *Making Native Space* (2002) for a detailed study of how these logics were enacted in nineteenth and early-twentieth-century British Columbia. Robert Nichols pushes these arguments yet further, asserting in *Theft is Property!* (2020) that colonial theft is constitutive of property relations as such.

8. In his account of the early colonial fishery in British Columbia, historian Douglas Harris argues persuasively that colonial authorities justified very small territorial allocations in reserves with the promise that Indigenous Peoples would have unrestricted access to local waterways for fishing. Once the reserves were established, however, Indigenous fishing access was curtailed dramatically and limited to an arbitrary and colonially defined category of subsistence in order to placate settler sports and commercial fishing lobbies (2008).

9. My point here is not to reduce all Indigenous commerce in the nineteenth century to colonial coercion, pure and simple, nor is it to ignore the complex histories of trade between Indigenous people and early European explorers and traders prior to the formal "settlement" of British Columbia. Rather, my goal is to emphasize that by the moment in which sustained museum acquisition was being pursued in the province in the latter half of the nineteenth and early twentieth centuries, Indigenous Peoples were by no means in control of the terms of commerce or, for that matter, secure in their lives or livelihoods (cf. Cole 1985).

10. Consider, for instance, Margaret Blackman's (1977) ethnohistorical argument that the potlatch ban led Haida people to dramatically intensify forms of community celebration and ceremonial exchange that were ostensibly permitted under Christianity, including large feasts at Christmas and Easter (52).

11. Nor are Indigenous perspectives on such contaminations uniform or homogenous. Anthropologist and curator Jennifer Kramer's 2006 study of art and ownership within the Nuxalk Nation, *Switchbacks*, illustrates this nicely, showing the great diversity of perspectives on how Nuxalk belongings, art, and artists should engage with and be engaged by settler institutions and subjects. Kramer narrates the perspective of one Nuxalk artist, for instance, who has been at times "accused of stealing Nuxalk culture by selling his art to outsiders," even though, from his perspective, the sale of Nuxalk art not only provides income to feed his family but also can symbolically "validate the Nuxalk Nations as a whole" through the value placed on its art *by* outsiders (114).

## Chapter Six

1. See the thesis of Lucy Bell, Sdaahl K'awaas, "*Xaad Kilang T'alang Dagwiieehldang*—Strengthening Our Haida Voice," for a detailed analysis of individual resources and medicines in Haida historical traditions and, in particular, in *Xaad Kil*, the Masset dialect of the Haida language.

2. In a further instance, Sdaahl K'awaas,'s discussion of Haida names is framed with the Haida phrase *Xaadas Kya'aang*, specifically, "Haida naming" (L. Bell 2016, 123).

3. In her 1988 ethnography of traditional political and ceremonial discourse in Gaw, Marianne Boelscher characterizes the Gaw Haida general term for potlatching as *gyaa 7isdla*, "giving things away," and distinguishes multiple historical forms of *gyaa 7isdla*, of which the foremost was the *waahlal*, "given upon the completion of a new cedar-plank longhouse, which either inaugurated or reaffirmed the rank of the lineage hosting the ceremony (1988, 66). Jisgang, Nika Collison, uses the Skidegate Haida term *'waahlGahl* to refer to the Haida potlatch more broadly.

## Outro

1. A caution here, however. As a prominent Conservative politician, Brazeau supported policies that were explicitly and overtly anti-Indigenous and hostile to Indigenous sovereignty, particularly during the tenure of Conservative prime minister Stephen Harper. The fact that he was used *as* a symbol of Indigenous violence (conflated with Conservative values) does not automatically mean that Brazeau himself should be considered *allied* with the radical anticolonial work of Indigenous Peoples in either the territories claimed by Canada or beyond them. It means, rather, that Brazeau's availability as a symbol exceeded his own personal politics, at least to an extent (cf. Anderson and Hokowhitu 2021).

2. The "Hill" referred to in phrase "The Thrill on the Hill" refers to Parliament Hill in Ottawa, seat of Canada's federal legislature.

3. Barker's point in this, it is worth adding, is not necessarily that this understanding of sovereignty is *correct*; rather, she uses it to demonstrate the ways in which sovereignty has become opened up to Indigenous resignification, which pushes the concept well beyond the confines of its Western European, Westphalian origins.

4. Of course, the word *xaada* already means "human," or, perhaps more accurately, "person," so to be human and to be Haida are already intimately linked, to say the least.

# References


Agamben, Giorgio. 1998. *Homo Sacer: Sovereign Power and Bare Life*. Translated by M. Raiola. Stanford, CA: Stanford University Press.

Agha, Asif. 2006. *Language and Social Relations*. Cambridge: Cambridge University Press.

Aiello, Rachel. 2022. "What Does the Trucker Convey Hope to Accomplish?" *CTV News*, January 28. www.ctvnews.ca/politics/article/what-does-the-trucker-convoy-hope-to-accomplish/.

Algonquins of Pikwanagan, the Algonquin Anishinaabeg Tribal Council, and Kitigan Zibi Anishinaabeg. 2022. "Press Release: The Algonquins of Pikwanagan, The Algonquin Anishinaabeg Tribal Council and Kitigan Zibi Anishinaabeg Do Not Support the Truckers Convoy and the Confederation Park Setup on the Algonquin Nation Lands/Territory." February 2. https://x.com/DylanWhiteduck/status/1488942789912059911/photo/1.

Amato, Sean. 2022. "'Thank You Truckers:' Edmonton Police Officer Makes Tearful Video Praising 'Freedom Convoy.'" *CTV News*, February 11. www.ctvnews.ca/edmonton/article/thank-you-truckers-edmonton-police-officer-makes-tearful-video-praising-freedom-convoy/.

Andersen, Chris, and Jean M. O'Brien. 2016. *Sources and Methods in Indigenous Studies*. London and New York: Routledge.

Anderson, Kim, and Brendan Hokowhitu. 2021. "'Pretty Boy' Trudeau Versus the 'Algonquin Agitator': Hitting the Ropes of Canadian Colonial Masculinities." In *Indigenous Celebrity: Entanglements with Fame*, edited by Jennifer Adese and Robert Alexander Innes, 146–62. Minneapolis: University of Minnesota Press.

Asch, Michael, ed. 1997. *Aboriginal and Treaty Rights in Canada: Essays on Law, Equality, and Respect*. Vancouver: University of British Columbia Press.

Ashforth, Adam. 1990. "Reckoning Schemes of Legitimation: On Commissions of Inquiry as Power/Knowledge Forms." *Sociology Lens* 3 (1): 1–22.

Assembly of First Nations and Canadian Museums Association. 1992. "Task Force Report on Museums and First Peoples." *Museum Anthropology* 16 (2): 12–20.

Austin, Ian, 2021. "Judge Rebukes Mounties' Handling of Fairy Creek Logging Protest." *New York Times*, October 1. www.nytimes.com/2021/10/01/world/canada/british-columbia-fairy-creek-protests.html.

Barker, Joanne. 2005. "For Whom Sovereignty Matters." In *Sovereignty Matters: Locations of Contestation and Possibility in Indigenous Struggles for Self-Determination*, edited by Joanne Barker, 1–32. Lincoln: University of Nebraska Press.

———. 2011. *Native Acts: Law, Recognition, and Cultural Authenticity*. Durham, NC: Duke University Press.

———. 2021. *Red Scare: The State's Indigenous Terrorist*. Berkeley: University of California Press.

Barman, Jean. 2007. *The West beyond the West: A History of British Columbia*. Toronto: University of Toronto Press.

Barrera, Jorge. 2021a. "Lost Children." *CBC News*, June 13. https://newsinteractives.cbc.ca/longform/kamloops-residential-school-children-dead.

———. 2021b. "Ottawa Says It's Not Liable for Cultural Damage Caused by Kamloops Residential School: Court Documents." *CBC News*, June 2. www.cbc.ca/news/indigenous/reparations-residential-school-1.6050501.

Basso, Keith H. 1979. *Portraits of "The Whiteman": Linguistic Play and Cultural Symbols Among the Western Apache*. Cambridge, UK: Cambridge University Press.

BBC News. 2021. "Canada Mourns as Remains of 215 Children Found at Indigenous School." May 29. www.bbc.com/news/world-us-canada-57291530.

BC Gov News. 2017. "Reconciliation Workshops Foster Greater Understanding." September 24. https://news.gov.bc.ca/releases/2017IRR0041-001628.

Bedard, Jusquan [Jaskwaan] Amanda. 2011. "Yahguudang.gang: Xaad Kil GwaayganGee." In *That Which Makes Us Haida—The Haida Language*, edited by Jusquan Amanda Bedard and Jisgang, Nika Collison, 88–97. Skidegate, BC: Haida Gwaii Museum Press.

Bell, Joshua. 2017. "A Bundle of Relations: Collections, Collecting, and Communities." *Annual Review of Anthropology* 46 (1): 241–59.

Bell, Lucy, Sdaahl K'awaas. 2016. "*Xaad Kilang T'alang Dagwiieehldang*—Strengthening Our Haida Voice." Master's thesis, University of Victoria.

Bell, Lucy, Sdaahl K'awaas, Collison, Jisgang Nika, and Neel, Lou-ann. 2019. *Indigenous Repatriation Handbook.* Victoria: Royal British Columbia Museum.

Bhandar, Brenna. 2018. *Colonial Lives of Property: Law, Land, and Racial Regimes of Ownership*. Durham, NC: Duke University Press.

Blackburn, Carole A. 2005. "Searching for Guarantees in the Midst of Uncertainty: Negotiating Aboriginal Rights and Title in British Columbia." *American Anthropologist* 107 (4): 586–96.

———. 2009. "Differentiating Indigenous Citizenship: Seeking Multiplicity in Rights, Identity, and Sovereignty in Canada." *American Ethnologist* 36 (1): 66–78.

Blackman, Margaret. 1977. "Ethnohistoric Change in the Haida Potlatch Complex." *Arctic Anthropology* 14 (1): 39–53.

———. 1992. *During My Time: Florence Edenshaw Davidson, a Haida Woman*. Seattle: University of Washington Press.

Boelscher, Marianne. 1988. *The Curtain Within: Haida Social and Mythical Discourse*. Vancouver: University of British Columbia Press.

Borrows, John. 1997. "Wampum at Niagara: The Royal Proclamation, Canadian Legal History, and Self-Government." In *Aboriginal and Treaty Rights in Canada: Essays on Law, Equality, and Respect*, edited by Michael Asch, 155–72. Vancouver: University of British Columbia Press.

———. 1999. "Sovereignty's Alchemy: An Analysis of Delgamuukw v. British Columbia." *Osgoode Hall Law Journal* 37 (3): 537–96.

———. 2015. "Aboriginal Title and Private Property." *The Supreme Court Law Review: Osgoode's Annual Constitutional Cases Conference* 71:91–134.

Bracken, Christopher. 1997. *The Potlatch Papers*. Chicago: University of Chicago Press.

Brown, Wendy. 2006. *Regulating Aversion: Tolerance in the Age of Identity and Empire*. Princeton, NJ: Princeton University Press.

———. 2010. *Walled States, Waning Sovereignty*. Princeton, NJ: Princeton University Press.

Bruyneel, Kevin. 2021. *Settler Memory: The Disavowal of Indigeneity and the Politics of Race in the United States*. Chapel Hill: University of North Carolina Press.

Butler, Judith. 2011. "Hannah Arendt's Challenge to Adolf Eichmann." *Guardian*, August 29. www.theguardian.com/commentisfree/2011/aug/29/hannah-arendt-adolf-eichmann-banality-of-evil.

Byrd, Jodi. 2011. *The Transit of Empire: Indigenous Critiques of Colonialism*. Minneapolis: University of Minnesota Press.

———. 2020. "What's Normative Got to Do with It?: Toward Indigenous Queer Relationality." *Social Text* 38 (4): 105–23.

Calder v. Attorney General of British Columbia. 1973. S.C.R. 313. https://www.canlii.org/en/ca/scc/doc/1973/1973canlii4/1973canlii4.html.

Canadian Museum of History. 2011. "Repatriation Policy." www.historymuseum.ca/wp-content/uploads/2015/09/REPATRIATION-POLICY.pdf.

———. n.d.-a. "Dance Mask." www.historymuseum.ca/collections/artifact/61031.

———. n.d.-b. "Edward Sapir." Archived April 21, 2024. https://web.archive.org/web/20240421045402/https://www.historymuseum.ca/cmc/exhibitions/tresors/ethno/etp1000e.html.

———. n.d.-c. "Panel Pipe." https://www.historymuseum.ca/collections/artifact/61719.

———. n.d.-d. "Pipe en argilite figurant le Corbeau, le Loup, la Baleine, l'Ours et l'Aigle, culture haïda, recueillie par Andrew A. Aaronson, 1879 = Argillite Pipe Featuring the Raven, Wolf, Whale, Bear and Eagle, Haida Culture, Collected by Andrew A. Aaronson, 1879." https://www.historymuseum.ca/collections/archive/3345927.

Canadian Press. 2024a. "Landmark Deal Recognizes Haida Nation's Title over Haida Gwaii." *CBC*, April 14. www.cbc.ca/news/canada/british-columbia/b-c-haida-gwaii-title-agreement-1.7173601.

———. 2024b. "10th Anniversary of Landmark Tsilhqot'in Decision Commemorated." *CBC*, June 26. www.cbc.ca/news/canada/british-columbia/tsilhqot%CA%BCin-decision-anniversary-1.7247955#:~:text=The%20Tsilhqot'in%2C%20representing%20six,land%20through%20Canada's%20highest%20court.

Canadian Trucking Alliance. 2022. "Canadian Trucking Alliance Statement to Those Engaged in Road/Border Protests." https://cantruck.ca/canadian-trucking-alliance-statement-to-those-engaged-in-road-border-protests/.

Carleton, Sean. 2021. "'I Don't Need Any More Education': Senator Lynn Beyak, Residential School Denialism, and Attacks on Truth and Reconciliation in Canada." *Settler Colonial Studies* 11 (4): 466–86.

Cattelino, Jessica. 2008. *High Stakes: Florida Seminole Gaming and Sovereignty*. Durham, NC: Duke University Press.

CBC News. 2021. "Edmonton's Oliver Square Changes Name after Community Consultation." August 2. www.cbc.ca/news/canada/edmonton/oliver-square-name-change-1.6126553#:~:text=Oliver%20Square%20has%20undergone%20a,already%20been%20replaced%20this%20weekend.

Chief Matthews School. 2010. "Newsletter: *Aajii kyee gan saa guudang aas.uu sahlgaan dang ga t'alang isdaang—Yahguudang dangad kiigaay dang gwii t'alang sdiihlda* (Giving Back the Name with Respect)." Old Massett, BC: Chief Matthews School.

Cole, Douglas. 1985. *Captured Heritage: The Scramble for Northwest Coast Artifacts*. Vancouver: University of British Columbia Press.

Cole, Douglas, and Ira Chaikin. 1990. *An Iron Hand upon the People: The Law Against the Potlatch on the Northwest Coast*. Seattle: University of Washington Press.

Coletta, Amanda. 2021. "An Unmarked Gravesite Drags a Not-so-Distant Horror Back into the Spotlight. Is This a Real Reckoning?" *Washington Post*, June 16. www.washingtonpost.com/world/2021/06/16/canada-kamloops-residential-school-children-graves/.

Coletta, Amanda, and Annabelle Timsit. 2022. "'Significant Element' from U.S. Involved in Self-Described 'Freedom Convoy' in Canada, Official Says." *Washington Post*, February 2. www.washingtonpost.com/world/2022/02/02/freedom-convoy-alberta-blockade-vaccine-mandate-protests/.

Collison, Jisgang Nika. 2011. "Xaayda XaadaGa GiiahlGalang, Story of the Haida People." In *That Which Makes Us Haida—The Haida Language*, edited by Jusquan Amanda Bedard and Jisgang, Nika Collison, 17–20. Skidegate, BC: Haida Gwaii Museum Press.

———. 2017. "Yahguudangang: The Act of Paying Respect." Talk given at the University of British Columbia, December 6. https://greencollege.ubc.ca/node/2249.

Collison, Jisgang Nika, and Nicola Levell. 2018. "Curators Talk: A Conversation." *BC Studies* 199:53–79.

Coulthard, Glen Sean. 2014. *Red Skin, White Masks: Rejecting the Colonial Politics of Recognition*. Minneapolis: University of Minnesota Press.

Coulthard, Glen, and Leanne Betasamosake Simpson. 2016. "Grounded Normativity/Placed-Based Solidarity." *American Studies Quarterly* 68 (2): 249–55.

Council of the Haida Nation. 2004. *Haida Gwaii Yah'guudang [Respect for This Place]: Haida Land Use Vision*. www2.gov.bc.ca/assets/gov/farming-natural-resources-and-industry/natural-resource-use/land-water-use/crown-land/land-use-plans-and-objectives/westcoast-region/haidagwaii-slua/haida_land_use_vision.pdf.

Cram, Stephanie. 2021. "Hudson Bay's Sale of Orange Shirts to Support Residential School Survivors Raises Questions." September 26. www.cbc.ca/news/canada/manitoba/hbc-orange-shirts-national-day-truth-and-reconciliation-1.6189924.

Crawford, Tiffany. 2022. "Mayor of Terry Fox's Hometown in B.C. Calls Out Vaccine Mandate Protestors for Defacing Statue." *Vancouver Sun*, January 29. https://vancouversun.com/news/mayor-of-terry-foxs-hometown-in-b-c-calls-out-vaccine-mandate-protesters-for-defacing-statue.

Crist, Valine. 2012. "Protecting Place Through Community Alliances: Haida Gwaii Responds to the Proposed Enbridge Northern Gateway Project." Master's thesis, University of Victoria.

Cuthand, Doug. 2022. "Cuthand: Authorities' Response to Convoy Protests Show White Supremacy in Action." *Saskatoon StarPhoenix*, February 4. https://thestarphoenix.com/opinion/columnists/cuthand-authorities-response-to-convoy-protests-shows-white-privilege-in-action.

Daigle, M. 2019. "The Spectacle of Reconciliation: On (the) Unsettling Responsibilities to Indigenous Peoples in the Academy." *Environment and Planning D: Society and Space*, 37 (4): 703–21.

Dalzell, Kathleen E. 1973. *The Queen Charlotte Islands*. Vol. 2, *Of Places and Names*. Madeira Park, BC: Harbour Publishing.

Delgamuukw v. British Columbia. 1997. 3 S.C.R. 1010. https://decisions.scc-csc.ca/scc-csc/scc-csc/en/item/1569/index.do.

Department of Justice Canada. n.d. "Implementing the United Nations Declaration on the Rights of Indigenous Peoples Act." Archived April 3, 2022. https://web.archive.org/web/ 20220403064534/https://www.justice.gc.ca/eng/declaration/index.html. (Site since modified.)

Dhillon, Jaskiran, and Will Parrish. 2019. "Exclusive: Canada Police Prepared to Shoot Indigenous Activists, Documents Show." *Guardian*, December 20. www.theguardian.com/world/2019/dec/20/canada-indigenous-land-defenders-police-documents.

Donald, D. T. 2004. "Edmonton Pentimento: Re-Reading History in the Case of the Papaschase Cree." *Journal of the Canadian Association for Curriculum Studies* 2 (1): 21–54.

Durkheim, Emile. 1995. *The Elementary Forms of Religious Life*. Translated by Karen Fields. New York: Free Press. First published 1912.

Ede, Amy. 2022. "The Convoy's Appropriations Are an Attack on Indigenous People." *Tyee*, February 18. https://thetyee.ca/Opinion/2022/02/18/Convoy-Appropriations-Attack-Indigenous-People/.

Edmonds, Penelope. 2010. "Unpacking Settler Colonialism's Urban Strategies: Indigenous Peoples in Victoria, British Columbia, and the Transition to a Settler-Colonial City." *Urban History Review / Revue d'histoire urbaine*, 38 (2): 4–20.

Edmonds, Penelope, and Amanda Nettelbeck, eds. 2018. *Intimacies of Violence in the Settler Colony: Economies of Dispossession around the Pacific Rim*. London: Palgrave Macmillan.

Elephant Cage Coffee. n.d. "Elephant Cage Coffee." https://www.facebook.com/p/Elephant-Cage-Coffee-Roasters-100069473760332/.

Enloe, Cynthia. 2000. *Maneuvers: The International Politics of Militarizing Women's Lives*. Berkeley and Los Angeles: University of California Press.

Epstein, Jake, and Kieran Press-Reynolds. 2022. "TikTok Video Shows Canadian Cop Telling Trucker Protester He Supports Them '100%' after Giving a Warning During a Traffic Stop." *Business Insider*, February 14. https://www.businessinsider.com/tiktok-video-canadian-cop-support-freedom-convoy-2022-2.

Forester, Brett. 2021 "B.C. Greenlit More Mounties on Wetsu'wet'en Territory before 3rd Raid." *APTN News*, December 2. www.aptnnews.ca/national-news/b-c-greenlit-mounties-wetsuweten-territory-3rd-raid/.

Fowlie, Jonathan, and Gordon Hoekstra. 2012. "Christy Clark Toughens Pipeline Stance as Enbridge Announced Safety Upgrades." *Vancouver Sun*, July 21. https://vancouversun.com/news/national/christy-clark-northern-gateway-pipeline-a-very-large-risk-with-very-small-benefit-for-bc.

Fraiman, Michael. 2021. "Trudeau Hits the Beach in Tofino. At Least He Isn't Surfing." *Maclean's*, October 1. https://macleans.ca/politics/trudeau-hits-the-beach-in-tofino-at-least-he-isnt-surfing/.

Freud, Sigmund. 1961. "Fetishism." In *The Standard Edition of the Complete Psychological Works of Sigmund Freud*, Vol. XXI, *The Future of an Illusion, Civilization and its Discontents and Other Works (1927–1931)*, edited and translated by James Strachey, 147–58. London: Hogarth Press and Institute of Psycho-analysis. First published 1927.

Gaayhllxid/Gíhlagalgang "Rising Tide" Haida Title Lands Agreement. 2024. www2.gov.bc.ca/assets/gov/environment/natural-resource-stewardship/consulting-with-first-nations/agreements/draft_haida_title_lands_agreement_27march2024_bilateral.pdf.

George III. 1763. Proclamation, issued October 7. Reprinted in *Revised Statutes of Canada* (RSC) 1985, App. II, No. 1.

Gill, Ian. 2010. *All That We Say Is Ours: Guujaaw and the Reawakening of the Haida Nation*. Vancouver: Douglas and McIntyre.

Gilmore, Rachel. 2022. "Some Trucker Convoy Organizers Have History of White Supremacy, Racism." *Global News*, January 29. https://globalnews.ca/news/8543281/covid-trucker-convoy-organizers-hate/.

Glass, Aaron. 2021. *Writing the Hamat'sa: Ethnography, Colonialism and the Cannibal Dance*. Vancouver: University of British Columbia Press.

Gordillo, Gastón. 2014. *Rubble: The Afterlife of Destruction*. Durham, NC: Duke University Press.

Gough, Barry M. 1984. *Gunboat Frontier: British Maritime Authority and Northwest Coast Indians, 1846–90*. Vancouver: University of British Columbia Press.

Government of British Columbia. 2024a. "Declaration on the Rights of Indigenous Peoples Act." www2.gov.bc.ca/gov/content/governments/indigenous-people/new-relationship/united-nations-declaration-on-the-rights-of-indigenous-peoples.

———. 2024b. "News Release: Haida Nation, B.C. Recognize Haida Aboriginal title, a Historic First in Canada." April 14. https://news.gov.bc.ca/releases/2024 PREM0020-000560.

Government of British Columbia and Council of the Haida Nation. 2010. "News Release: B.C., Haida Nation Restore Name 'Haida Gwaii' to Islands. June 17. https://archive.news.gov.bc.ca/releases/news_releases_2009-2013/2010prem0125-000719.htm.

Government of Canada. 2014. "Joint Review Panel for Northern Gateway Project." https://www.canada.ca/en/news/archive/2014/06/joint-review-panel-northern-gateway-project.html.

———. 2017. "First Nations in Canada." www.rcaanc-cirnac.gc.ca/eng/1307460755710/1536862806124.

———. 2024. "National Day for Truth and Reconciliation." www.canada.ca/en/canadian-heritage/campaigns/national-day-truth-reconciliation.html.

Gray, Robin R. R. (T'uu'tk). 2015. "Ts'msyen Revolution: The Poetics and Politics of Reclaiming." PhD diss., University of Massachusetts, Amherst.

———. 2022. "Rematriation: Ts'msyen Law, Rights of Relationality, and Protocols of Return." *Native American and Indigenous Studies* 9 (1): 1–27.

Green, Joyce, and Gina Starblanket. "Opinion: Freedom Convoy Given Far More Space than Indigenous Protests." *Regina Leader-Post*, February 22. https://leaderpost.com/opinion/opinion-freedom-convoy-given-far-more-space-than-indigenous-protests.

Haida Nation. 2005. *Haida Land Use Vision: Haida Gwaii Yah'Guudang [Respecting Haida Gwaii]*. www.haidanation.ca.

Haida Nation v. British Columbia (Minister of Forests). 2004. SCC 73, [2004] 3 S.C.R. 511. https://decisions.scc-csc.ca/scc-csc/scc-csc/en/item/2189/index.do.

Hall, Stuart. 2017. *The Fateful Triangle: Race, Ethnicity, Nation*. Cambridge, MA: Harvard University Press.

Harper, Stephen. 2008. "Statement of Apology to Former Students of Indian Residential Schools." www.rcaanc-cirnac.gc.ca/eng/1100100015644/1571589171655.

Harris, Cole. 2002. *Making Native Space: Colonialism, Resistance, and Reserves in British Columbia*. Vancouver: University of British Columbia Press.

Harris, Douglas. 2008. *Landing Native Fisheries: Indian Reserves and Fishing Rights in British Columbia, 1849–1925*. Vancouver: University of British Columbia Press.

Hart, Gwaliga, dir. 2017. *Giving Back the Name with Respect*. Longhouse Productions in association with StoryHouse Productions. 23 min. https://worldfilmpresentation.com/film/giving-back-name-respect.

Hawker, Ron. 1989. "The Johnson Street Gang: British Columbia's Early Indian Art Dealers." *British Columbia Historical News: Journal of the B.C. Historical Foundation* 22 (1): 10–14.

Indigenous Relations Academy. n.d. "Indigenous Relations Academy, Powered by Indigenous Corporate Trainings, Inc." https://www.indigenousrelationsacademy.com/.

Jobs and Growth Act, 2012 (Bill C-45), S.C. 2012. https://www.parl.ca/DocumentViewer/en/41-1/bill/C-45/royal-assent.

Joint Review Panel for the Enbridge Northern Gateway Project. 2012a. *Hearing Order OH-4-2011, Volume 54*. Old Massett, June 1. https://ceaa-acee.gc.ca/050/documents/p21799/85712E.pdf.

———. 2012b. *Hearing Order OH-4-2011, Volume 55*. Old Massett, June 2. https://ceaa-acee.gc.ca/050/documents/p21799/85713E.pdf.

———. 2012c. *Hearing Order OH-4-2011, Volume 56*. Skidegate, June 13. https://ceaa-acee.gc.ca/050/documents/p21799/85714E.pdf.

———. 2012d. *Hearing Order OH-4-2011, Volume 57*. Skidegate, June 14. https://ceaa-acee.gc.ca/050/documents/p21799/85715E.pdf.

Justice, Daniel Heath, and Jean O'Brien, eds. 2021. *Allotment Stories: Indigenous Land Relations under Settler Siege*. Minneapolis: University of Minnesota Press.

Kauanui, J. Kēhaulani. 2014. "A Sorry State: Apology Politics and Legal Fictions in the Court of the Conqueror." In *Formations of Colonialism*, edited by Alyosha Goldstein, 110–34. Durham, NC: Duke University Press.

———. 2016. "A Structure, Not an Event": Settler Colonialism and Enduring Indigeneity." *Lateral* 5 (1).

———. 2018a. *Paradoxes of Hawaiian Sovereignty: Land, Sex, and the Colonial Politics of State Nationalism*. Durham, NC: Duke University Press.

———. 2018b. *Speaking of Indigenous Politics: Conversations with Activists, Scholars, and Tribal Leaders*. Minneapolis: University of Minnesota Press.

Kierans, Ciara, and Kirsten Bell. 2017. "Cultivating Ambivalence: Methodological Considerations for Anthropology." *HAU: Journal of Ethnographic Theory* 7 (2): 23–44.

Kii'iljus (Barbara J. Wilson), and Luu Gaahlandaay (Kevin J. Borserio). 2011. "Gam tluu tllgaay aa kiix*a* Gang ga, There Is No Land Strange." In *That Which Makes Us Haida—The Haida Language*, edited by Jusquan Amanda Bedard and Jisgang, Nika Collison, 187–96. Skidegate, BC: Haida Gwaii Museum Press.

Kisin, Eugenia. 2024. *Aesthetics of Repair: Indigenous Art and the Form of Reconciliation*. Toronto: University of Toronto Press.

Knight, Emma. 2017. "Unpacking the Museum Register: Institutional Memories of the Potlatch Collection Repatriation." *Museum Worlds: Advances in Research* 5:35–47.

Koffman, David. 2012. "Jews, American Indian Curios, and the Westward Expansion of Capitalism." In *Chosen Capital: The Jewish Encounter with American Capitalism*, edited by Rebecca Kobrin, 168–86. New Brunswick, NJ: Rutgers University Press.

Kramer, Jennifer. 2006. *Switchbacks: Art, Ownership, and Nuxalk National Identity*. Vancouver: University of British Columbia Press.

Krmpotich, Cara. 2014. *The Force of Family: Repatriation, Kinship, and Memory on Haida Gwaii*. Toronto: University of Toronto Press.

Kunst'aa Guu—Kunst'aayah Reconciliation Protocol. 2009. www.haidanation.ca.

Laclau, Ernesto. 2005. *On Populist Reason*. London and New York: Verso.

Lamoureux, Mack, and Anya Zoledziowski. 2021. "An Anti-Vax Conspiracy Theory Video Went Viral. An Indigenous Community Paid the Price." *Vice*, October 20. www.vice.com/en/article/conspiracy-black-lake-pat-king/.

Leathem, Hilary Morgan V. 2019. "Manifestations that Matter: A Case of Oaxacan Ruin Possession." *Archaeological Review from Cambridge* 34 (2): 92–110.

———. 2022. "Heritage (Dis)possessed: Haunting, Theft, and the Making of Monumental History in Oaxaca, Mexico." PhD diss., University of Chicago.

———. 2025. "Looting Made Legal: Settler-Colonial Logics of Erasure and the Making of Phantasmal Patrimony." *Current Anthropology* 66 (2): 156–82.

Leathem, Hilary Morgan V., and Joseph Weiss. 2022. "Sovereign Graffiti on Haida Gwaii: A Photo Essay." *BC Studies* 214:9–27.

Ledbetter, Carly. 2017. "The Meaning behind Canadian Prime Minister Justin Trudeau's Tattoo." *Huffington Post*, March 29. https://www.huffingtonpost.co.uk/entry/justin-trudeau-tattoo_n_58d919abe4b03787d35a6a11.

Levi-Strauss, Claude. 1987. *Introduction to the Work of Marcel Mauss*. Translated by Felicity Baker. London: Routledge & Kegan Paul.
Liboiron, Max. 2021. *Pollution is Colonialism*. Durham, NC: Duke University Press.
Lonetree, Amy. 2012. *Decolonizing Museums: Representing Native America in National and Tribal Museums*. Chapel Hill: University of North Carolina Press.
Lutz, Catherine, ed. 2002. *Homefront: A Military City and the American Twentieth Century*. Boston: Beacon Press.
———. 2009. *The Base of Empire: The Global Struggle against U.S. Military Posts*. New York: NYU Press.
Lyons, Scott R. 2010. *X-Marks: Native Signatures of Assent*. Minneapolis: University of Minnesota Press.
Macdonald, Nancy. 2016. "Skin-Deep: The Awkwardness of Justin Trudeau's Haida Tattoo." *Maclean's*, October 27. https://macleans.ca/politics/skin-deep-the-awkwardness-of-justin-trudeaus-haida-tattoo/.
Mackey, Eva. 2002. *The House of Difference: Cultural Politics and National Identity in Canada*. Toronto: University of Toronto Press.
———. 2016. *Unsettled Expectations: Uncertainty, Land, and Settler Decolonization*. Halifax and Winnipeg: Fernwood Press.
Mannoni, Octave. 2003. "I Know Well, but All the Same . . ." In *Perversion and the Social Relation*, edited by Molly Anne Rothenberg, Dennis A. Foster, and Slavoj Žižek, 68–92. Durham, NC: Duke University Press.
Mas Gak (Don Ryan). 1994. Foreword to *Eagle Down Is Our Law: Witsuwit'en Law, Feasts, and Land Claims*, by Antonia Mills, xi–xiii. Vancouver: University of British Columbia Press.
Mas, Susana. 2015. "Truth and Reconciliation Chair Says Final Report Marks Start of a 'New Era.'" *CBC News*, December 15. www.cbc.ca/news/politics/truth-and-reconciliation-final-report-ottawa-event-1.3365921.
Masco, Joseph. 1995. "'It Is a Strict Law That Bids Us Dance': Cosmologies, Colonialism, Death, and Ritual Authority in the Kwakwaka'wakw Potlatch, 1849 to 1922." *Comparative Studies in Society and History* 37 (1): 41–75.
Massie, Gillian. 2021. "Hudson Bays Orange Shirt Links Capitalism with Colonialism." *The Carillon*, October 7, 2021. https://carillonregina.com/hudson-bays-orange-shirts-link-capitalism-with-colonialism/.
Maynard, Robin, and Leanne Betasamosake Simpson. 2022. *Rehearsals for Living*. New York: Haymarket.
McMullen, Frank Francis Gerald. 1998. "When You Come to a Fork in the Road Take It: Negotiating Crisis and Transition in a Northern Village." Master's thesis, University of Northern British Columbia.
McNeil, Kent. 1998. "Defining Aboriginal Title in the 90's: Has the Supreme Court Finally Got It Right?" Twelfth Annual Robarts Lecture, March 25, 1998, York University, Toronto.
———. 2016. "The Doctrine of Discovery Reconsidered: Reflecting on Discovering Indigenous Lands: The Doctrine of Discovery in the English Colonies, by Robert J. Miller, Jacinta Ruru, Larissa Behrendt, and Tracey Lindberg, and

Reconciling Sovereignties: Aboriginal Nations and Canada, by Felix Hoehn." *Osgoode Hall Law Journal* 53 (2): 699–728.

Meissner, Dirk. 2021 "Kamloops Residential School Survivor Says Canadian Outpouring of Support Can Bring Healing." *Globe and Mail* (Toronto), June 2. www.theglobeandmail.com/canada/article-kamloops-residential-school-survivor-says-canadian-outpouring-can/.

Mickleburgh, Rod. 2012. "B.C. Natives Willing to Go 'To the Wall' against Enbridge Pipeline." *Globe and Mail* (Toronto), July 30. www.theglobeandmail.com/news/british-columbia/bc-natives-willing-to-go-to-the-wall-against-enbridge-pipeline/article4449911/.

Miller, Bruce. 2003. *Invisible Indigenes: The Politics of Nonrecognition*. Lincoln: University of Nebraska Press.

Miller, Robert J. 2019. "The Doctrine of Discovery." *Indigenous Peoples' Journal of Law, Culture, and Resistance* 5:35–42.

Milloy, John S. 1999. *A National Crime: The Canadian Government and the Residential School System*. Winnipeg: University of Manitoba Press.

Miyazaki, Hirokazu. 2004. *The Method of Hope: Anthropology, Philosophy, and Fijian Knowledge*. Stanford, CA: Stanford University Press.

Moreton-Robinson, Aileen. 2009. "Imagining the Good Indigenous Citizen: Race War and the Pathology of Patriarchal White Sovereignty." *Cultural Studies Review* 15 (2): 61–79.

———. 2015. *The White Possessive: Power, Property and Indigenous Sovereignty*. Minneapolis: University of Minnesota Press.

———. 2021. "Incommensurable Sovereignties: Indigenous Ontology Matters." In *Routledge Handbook of Critical Indigenous Studies*, edited by Brendan Hokowhitu, Aileen Moreton-Robinson, Linda Tuhiwai-Smith, Chris Andersen, and Steve Larkin, 257–68. Abingdon, UK: Routledge.

Murdock, George Peter. 1934. *Our Primitive Contemporaries*. New York: Macmillan Company.

Nadasdy, Paul. 2003. *Hunters and Bureaucrats: Power, Knowledge, and Aboriginal-State Relations in the Southwest Yukon*. Vancouver: University of British Columbia Press.

———. 2007. "The Gift in the Animal: The Ontology of Hunting and Human-Animal Sociality." *American Ethnologist* 34 (1): 25–43.

———. 2017. *Sovereignty's Entailments: First Nations State Formation in the Yukon*. Toronto: University of Toronto Press.

National Energy Board. 2013. *Considerations: Report of the Joint Review Panel for the Enbridge Northern Gateway Project*, Vol. 2. Calgary: National Energy Board.

Navaro-Yashin, Yael. 2009. "Affective Spaces, Melancholic Objects: Ruination and the Production of Anthropological Knowledge." *Journal of the Royal Anthropological Institute* 15 (1): 1–18.

NetNewsLedger. 2020. "RCMP Patrols Wet'suwet'en Cultural Site with Assault Rifles." *NetNewsLedger*, June 29. www.netnewsledger.com/2020/06/29/rcmp-patrol-wetsuweten-cultural-site-with-assault-rifles/.

Newell, Dianne. 1993. *Tangled Webs of History: Indians and the Law in Canada's Pacific Coast Fisheries*. Toronto: University of Toronto Press.

Nichols, Robert. 2020. *Theft is Property!: Dispossession and Critical Theory*. Durham, NC: Duke University Press.
Nikiforuk, Andrew. 2019. "When Indigenous Assert Rights, Canada Sends Militarized Police." *Tyee*, January 29. https://thetyee.ca/Analysis/2019/01/17/Indigenous-Rights-Canada-Militarized-Police/.
Onishi, Norimitsu. 2024. "On Small Islands off Canada's Coast, a Big Shift in Power." *New York Times*, July 5. https://www.nytimes.com/2024/07/04/world/canada/canada-indigenous-rights-haida.html.
paperson, la. 2017. *A Third University Is Possible*. Minneapolis: University of Minnesota Press.
Peerless, Sarah. 2013. "Family Questions Trespass Notice from Masset Military." *Haida Gwaii Observer*, July 15. https://www.haidagwaiiobserver.com/news/family-questions-trespass-notice-from-masset-military-6328983.
Penikett, Tony. 2006. *Reconciliation: First Nations Treaty Making in British Columbia*. Vancouver: Douglas & McIntyre.
Platt, Brian. 2020. "O'Toole Would Criminalize Blocking 'Critical' Infrastructure, Allow Police to Clear Blockades without Injunction." *National Post*, February 20. https://nationalpost.com/news/politics/otoole-says-he-would-criminalize-blocking-critical-infrastructure-allow-police-to-clear-blockades-without-an-injunction.
Povinelli, Elizabeth. 2002. *The Cunning of Recognition: Indigenous Alterities and the Making of Australian Multiculturalism*. Durham, NC: Duke University Press.
———. 2011. *Economies of Abandonment: Social Belonging and Endurance in Late Liberalism*. Durham, NC: Duke University Press.
———. 2016. *Geontologies: A Requiem for Late Liberalism*. Durham, NC: Duke University Press.
Prata, Rosie. 2016. "Haida Artist Behind Trudeau's Tattoo: 'I'm Just Appalled.'" *Canadian Art*, November 10. https://canadianart.ca/features/robert-davidson-trudeau-tattoo-statement/.
Pruden, Jana G. 2021. "Discovery of Children's Remains at Kamloops Residential School 'Stark Example of Violence' Inflicted upon Indigenous Peoples." *Globe and Mail* (Toronto), May 31. www.theglobeandmail.com/canada/article-bodies-found-at-kamloops-residential-school-site-in-bc/.
R. v. Sparrow. 1990. 1 S.C.R. 1075. https://decisions.scc-csc.ca/scc-csc/scc-csc/en/item/609/index.do.
R. v. Van der Peet. 1996. 2 S.C.R. 507. https://decisions.scc-csc.ca/scc-csc/scc-csc/en/item/1407/index.do.
Rancière, Jacques. 2004. *Disagreement: Politics and Philosophy*. Translated by Julie Rose. Minneapolis: University of Minnesota Press.
RBC. 2013. *RBC Aboriginal Partnership Report: A Chosen Journey*. https://www.rbc.com/newsroom/pdf/2013-rbc-aboriginal-partnership-report.pdf.
Reconciliation Canada. n.d. "How to Get Involved." Accessed May 1, 2024. https://www.indigenousrelationsacademy.com/. (Site discontinued).
Renner, Serena. 2024. "On Haida Gwaii, A Colonial Government Is No Longer Lord of the Land." *Narwhal*, April 24. https://thenarwhal.ca/haida-get-their-land-back/.

Reuters Fact Check. 2022. "Fact Check: Video of Indigenous Group Is Not Related to 2022 'Freedom Convoy.'" *Reuters*, January 27. www.reuters.com/article/factcheck-indigenous-convoy/fact-check-video-of-indigenous-group-is-not-related-to-2022-freedom-convoy-idUSL1N2U72WJ/.

Richland, Justin. 2021. *Cooperation without Submission: Indigenous Jurisdictions in Native Nation-US Engagements*. Chicago: University of Chicago Press.

Rifkin, Mark. 2009. "Indigenizing Agamben: Rethinking Sovereignty in Light of the 'Particular' Status of Native Peoples." *Cultural Critique* 73 (Fall 2009): 88–124.

———. 2014. *Settler Common Sense: Queerness and Everyday Colonialism in the American Renaissance*. Minneapolis: University of Minnesota Press.

Royal British Columbia Museum. 2018. "Indigenous Collections and Repatriation Policy." https://royalbcmuseum.bc.ca/media/5331.

Royal Ontario Museum. 2018. "Repatriation of Canadian Indigenous Objects." www.rom.on.ca/sites/default/files/sites/default/files/imce/policies2018/repatriation-indigenous-objects-2018.pdf.

Rutherford, Danilyn. 2012. *Laughing at Leviathan: Sovereignty and Audience in West Papua*. Chicago: University of Chicago Press.

Sahlins, Marshall. 1974. *Stone Age Economics*. New York: Aldine de Gruyter.

———. 1981. *Historical Metaphors and Mythical Realities: Structure in the Early History of the Sandwich Islands Kingdom*. Ann Arbor: University of Michigan Press.

Schmitt, Carl. 1988. *The Crisis of Parliamentary Democracy*. Translated by Ellen Kennedy. Cambridge, MA: MIT Press.

———. 2005. *Political Theology: Four Chapters on the Concept of Sovereignty*. Chicago: University of Chicago Press.

Schober, Elisabeth. 2016. *Base Encounters: The US Armed Forces in South Korea*. London: Pluto Press.

Sewid-Smith, Daisy (My-yah-nelth). 1979. *Prosecution or Persecution*. Cape Mudge, BC: Nuyumbalees Society.

Simpson, Audra. 2014. *Mohawk Interruptus: Political Life Across the Borders of Settler States*. Durham, NC: Duke University Press.

———. 2016. "The State Is a Man: Theresa Spence, Loretta Saunders, and the Gender of Settler Sovereignty." *Theory & Event* 19 (4).

———. 2017. "The Ruse of Consent and the Anatomy of 'Refusal': Cases from Indigenous North America and Australia." *Postcolonial Studies* 20 (1): 18–33.

Simpson, Leanne Betasamosake. 2012. "Aambe! Maajaadaa! (What #IdleNoMore Means to Me)." https://decolonization.wordpress.com/2012/12/21/aambe-maajaadaa-what-idlenomore-means-to-me/.

———. 2016. "Indigenous Resurgence and Co-Resistance." *Critical Ethnic Studies* 2 (2): 19–34.

———. 2017. *As We Have Always Done: Indigenous Freedom through Radical Resistance*. Minneapolis: University of Minnesota Press.

———. 2021. *A Short History of the Blockade: Giant Beavers, Diplomacy, and Regeneration in Nishnaabewin*. Edmonton: University of Alberta Press.

———. 2022. "A Short History of the Blockade." Talk given at Wesleyan University, April 14.

Stearns, Mary Lee. 1981. *Haida Culture in Custody: The Masset Band*. Seattle: University of Washington Press.

Stoler, Ann Laura. 2016. *Duress: Imperial Durabilities in Our Times*. Durham, NC: Duke University Press Books.

Stoymenoff, Alexis. 2012. "Haida Nation Leader Outraged over 'Libelous' Enbridge Documents." *Vancouver Observer*, January 10. www.vancouverobserver.com/sustainability/2012/01/10/haida-nation-leader-outraged-over-%c3%a2%e2%82%ac%c5%93libelous%c3%a2%e2%82%ac%c2%9d-enbridge-documents.html.

Sturm, Circe. 2011. *Becoming Indian: The Struggle over Cherokee Identity in the Twenty-First Century*. Albuquerque: University of New Mexico Press.

Supernant, Kisha, and Sean Carlton. 2022. "Fighting 'Denialists' for the Truth about Unmarked Graves and Residential Schooling. *CBC News*, June 3. https://www.cbc.ca/news/opinion/opinion-residential-schools-unmarked-graves-denialism-1.6474429.

Swanton, John Reed. 1905. *Contributions to the Ethnology of the Haida*. Leiden: E. J. Brill.

Takeda, Louise. 2015. *Island Spirit Rising: Reclaiming the Forests of Haida Gwaii*. Vancouver: University of British Columbia Press.

Tasker, John Paul. 2021. "Lynn Beyak, the Senator Who Defended Residential Schools, Is Retiring." *CBC News*, January 25. www.cbc.ca/news/politics/beyak-retirement-1.5886435.

Taylor, Charles. 1994. *Multiculturalism and the "Politics of Recognition."* Princeton, NJ: Princeton University Press.

Tengan, Ty P. Kāwika. 2008. *Native Men Remade: Gender and Nation in Contemporary Hawai'i*. Durham: Duke University Press.

Tennant, Paul. 1990. *Aboriginal Peoples and Politics: The Indian Land Question in British Columbia, 1849–1989*. Vancouver: University of British Columbia Press.

Thomas and Saik'uz First Nation v. Rio Tinto Alcan Inc. 2022. BCSC 15. www.canlii.org/en/bc/bcsc/doc/2022/2022bcsc15/2022bcsc15.html.

Tobe, Sarah. 1999. "Victoria's Curio Dealers." *The Scribe: The Journal of the Jewish Historical Society of B.C.* 19 (1): 9–18.

Tribal Trade. n.d. "Events and Workshops." https://tribaltradeco.com/pages/indigenous-workshops.

Trouillot, Michel Rolph. 1995. *Silencing the Past: Power and the Production of History*. Boston: Beacon Press.

Trudeau, Justin. 2021. "Statement by the Prime Minister on the National Day for Truth and Reconciliation." September 30. www.pm.gc.ca/en/news/statements/2021/09/30/statement-prime-minister-national-day-truth-and-reconciliation.

Truth and Reconciliation Commission. 2015. *Canada's Residential Schools: The Final Report of the Truth and Reconciliation Commission of Canada.* Vol. 1, *The History, Part 1: Origins to 1939*, and *Part 2: 1939 to 2000.* Montreal and Kingston: McGill-Queen's University Press.

Tsilhqot'in Nation v British Columbia. 2014. SCC 44, [2014] 2 S.C.R. 7. https://decisions.scc-csc.ca/scc-csc/scc-csc/en/item/14246/index.do.

Tuck, Eve. 2010. "Breaking Up with Deleuze: Desire and Valuing the Irreconcilable." *International Journal of Qualitative Studies in Education* 23 (5): 635–50.

Tuck, Eve, and K. Wayne Yang. 2012. "Decolonization Is Not a Metaphor." *Decolonization: Indigeneity, Education & Society* 1 (1): 1–40.

Tuck, Lon. 1978. "Bringing Back the Frontier." *Washington Post*, December 23. https://www.washingtonpost.com/archive/lifestyle/1978/12/24/bringing-back-the-frontier/981b6cfb-4316-4a67-a65c-3f92d158e8dc/.

Tully, James. 1995. *Strange Multiplicity: Constitutionalism in an Age of Diversity*. Cambridge, UK: Cambridge University Press.

Umeek/E. Richard Atleo. 2011. *Principles of Tsawalk: An Indigenous Approach to Global Crisis*. Vancouver: University of British Columbia Press.

U'mista Cultural Centre. n.d. "The History of the Potlatch Collection." www.umista.ca/pages/collection-history.

Union of BC Indian Chiefs. n.d. "Background to the McKenna McBride Royal Commission." https://collections.ubcic.bc.ca/s/ourhomesarebleeding/page/background.

Unist'ot'en. 2020. "Reconciliation Is Dead. Revolution Is Alive." February 13. https://unistoten.camp/reconciliationisdead/.

———. n.d.-a. "Unist'ot'en." https://unistoten.camp/.

———. n.d.-b. "A Timeline of the Campaign: A Timeline." https://unistoten.camp/timeline/timeline-of-the-campaign/.

*United Nations Declaration on the Rights of Indigenous Peoples* (UNDRIP). Resolution 61/295, Adopted by the General Assembly on 13 September, 2007.

United Nations Declaration on the Rights of Indigenous Peoples Act. S.C. 2021, c. 14. https://laws-lois.justice.gc.ca/eng/acts/U-2.2/page-1.html#h-1301577.

University of British Columbia. 2021. "Indigenous Strategic Plan." https://indigenous.ubc.ca/indigenous-engagement/indigenous-strategic-plan/.

Van den Brink, J. H. 1974. *The Haida Indians: Cultural Change Mainly between 1876–1970*. Leiden: Brill.

Venn, David. 2021. "Colonization Is a 'Book,' Not a 'Chapter' in Indigenous History, Says Nunavut MP." *Toronto Star*, June 7. www.thestar.com/news/canada/2021/06/07/colonization-is-a-book-not-a-chapter-in-indigenous-history-says-nunavut-mp.html?rf.

Vimalassery, Manu, Juliana Hu Pegues, and Alyosha Goldstein. 2016. "Introduction: On Colonial Unknowing." *Theory & Event* 19 (4).

Wakeham, Pauline. 2008. *Taxidermic Signs: Reconstructing Aboriginality*. Minneapolis: University of Minnesota Press.

Weber, Max. 1994. "The Profession and Vocation of Politics." In *Weber: Political Writings*, edited by Peter Lassman and Ronald Speirs, 309–69. Cambridge, UK: Cambridge University Press.

Webster, Gloria Cranmer. 1992. "From Colonization to Repatriation." In *Indigena: Contemporary Native Perspectives*, edited by Gerald McMaster and Lea-Ann Martin, 25–37. Vancouver: Douglas & MacIntyre.

Weiss, Joseph. 2015. "Challenging Reconciliation: Indeterminacy, Disagreement, and Canada's Indian Residential Schools' Truth and Reconciliation Commission." *International Journal of Canadian Studies* 51:27–55.

———. 2018. *Shaping the Future on Haida Gwaii: Life Beyond Settler Colonialism*. Vancouver: University of British Columbia Press.

———. 2020. "Giving Back the "Queen Charlotte Islands": The Politics of Names and Naming between Canada and the Haida Nation." *Native American and Indigenous Studies* 7 (1): 62–86.

———. 2021. "The Era of Endless Repatriation: Respectful Relationality and the Reconfiguration of Colonial Authority." *Anthropologica* 63 (2): 1–26.

———. 2024. "Settler Shock: Colonial Fetishism and the Disavowal of Violence in Contemporary Canada." *Public Culture* 36 (1): 75–95.

West Coast Environmental Law. 2012. "First Nations That Have Declared Opposition to Proposed Enbridge Tanker & Pipeline Project." https://www.wcel.org/publication/first-nations-have-declared-opposition-proposed-enbridge-tanker-pipeline-project.

White, Frederick H. 2006. "Was New Spain Really First? Rereading Juan Perez's 1774 Expedition to Haida Gwaii." *Canadian Journal of Native Studies* 26 (1): 1–24.

Wolfe, Patrick. 2006. "Settler Colonialism and the Elimination of the Native." *Journal of Genocide Research* 8 (4): 387–409.

———. 2013. "Recuperating Binarism: A Heretical Introduction." *Settler Colonial Studies* 3 (4): 257–79.

Wood, Patricia Burke, and David Rossiter. 2022. *Unstable Properties: Aboriginal Title and the Claim of British Columbia*. Vancouver: University of British Columbia Press.

Woolford, Andrew. 2006. *Between Justice and Certainty: Treaty Making in British Columbia*. Vancouver: University of British Columbia Press.

Yellowhead Institute. 2019. *Land Back: A Yellowhead Institute Red Paper*. https://redpaper.yellowheadinstitute.org/.

Zimonjic, Peter. 2021. "'The Fault of Canada': Trudeau Addresses Commons on Discovery of Remains at B.C. Residential School." *CBC News*, June 1. www.cbc.ca/news/politics/trudeau-house-commons-debate-residential-school-kamloops-1.6049312.

Zoledziowski, Anya. 2022. "Indigenous Leaders Are Denouncing the 'Freedom Convoy' for 'Hateful, Racist' Conduct." *Vice*, February 16. www.vice.com/en/article/indigenous-leaders-are-condemning-the-freedom-convoy-for-hateful-racist-conduct/.

# *Index*

Page numbers in *italics* indicate illustrations.

www.ingramcontent.com/pod-product-compliance
Lightning Source LLC
Chambersburg PA
CBHW032348280326
41935CB00008B/489

* 9 7 8 1 4 6 9 6 9 3 7 3 6 *